City of Disorder

City of Disorder

*How the Quality of Life Campaign
Transformed New York Politics*

Alex S. Vitale

NEW YORK UNIVERSITY PRESS
New York and London

NEW YORK UNIVERSITY PRESS
New York and London
www.nyupress.org

Library of Congress Cataloging-in-Publication Data
Vitale, Alex S.
City of disorder : how the quality of life campaign transformed
New York politics / Alex S. Vitale.
p.   cm.
Includes bibliographical references and index.
ISBN-13: 978-0-8147-8817-2 (cloth : alk. paper)
ISBN-10: 0-8147-8817-3 (cloth : alk. paper)
1. Quality of life—New York (State)—New York. 2. Quality of
life—Sociological aspects—New York (State)—New York.
3. Quality of life—Political aspects—New York (State)—New York.
4. New York (N.Y.)—Politics and government.   I. Title.
HN60.V58 2008
306.2'809747109045—dc22   2007043257

New York University Press books are printed on acid-free paper,
and their binding materials are chosen for strength and durability.

Manufactured in the United States of America

10 9 8 7 6 5 4 3 2 1

In memory of my father, Lawrence S. Vitale

Contents

Preface

From 1990 to 1993 I directed civil rights policy for the San Francisco Coalition on Homelessness, and during that time I witnessed the beginning of what would become a national backlash against homeless people. San Francisco Mayor Art Agnos had made extensive efforts to address what appeared at first to be a short-term problem made worse by the economic slowdown of the early 1980s and then exacerbated by the 1989 Loma Prieta earthquake, which damaged a significant amount of the city's low-cost housing. Within a few years, however, the problem had become worse, with homeless people encamped throughout the city, undermining the usability of parks, sidewalks, and other public spaces. The mayor's response was to begin to target homeless people in certain high-visibility areas of the city such as Golden Gate Park, the Civic Center, and Union Square. Through aggressive ticketing by police and outreach efforts by social workers, he attempted to restore order to those parts of the city. His efforts, however, were unsuccessful, as he lacked both the housing and services to move people off the streets and the willingness to fully engage the police in a program of harassment, intimidation, and arrests.

By 1992, public frustration with Agnos's failure to "solve" homelessness through either progressive or regressive means resulted in his ouster. He was replaced by the city's police chief, Frank Jordan, who campaigned on a platform of removing the homeless and restoring order through aggressive policing. In 1993 he initiated the "Matrix" program, which gave the police new authority and political backing for a concerted crackdown on public homelessness. Encampments were removed from public parks and plazas; thousands of tickets were issued for minor legal violations; and hundreds of homeless people were sent to jail.

Despite these aggressive efforts to restore order, the number of people without a place to live continued to increase and public order remained impaired, with the problem often being shifted from the central city to outlying neighborhoods. Although Jordan's backlash brought limited relief to a handful of targeted areas, it also engendered misery, anger, and hopelessness in thousands of homeless people.

Acknowledgments

I moved to New York in 1993 to attend the CUNY Graduate Center just in time to see this same process play out in the transition from the liberal administration of David Dinkins to the neoconservative administration of Rudolph Giuliani. Once again, homeless people were portrayed as the cause of urban blight, and aggressive policing was held out as the solution. This book is an attempt to explain how this dynamic of urban politics emerged in the hopes that a new progressive urban politics will emerge that reestablishes both order and security for urban neighborhoods and restores dignity to those left out of the new global economy.

This book would not have been possible without the support of many friends and colleagues who read drafts, suggested new lines of inquiry, and provided much needed encouragement. I would like to thank Leslie Kauffman, Steven Duncombe, Robert Cherry, and Kelly Moore, each of whom made crucial contributions to the structure of the book and the ideas it contains, though of course any mistakes or omissions are solely my own. I would most like to thank my wife, Elizabeth Palley, who gave up many weekends helping with the preparation of the manuscript and keeping me focused on its completion.

I would also like to give special thanks to research librarians at the New York Public Library's Research Division, the City Hall Library of New York City, Brooklyn College, and the Jefferson Market and Tompkins Square branches of the New York Public Library. This project involved hundreds of hours of library research utilizing clipping files, archives, microfilmed newspapers, and other sources. These librarians do heroic work in underfunded institutions for low pay and little public recognition.

I received support for this project from the PSC-CUNY Research Fund and the office of the Provost of Brooklyn College. Portions of chapter 6 appeared previously in vol. 15, no. 2, of *Policing and Society.*

Finally, I would like to thank the many people from neighborhoods, organizations, and city agencies throughout the city who agreed to take time out of their busy schedules to explain the workings of their daily lives. I hope this book will be of some use to them.

Introduction

During the 1980s and early 1990s, the quality of everyday life in New York City underwent dramatic changes, suffering the twin scourges of rising crime and disorder. In 1991, the city's crime rate peaked at its highest level ever, with more than two thousand homicides, and homeless encampments, panhandlers, and drug dealers became a normal part of the urban landscape. Then in a major shift, by the year 2000, homelessness was largely erased from public view, and crime had dropped to the lowest level in forty years. Somehow, the quality of daily life for millions of New Yorkers had been restored. There was, however, a darker side to this miraculous transformation. By 2004, homelessness reached its highest levels since the Great Depression, with both more than 100,000 New Yorkers relying on emergency shelter at some point during the year and new aggressive policing tactics, which resulted in the incarceration of tens of thousands of people for a wide variety of minor offenses such as drinking or urinating in public, blocking subway stairways, and sleeping in public parks.

This transformation in the quality of life in New York and many other American cities was more than the creation of some new policing tactics or the construction of a new philosophy of the socially marginal. Rather, it was a melding of the two into a coherent new approach toward social control. This "quality-of-life" paradigm emerged as a set of concrete social control practices united by a political philosophy that explained the nature of homelessness and disorder as one of personal responsibility and established punitive methods for restoring social order and public civility. In the process, it changed the way that cities dealt with welfare reform, community development, and policing practices in general.

The quality-of-life paradigm is a way of reorienting the efforts of city government away from directly improving the lives of the disenfranchised and toward restoring social order in the city's public spaces. This paradigm blames the current crisis on permissive social policies and calls for the implementation of a variety of punitive social control practices directed at minor incivilities as the way to restore neighborhood stability. While the previous paradigm of urban liberalism placed a premium on social tolerance, government planning, and rehabilitation, the new paradigm was driven by a concern with social intolerance, market- and volunteer-driven mechanisms of social change, and punitiveness.

The quality-of-life agenda did more than just criminalize homeless people. It helped transform the way these cities addressed a whole range of social problems. Prostitution, graffiti, and young men hanging out on street corners, as well as panhandlers and squeegee men, were viewed as a source rather than a symptom of urban decline. The government's response was to treat these groups as a major threat to public order and to place them at the center of new aggressive policing tactics and punitive social policies. Part of the innovation of "quality of life" is how it grouped and used punitive tactics rather than rehabilitative or structural reforms.

Society at large usually is indifferent to the means that the police use to maintain order on the edges of society. The police have always treated those on the margins of society in a repressive manner. Vagrancy and loitering laws, roundups of drunks and prostitutes, and the meting out of street justice in the form of physical attacks and personal indignities in a hidden late-night world of alleys, park benches, and skid-row sidewalks have been routine elements of urban life since the creation of police forces more than 150 years ago. Yet the daily lives of social outcasts have rarely been the focus of social movements, political speeches, or popular culture. What made the criminalization of homelessness in the 1990s new was that it transcended this popular disinterest. That is, the public attitude toward the issue of homeless and socially marginal people changed from passive sympathy to active antagonism. In the process, much of the political landscape of urban America was transformed.

This book is about the rise, dynamics, and consequences of a punitive approach to the urban social problems that developed in many American cities during the 1980s and 1990s. As homelessness, crime, and public disorder began to emerge as major social problems in the 1980s, local politicians, economic elites, and local community groups looked for new ways of restoring stability to the urban environment. As part of this process, a new philosophy of urban social control developed that emphasized the centrality of maintaining order through aggressive zero-tolerance policing and other punitive social policy measures. These were designed to enforce public civility through the fear of negative sanctions rather than simply the provision of enhanced economic opportunities and social services. The result has been the broad criminalization of homeless and other socially marginal people and the abandonment of the liberal ideals of reducing economic and social inequality which guaranteed basic universal human rights, and promoted social tolerance.

This process can be most clearly seen through the lens of the homelessness crisis. In response to the explosive growth in the number of homeless people across the country in the 1980s, cities created new policies that restricted a wide variety of behaviors associated with them, including panhandling, sleeping in parks, and sitting on sidewalks. These policies were joined under the rubric of quality-of-life improvements to emphasize their focus on visible forms of disorder that directly affect the everyday lives of urban residents from all social strata. The term *quality of life* has come to mean more than a set of policies, however; it also is a new way of thinking about urban social problems that attributes neighborhood decline to the presence of visible disorder. Rather than focusing on structural solutions to homelessness, unemployment, and crime, the new paradigm redefines these problems as one of individualized moral failure leading to neighborhood disorder and decline. Mass homelessness is thus transformed from a social problem of housing and social services to a law enforcement problem of maintaining order. The result has been a rejection of urban liberal politics in much of urban America.

As homelessness dramatically expanded in the 1980s, it evoked a variety of individual, community, and governmental responses. People were motivated to volunteer in soup kitchens, give out clothing, stock food pantries, and give money to panhandlers on the streets. The government produced a number of emergency responses, including shelters, soup kitchens, and a variety of social services designed to get people back on their feet. In these early days, homelessness was often viewed through the lens of the early 1980s recession and was therefore seen as a short-term economic problem that would improve along with the economy. Little effort was made to invest in more substantial responses such as housing and residential mental health and drug treatment facilities or to look at the ways in which housing and labor markets were being altered by both global and local political and economic factors.

As the recession gave way to the economic expansion of the late 1980s, the problem of homelessness became more obstinate and odious. The number of homeless people grew, and their impact on the daily life of the city became more problematic as subways, sidewalks, and parks became the living rooms for tens of thousands of people. At the same time, these people's connection to any specific economic downturn became harder to discern. Government and individual responses slowly became more routinized and structured. Emergency shelters became long-term shelters or transitional housing. Soup kitchens had to rely more and more on large government budgets to hire professional staffs rather than using volunteers.[1] Although people continued to give their time and money, only a few sought to develop long-term solutions, preferring instead to respond in some small way to the cries for help ringing throughout America's cities.

As the 1980s drew to a close and homelessness continued to pervade the urban environment along with the intertwined scourges of drugs and crime, a siege mentality emerged in the cities. Local residents felt that their public spaces were becoming unusable. Residents awoke to find people sleeping on their front stoops; merchants found encampments in their doorways and panhandlers on their sidewalks at all hours; and the city's subway system and parks became massive homeless shelters for thousands of people. Physical and social disorder in the form of the remains of cardboard beds, human waste, panhandling, and the ghostly presence of the mentally ill wandering the streets became omnipresent assaults on the population's sensibilities. The focus gradually shifted from how to help homeless people to how to reduce the impact of homelessness on the rest of society. As a result, society's charitable impulses turned from restoring the homeless to restoring communities. Urban residents, politicians, and business leaders began to demand that the visible symptoms of the growing urban crisis—crime, disorder, and homelessness—be directly and immediately resolved through punitive means.

The Rise of Disorder

The city that was the most dramatically affected by demands for improving the quality of daily life was New York. Whereas other cities— such as San Francisco, Los Angeles, Seattle, Baltimore, and Chicago—

experienced similar political upheavals in the face of growing disorder, New York's changes were the most pronounced. During the 1980s, New Yorkers witnessed a continuous rise in the level of disorder in public spaces. Tens of thousands of homeless people could be found in all parts of the city, both above and below ground. Estimates of the number of people living in shelters and on the streets have been difficult to gauge, in part owing to the extent and scope of the problem, but the most reliable figures are the number of people relying on emergency shelters on any given night. In October 1986, New York City's Human Resources Administration, which operates the shelter system, stated that 4,500 families and 9,000 single adults had entered the system, with an average of 450 new families seeking shelter each month.[2] Less than a year later, the numbers were 9,000 single adults and more than 5,000 families.[3] These numbers continued to increase throughout the late 1980s and early 1990s. Homeless advocates estimated that an average of 50,000 people were homeless at one time during this period, and 200,000 were living with friends and relatives or in substandard housing.[4]

Most of these people stayed in shelters, meaning that they were not a visible presence at night. In many cases, however, even those staying in the shelter system were forced out in the early morning to fend for themselves until the early evening. A significant number of these people spent their days working, searching for work, and navigating the social welfare bureaucracy. Many thousands, however, left the shelter system each morning and went into the surrounding neighborhoods looking for opportunities to make money, engaging in substance abuse, and, in some cases, wandering aimlessly. Even more distressing were the thousands of people not using the shelter system. Each night, the subway alone housed thousands of people in stations, tunnels, and subway cars. Many of them set up full-time residences in out-of-the-way corners of stations or deep in the labyrinth of tunnels and service rooms below ground. Those above ground slept where they could, alone or in groups. The most noticeable were the large encampments in which sometimes dozens of people set up makeshift tents in abandoned lots, under freeways, or even in public parks. These camps usually were characterized by the presence of drug use, trash, and human waste. Since the mentally ill and hard-core substance abusers were the groups most likely to avoid the regimented and sometimes dangerous shelters, those sleeping on the streets were more likely to be a source of aggressive panhandling, intoxicated or mentally ill behavior, and petty crime.

As homelessness grew, neighborhoods throughout the five boroughs were confronted with people living in their parks, subway stations, and even doorways. Automated teller machines and the fronts of all-night markets were favorite spots for round-the-clock panhandling and sleeping, with occasional late-night battles over the prime spots. Many residents had to walk a daily gauntlet of homeless people at the store and at the bank and sleeping on the sidewalk and in the subway. In addition to the constant requests for handouts, the visible presence of so many disheveled people and their possessions became a landscape of disorder, despair, and, in some cases, fear.

These conditions worsened throughout the late 1980s, but 1989 was a watershed year that both typified the period and displayed some of its worst characteristics. The city estimated that ten thousand homeless mentally ill people were on the streets of New York that year.[5] That spring, the shelter system housed more than eleven thousand single adult and close to five thousand families, with advocates claiming there were twenty thousand to thirty thousand more on the streets.[6] The transit authority counted one thousand people living in its stations on a single winter night, not including people sleeping on trains or hidden away in the tunnels.

That year, the city was filled with quotidian indignities for both the housed and the homeless. In particular, there were three social landscapes that exemplified the extent of the problem and the seeming inability to do anything substantive about it. Each of these shows the central role of homelessness in unraveling New York City's social fabric.

West Ninety-sixth Street

A paradigmatic sign of the disorder crisis of 1989 was the arrest of Larry Hogue on Manhattan's West Ninety-sixth Street for vandalizing a church on that block. A homeless veteran with serious psychiatric and substance abuse problems, Hogue had been a fixture on that street since the mid-1980s, using his monthly disability check to buy alcohol, crack, and other drugs. At his best, he slept and wandered the streets as a ghostlike presence. When high on crack or other drugs, however, he was often a raging menace, threatening passersby, vandalizing cars and buildings, and occasionally assaulting local residents. He was arrested in 1989 after he caused $10,000 to $20,000 in damage by throwing bricks through the stained-glass windows at the First Church of Christ,

Scientist, at 1 West Ninety-sixth Street. After being psychologically evaluated, he was deemed mentally incompetent to be held accountable for his actions, and after being medically stabilized and treated for his drug use, he was judged to be stable enough to take care of himself without harming himself or others and was discharged back onto the streets.

This was not the first or last time this would happen. Hogue was arrested nine times in the twenty years from 1972 to 1992, and he was sentenced to prison six times, with sentences ranging from five days to a year. During that same period, he was hospitalized more than twenty times in city facilities and several more times at VA hospitals. The most serious incident involving Hogue occurred in 1988 when he assaulted a sixteen-year-old girl and pushed her in front of a moving truck, leading to another temporary involuntary hospital commitment. In 1994 he was arrested again for throwing slabs of concrete through the windshield of an occupied car.

During this period, residents around West Ninety-sixth Street were continually threatened by Hogue's presence in the neighborhood, often feeling that it was not safe to walk down their own block when he was around, for fear of his constant verbal and even physical harassment. They felt incapable of doing anything about this, because each time Hogue was arrested or committed, he was soon released and allowed to return to the same street. Mental health officials pointed out that with the loss of almost half the city and state's mental health beds since the 1960s, there was nowhere to put people with minor psychological problems exacerbated by regular substance abuse. According to psychiatrist Gregory A. Miller, who frequently treated Hogue, "The system is so overburdened that even the mentally ill addicts that beg for treatment do not get it, much less those that resist treatment. What it boils down to is that we as a society have decided to ignore the problem and then get mad when someone is out on the street."[7]

Tompkins Square Park

One of the most contentious and notorious signs of the declining quality of public life in 1989 could be seen in Tompkins Square Park on the Lower East Side of Manhattan. Beginning the previous summer, a mixture of young street kids, homeless men, and drug dealers and users had taken over the park. Local residents complained that they could not use the park and that the noise from the people congregated there kept them up at night despite an existing midnight curfew. The situation became worse as people living in the park set up makeshift tents, lit fires in trash barrels, and accumulated large amounts of possessions in boxes and shopping carts. Noise, trash, discarded drug paraphernalia, and even human waste came to overpower the park and its surroundings. Residents formed new neighborhood groups designed to pressure the city to take action, which it did on August 6, 1988. That night, police evicted people in the park after midnight, sparking a riot as park dwellers, along with many community supporters, resisted the eviction and police attacked them in large numbers. Dozens of police, rioters, and passersby were injured in the confrontation that lasted until the early hours of the morning.

The neighborhood was deeply divided by the eviction. Mayor Edward Koch rescinded the curfew in the face of organized community opposition to it because of the absence of an adequate alternative place for the people to go to. But by the summer of 1989 the park was again besieged by the overlapping populations of homeless people, drug dealers, and street kids. Another round of community organizing resulted in the police's restricting the use of tents or other structures by the hundreds of people living there. This low-level harassment of the park dwellers satisfied neither side of the divided community. It failed to provide real alternatives for the people there, and it failed to remove them from the park. This halfhearted approach further polarized the community and highlighted the city's inability to develop real services for single homeless adults with mental health and substance abuse problems. By the summer of 1991, even many supporters of the homeless, who had preferred an expansion of services instead of evictions, were ready to support the closure and renovation of the park as a way of displacing the problem from their midst. On June 2, Mayor David Dinkins did just that, closing the park for more than a year in order for it to be rehabilitated. Since then, the park has been closed each night at midnight, and no sleeping materials or tents are allowed during the day.

Subways

Conditions in the city's subway system also were at a low point in 1989. The New York Transit Authority (TA) estimated that more than two thousand people were living in the system's stations and trains, but advocates maintained that the number was several times larger. Indeed, conditions were so bad in some areas that the TA believed that it was at least partially responsible for the first fall in ridership levels since the fiscal crisis of the mid-1970s. Riders complained about the usability of cars occupied by sleeping people who had not bathed or had soiled themselves. Entry areas were populated by people disabling the turn-stiles in hopes of obtaining errant tokens for resale. Benches throughout the system were turned into beds, especially on cold winter nights. Pan-handling was endemic as well, especially during heavily traveled day-time hours. And more than two dozen homeless people died in the sys-tem that year after being hit by trains or electrocuted by the third rail while looking for shelter in tunnels.

The situation became so bad that in October the TA announced the creation of new rules for the system that prohibited blocking stairs or platforms, sleeping while lying down, trespassing in the tunnels, and panhandling, as well as the stricter enforcement of existing rules pro-hibiting public drinking and intoxication, vandalism, smoking, and lit-tering. Operation Enforcement, as it was called, was designed to restore order to the subway by strict "zero-tolerance" enforcement of minor vi-olations. The hope was that this would give officers the tools to root out those who were making the subway less usable and, in the process, set a tone of law and order that would draw back the riding public. This initial effort, however, was unsuccessful due to the lack of support by New York's governor, Mario Cuomo, and many police officers, as well as resistance from homeless advocates who brought a number of lawsuits against the effort. As a result, thousands of people continued to live in the subway system.

The Quality-of-Life Response

By the early 1990s, the unabated increase of public disorder caused a dramatic shift in social policies and urban politics that ushered in an ur-ban political backlash in New York and many other American cities. This is not to say that before 1990 all homeless policies were therapeu-tic and that after 1990 all were punitive. Nonetheless, during the early 1990s, there was a radical change in emphasis toward punitiveness that could be seen all across the country. The National Law Center on Homelessness and Poverty identified forty-two cities that developed new antihomeless measures in 1994, compared with only nine cities in 1991.

The report indicated that the adoption of punitive measures was widespread and occurred in both historically liberal cities such as San Francisco, Santa Cruz, and Seattle, and conservative cities such as San Diego, Houston, and Denver. It also showed that these actions were often taken with broad grassroots support, as evidenced by the success of ballot measures and political candidates who championed the new punitiveness.[8]

In 1991, the Miami police regularly arrested homeless people for sleeping, eating, and urinating in public. In 1994, they used bulldozers to demolish a homeless shantytown in downtown Bicentennial Park. Later that year, they also passed new laws restricting "aggressive solicitation" and "pedestrian interference." In fact, these attacks became so intense that a federal court in *Pottinger v. City of Miami* (1991) ruled that the city's intent was to criminalize the essential acts of homeless people who had no alternative, given the almost complete lack of a homeless shelter system, and that the city must establish safe zones where the police would be prevented from harassing people living outdoors.

In 1993, the city of Seattle created a new ordinance making it illegal to sit or lie down on the sidewalk in many public places, including the central business district. Police, working closely with area merchants, also began rigorously enforcing obstruction, begging, and trespassing laws. The result was hundreds of arrests and numerous large "sweeps" of public places in the central city.

In 1993, a number of local groups in Santa Monica, California, proposed a local ordinance banning both camping in any public place and abusive solicitation. After a broad mobilization in support of the ordinance, the city council passed it in 1994, as well as tough restrictions on the public distribution of free food. The effect of these measures was to criminalize the basic social and bodily acts of homeless people, forcing them to choose among jail, an overcrowded shelter system, or moving to another town, with similar consequences.

One of the clearest examples of the new backlash was the creation of the Matrix Program in San Francisco in 1993. Matrix relied on a wide variety of enforcement tools against public disorder, including the zero-tolerance enforcement of existing nuisance laws, the resurrection of nineteenth-century municipal statutes, and reinterpretations of existing state laws, local ordinances, health codes, and park regulations. Matrix resulted in the arrests of hundreds of people for sleeping in parks, panhandling, loitering, urinating outdoors, and serving free food in public. More significantly, it generated thousands of citations that quickly became arrest warrants when people failed to make their court appearances or to pay their sometimes sizable fines. In an effort to increase the tools available to the police, the mayor (and former police chief), Frank Jordan, supported a local initiative to criminalize "aggressive panhandling," which the voters passed in 1994 and the police used to sweep central commercial areas.

New York City, which like San Francisco represented the pinnacle of liberal approaches to social problems, stepped up its punitive measures against the homeless in 1990 with the ejection of large numbers of homeless people from the state-run subway system. This effort was led by William Bratton, the chief of the New York City Transit Police. In 1991, Mayor David Dinkins, a liberal Democrat, expanded this approach with the sweeping of Tompkins Square Park and numerous other public encampments. In 1993, Mayor Dinkins also initiated a police enforcement effort targeting "squeegee men," who wash car windows at intersections for spare change. The move toward punitiveness did not begin in earnest, however, until Rudolph Giuliani took over as mayor in 1994. Giuliani immediately brought in William Bratton to be commissioner of the New York Police Department (NYPD), and together they developed a number of new tactics to drive the homeless from public space.

Giuliani reformulated the homeless problem as a disorder problem by framing the issue in terms of "quality of life," which allowed him to treat homelessness as a criminal justice issue and not a social services one. He switched the focus of urban social policy from improving housing, employment, social services, and fighting poverty, to using the police to control public disorder. Rather than expanding access to affordable housing or social services or improving labor market opportunities for those with limited skills, Giuliani dramatically expanded the size and role of the police department. The NYPD became the agency of first resort for complaints about the declining quality of community life, including homelessness. This approach concentrated on the impact of homelessness and other low-level disorders on residents and neighborhoods rather than focusing on the plight of the people who were the source of this disorder. The police department's primary new directive on homelessness, "Police Strategy No. 5: Reclaiming the Public Spaces of New York," addressed the policing of specific behaviors such as street peddling, panhandling, and squeegee cleaning, rather than explicitly targeting the status of being homeless: "Over the years, enjoyment of public space has been curtailed. Aggressive panhandling, squeegee cleaners, street prostitution, 'boombox cars,' public drunkenness, reckless bicyclists, and graffiti have added to the sense that the entire public environment is a threatening place."[9] These behaviors were mainly but not exclusively associated with people living on the streets. As a result, these behaviors became code words for the presence of homeless people, and in the process, rather than focusing on homeless people as such, this directive and its enactment established a new way of thinking about homeless people as causes of disorder, thereby facilitating the criminalization of a whole range of socially marginal people.

Explaining the Rise of Quality-of-Life Policing

These punitive measures were a significant departure from earlier approaches to homelessness, which relied largely on short-term emergency responses and therapeutic strategies. In the early years of Mayor David Dinkins's administration, New York City focused on maintaining the city's mammoth emergency shelter system and creating permanent and transitional housing, as well as a network of social services. Rhetorically, Dinkins emphasized the plight of homeless families and children in an attempt to portray them as the deserving poor. But two years into Dinkins's term of office, he began to move away from his liberal policies of housing development and social services and to experiment with more punitive measures. He failed, however, to embrace this new punitive effort completely, enacting it only sporadically. Perhaps more important, he failed to fashion it into a public ideology. Consequently, Rudolph Giuliani was able to unseat him as mayor by clearly articulating a vision of restoring order and bringing prosperity to the city, its neighborhoods, and its public spaces through aggressive zero-tolerance policing. Giuliani was politically successful because he managed to harness the widespread concern of business leaders and neighborhood residents about the declining quality of life in the city by promising to quickly and effectively address visible disorderly behavior. He argued that by reversing the visible symptoms of social and physical disorder, urban spaces would be economically revitalized. This contention appealed to residents who similarly viewed the problems of disorder as symptomatic of a city out of control: economically in the form of rising rents and declining wages, socially in the form of growing crime and disorder, and physically in the form of increased filth and decaying public infrastructures.

When Giuliani took office in 1994, he turned Dinkins's policing experiments into major citywide operations. He evicted dozens of homeless encampments, displaced squeegee men, and ordered the police to harass homeless people through the zero-tolerance enforcement of minor infractions. In the shelter system he attempted to transform the rules of accountability for homeless people by charging them for staying in shelters and threatening them with eviction from the shelter system, loss of benefits, and even separation from their families for failing to abide by work requirements calling for people to work twenty hours a week. "Tough love" replaced housing and services as a new strategy for addressing homelessness and restoring order.

"Quality of Life" as a New Paradigm of Social Control

This book tries to answer one central question: What social forces lead to the rise of this new quality-of-life paradigm of urban social control? To answer this question, I describe the economic development strategies, policing practices, and social welfare policies that constituted urban liberalism in the 1970s and 1980s in relation to the problem of homelessness and other forms of disorder. The quality-of-life paradigm represents a general shift in social policies away from the prior paradigm of urban liberalism, along three axes. The first axis is a transition from socially inclusive, rehabilitation-oriented policies to socially exclusive, punitive ones. The second is a rejection of government-centered approaches to social problems in favor of market- and community-based efforts, and the third is a move away from the social tolerance of individual and group differences and toward a communitarian outlook that privileges majoritarian views of appropriate public behavior at the expense of the socially marginalized.

To explain why this transformation occurred in the late 1980s and early 1990s, I use New York City as a case study through which to examine the economic, political, and social factors contributing to the breakdown of urban liberalism and the rise of the new quality-of-life paradigm. Although New York is not representative of all American cities, it is the premier example of a process that happened to a lesser degree in many other major liberal cities, including San Francisco, Seattle, Los Angeles, and Chicago. Like New York, these cities share a long-term investment in the political paradigm of urban liberalism, with its commitment to corporate-focused entrepreneurial economic development strategies, a social services orientation to social problems, a reliance on expert-driven centralized planning of land use and social services coordination, and a legacy of social tolerance.

I look at a number of different neighborhoods within New York City to see how the transformation from urban liberalism to "quality of life" was carried out. The new paradigm was able to garner support from a wide range of social actors from different races and classes. Business groups were motivated to increase retail and tourist business by reestablishing public order. Middle-class community activists—many with roots in the social movements of the 1960s and 1970s—mobilized to defend their neighborhoods from disorder. Minority neighborhoods were supportive of new policing strategies that would fight crime and involve community residents in the process. All these constituencies were frustrated by the inability of urban liberal politicians to reduce visible homelessness and restore civility to public spaces.

1

Conceptualizing the Paradigm Shift

How can we understand this shift in the social regulation of marginal populations in New York in the 1990s? Two discourses have emerged in the last twenty years to explain this process. In one, criminologists ask whether this transformation is part of a process of growing criminalization and punitiveness toward those who violate the law and community norms or is merely a more effective form of policing and criminal justice administration developed in response to popular calls for enhanced security. In the other discourse, urbanists debate whether or not quality-of-life politics developed as a response to a decline in public civility or gentrification and disorder emerging as a result of growing inequality. These two fields of study are a logical starting point for a framework to interpret the complex social, political, and economic changes associated with the rise of quality-of-life politics.

Criminology

Criminologists are concerned with why, over the last thirty years, the orientation of American society has become more punitive toward crime and disorder. More people are in jail for longer periods; more police are patrolling the streets; and support for the death penalty remains widespread. Currently, a staggering two million people are incarcerated in the United States, and another four million are on probation or parole. Since the 1980s, numerous states have imposed heavier penalties for a variety of violent and nonviolent crimes and increased their use of the death penalty. This is in marked contrast to the predictions of classical sociological and criminological theorists, who argue that the natural social progression is to find more integrative methods of dealing with deviance and to move away from more punitive methods. These theorists generally contend that as society became more complex, educated, and wealthy, criminal justice policies would become more restitutive and reintegrative rather than punitive and exclusionary. What can explain this seeming contradiction?

The story of urban policing is similar. While there has been an overall reduction in police violence since the social unrest of the 1960s and 1970s, the 1990s turned away from community policing and refocused on maintaining order, including the utilization of zero-tolerance strategies, aggressive stop-and-frisk operations, and large-scale sweeps of minor offenders. In addition, SWAT and other paramilitary units have grown in prominence, and the overall size and scope of urban police departments have increased even before new terrorism concerns arose. Why have the police taken a more punitive posture in the last decade, and how is this tied to broader criminological trends?

Advocates of more restrictive policing methods argue that they are in direct response to the growth of crime and disorder. In their book *Fixing Broken Windows,* George Kelling and Catherine Coles lay much of the blame on the social tolerance of unregulated individualism following the social upheavals of the 1960s.[1] Building on Amita Etzioni's new communitarianism,[2] they contend that this dangerous move in favor of individual rights came at the expense of the communities' needs and that the privileging of the individual has contributed to the breakdown of community stability. According to Kelling and Coles, the rise of new policing methods is in direct response to the recent

> emphasis on individual needs and rights, and the belief that such rights were absolute; a rejection, or at least a serious questioning, of middle-class morality; the notion that stigmatizing individuals as criminals or deviants turned them into criminals or deviants; and the positing of solutions such as mental hospitals, therapies, and other interventions as more invidious than the problems they were designed to address. In the judicial arena, the courts developed a corresponding body of legal precedent in which constitutional protections for the fundamental rights and liberties of individuals were expanded and elevated to a position of far greater significance than either the responsibilities of individuals, or community interests.[3]

For Kelling and Coles, the rise of unregulated individualism is at the root of the quality-of-life crisis, and the water that has given life to those roots is liberal permissiveness. This is similar to Fred Siegel's and Jim Sleeper's arguments that the origin of urban disorder and decline was the rise of liberal permissiveness toward extreme social movements and minority groups.[4] All these theorists consistently point to liberal judicial rulings that, they maintain, have unleashed anomic incivilities by failing to regulate the human potential for antisocial and destructive behaviors.

They see this criminalization of homelessness and the rise of quality-of-life policing as a necessary counteraction to the growth of unregulated social behaviors that threaten to destabilize local neighborhoods and entire cities. Quality of life comes to stand for the middle-class desires for order that have been ignored by liberal legal, political, and cultural actors. According to Kelling and Coles, Siegel, and Sleeper, the middle class chose the police as the tool to restore these values, by directly confronting these unregulated incivilities. In essence, this is a return to a social control theory of social regulation in which the police become the primary labelers of appropriate behaviors and provide the necessary negative sanctions to reinforce them.

But is the emergence of this new individualism really the result of the judicial actions taken by liberal elites engaged in social engineering? Another way of understanding the anticommunal individualism of this period is to look at the economic forces driving individualism and social deregulation. David Garland pursued this approach in his analysis of social changes over the last thirty years that describes the new punitiveness.[5] These changes include the decline of the rehabilitative ideal, the reemergence of punitive sanctions, a focus on victims, an aversion to risk, the expansion of the criminal justice system, and the commercialization of crime control. Some of these changes predate many aspects of the new quality-of-life movement and therefore represent a national punitive context for the changes in urban areas.

Garland argues that the origin of the new anomic individualism is not the rise of a liberal regime of expanding formal rights. Instead, it is tied to the economics of "late modernism," which Garland characterizes as more flexible production and distribution, the increase in two-wage families, the suburbanization of work and living, the rise of electronic mass media, and the democratization of social and cultural life. These changes have been combined with a political realignment favoring economic liberalism and social austerity. The result is a new social condition of an increasing sense of risk as people's social and economic lives become less stable. Not surprisingly, the cultural response to this condition is, on the one hand, a desire for greater individual freedom of expression, consumption, and lifestyle and, on the other hand, a desire for risk aversion in the form of increasing demands for security, orderliness, and control.

This reconceptualization of liberalism is more than just a series of social movements and court decisions granting additional individual and minority-group rights. It defines postwar liberalism as an expression of a larger economic shift away from a mass society of undifferentiated consumers and workers toward a society made up of individuals maximizing both their productivity and their formation of identity through flexible specialization. The effect of this process on geographic communities is disintegrative. British criminologist Jock Young describes it as a shift from social inclusiveness to social exclusion, whereas the old approach was characterized by a growing social tolerance of difference:

> The post-war years came to fruition in the permissive 1960s. Just as citizenship in the legal and political sense became extended by class, by age, by race and by gender, so the limits of normality, permissible behavior within the social contract, were pushed forward. More and more areas of behavior which were once seen as offences, *by definition* outside the social contract, became embraced by it. (emphasis in original)[6]

For Young, this was a paternal liberalism that treated the socially marginal as needing individual assistance to help them become better integrated into the society, rather than addressing the structural roots of inequality.

According to Young, modern society has become more tolerant of diversity but less tolerant of difficulty. As the new paradigm developed, therefore, it focused less on destroying diversity than on consuming it, and at the same time, it threw out those parts that it found difficult. The superficial trappings of diversity were embraced as long as they did not produce any major inconvenience. The result is a kind of social "bulimia" that deals with social tension by purging the symbolic and superficial source of the problem without addressing the actual cause. This process of assessing difficulty has developed into what Young describes as an "actuarial society" in which social actors are constantly assessing risk:

The actuarial stance is calculative of risk, it is wary and probabilistic, it is not concerned with causes but with probabilities, not with justice but with harm minimization, it does not seek a world free of crime but one where the best practices of damage limitation have been put in place; not a utopia but a series of gated havens in a hostile world.[7]

Young makes it clear that this new paradigm rejects the hopefulness of liberal social interventions carried out in the interests of the society as a whole, in favor of more parochial and individual calculations. It represents a profoundly conservative approach that undermines progressive attempts to increase equality and social integration.

Young argues that the rise in punitive social control policies is tied to two related developments: the increased individualism of the 1960s and 1970s and the economic restructuring of cities during the 1980s and 1990s. Both of these stem from a general process of disaggregation. Individualism takes the form of a kind of "personal exclusiveness" characterized by the breakdown of traditional connecting and regulating institutions such as the family and the community, producing individualized identities and desires. This is a Durkheimian vision of an anomic individualism that leads some people to pursue their unregulated desires at the expense of others in the form of increased street crime. The economic restructuring of society is tied to the post-Fordist economic model in which production and demand are increasingly disaggregated and individualized. Young contends that a new consumer economy has been created that decentralizes production and thereby leads to unemployment, underemployment, and contingency in the workforce.

The combination of these developments has led to a great deal of relative deprivation. Although people's individual desires have been increased, the ability of all but the most wealthy to satisfy them has been diminished. The result is both more crime and more resentment of criminals. As Young argues,

What I am suggesting is that both the causes of criminal violence and the punitive response towards it spring from the same source. The obsessive violence of the macho street gang and the punitive obsession of the respectable citizen are similar not only in their nature but in their origin. Both stem from the dislocations in the labor market: the one a market which excludes participation as a worker but encourages voraciousness as a consumer, the other from a market which includes, but only in a precarious fashion.[8]

The causes of the new punitiveness are therefore tied to both the actual rise in crime and the rise in insecurity among those in the middle and, to a lesser degree, the upper classes. And both of these are tied to the changing labor market and the rise in individualism.

Young and Garland make important theoretical contributions to our understanding of the cultural nature of the current backlash. We clearly are living in an actuarial moment in which assessments of personal risk have replaced concerns about society's collective well-being. Conversely, our view of those who pose a risk have turned from an interest in addressing the needs of individuals existing outside societal norms to viewing that group as a collective "dangerous class" to be avoided and excluded. In addition, we can see that the failure of the state to address the underlying crime and disorder problems is a significant contributor to the punitive backlash as communities become frustrated with the declining conditions of everyday life.

Urban Studies

One of the more interesting urban phenomena of the last twenty years is the rise of neoconservative politicians in many traditionally Democratic cities. New York City, in particular, has elected Republicans as mayor in the last four elections, despite the city's being about 80 percent Democratic. Many urban scholars have been interested in this apparent abandonment of liberalism in New York and other major cities. Some have concentrated on the role of race and disorder in undermining liberalism, while others have highlighted the effects of globalization in destabilizing the liberal project of social reform, increased equality, and social tolerance. Both sets of scholars point out that liberal urban politicians failed to take into full account the effects of their economic and social policies on the city's long-term stability.

Some critiques of liberalism have stressed the ways in which liberalism's tolerance of radical demands by racial minorities during the civil rights era hurt white support for liberalism's economic and social agenda. In his book *Canarsie*, Jonathan Rieder describes how white Italian and Jewish residents of the Brooklyn neighborhood of Canarsie came together to fight the busing of minority children into schools in their neighborhood. He shows that these residents' historic connection to the ideals of New Deal liberalism were undermined by their desire to protect their neighborhood from the destabilizing process of integration. They accused the city of social engineering, which they believed threatened the life of their community.[9]

Rieder's main contention is that it was the liberals' attempt to use government to increase blacks' economic and social equality that created whites' racial resentment. Canarsie's residents felt that they were being asked to sacrifice their schools, homes, and neighborhood for the advancement of another group. This was especially troubling because they already felt under siege from their own declining economic status. During the 1970s, New York and other major cities were losing middle-class manufacturing jobs, which put a squeeze on many white-ethnic communities.

Rieder outlines how the rise of crime and political disorder in the 1960s began weakening liberalism, especially along racial lines. As crime increased and blacks made more radical demands on government, middle- and working-class whites turned away from liberalism's embrace of racial inclusiveness. Evidence of this can be seen in Canarsie's support for Richard Nixon in 1968 and 1972, despite having voted for Democrats since the New Deal. This process, however, was reversed in the mid-1970s when Canarsie residents voted for Jimmy Carter and continued to vote for Democrats in neighborhood elections. Although they had become disaffected from liberalism, they were not yet ready to abandon it altogether and voted for Democratic mayoral candidates, including Koch in the 1980s and Dinkins in 1989. It took the social crisis of homelessness, combined with concern about crime and race to finally and fully destabilize urban liberalism in Canarsie and other white working-class neighborhoods.

Rieder's emphasis on the role of race in undermining liberalism is echoed by Jim Sleeper and Fred Siegel, each of whom claims that liberals were too tolerant of the more extreme demands made by black militants in the late 1960s and early 1970s.[10] As an example, they point to the effort by blacks to take local control of the schools in the black Ocean Hill–Brownsville neighborhood in Brooklyn. Many whites viewed this effort as an assault on the mostly white teachers' union and as a threat to the overall standards of the public school system. They accused New York City Mayor John Lindsay of failing to take action more quickly to regain control of the schools and reestablish a sense of order. This was a crucial moment for liberalism. Up to that point, the teachers' union had been viewed as a liberal organization in city politics, but the racialized split between black parents and white teachers drove them to be more conservative. In both 1993 and 1997, the teachers' union failed to endorse the liberal and African American David Dinkins in his races against Rudolph Giuliani, despite Giuliani's repeated criticism of the teachers and the Board of Education.

Siegel claims that this racial resentment became the basis of a new neoconservative urban politics ushered in by Rudolph Giuliani. According to Siegel, whites began to view liberalism as a political philosophy that tolerated political and social extremism, which was socially and economically threatening to middle-class whites. Siegel also criticizes liberals' reliance on the courts to win enhanced social freedoms, accusing groups like the Coalition for the Homeless and the American Civil Liberties Union (ACLU) of trying to win cases in the courts that they could not convince the public were worthwhile. According to Siegel, this gave these groups an elitist and antidemocratic appearance, and his bypassing of public opinion also alienated many community residents from liberalism's allegiance to social tolerance and a rights-based view of social interaction.

When Giuliani ran for office in 1989, he appealed directly to these disaffected white, formerly liberal voters. He even received support from the local Liberal Party and numerous well-known white liberals such as neighborhood activist Fran Reiter from the Upper West Side and journalist Wayne Barrett of the *Village Voice*.[11] In 1993, Giuliani campaigned on a platform of retaking control of the city from welfare recipients, criminals, and the homeless. These were code words for poor minorities, whom, the argument goes, liberal politicians had "coddled" with their poorly designed social programs, which had created a climate of sloth and permissiveness that encouraged unregulated or anomic individualism. Siegel criticizes what he calls the "riot ideology" in which blacks threaten social instability if their social policy demands are not met and argues that it was Giuliani's lack of tolerance of these demands that saved the city from the crime, homelessness, and incivility that were destroying it.

Other urbanists explain this transformation by emphasizing economic pressures on urban neighborhoods and cities that disrupted their social stability and encouraged a backlash against those whom they associated with the new conditions, namely, the homeless and disorderly. British geographer Neil Smith looks from this perspective at the role of race in the neighborhood-level backlashes against urban liberalism.[12] Unlike Rieder, Sleeper, and Siegel, who maintain that it was the liberal tolerance of extremist racial demands that hurt liberalism, Smith argues that local government, community activists, and property owners turned race into a social marker of the "dangerous classes," which led to a criminalization of the disorderly and homeless as part of a broader politics of reaction. He compares the early-1990s New York with nineteenth-century Paris after the Commune, in which middle-class residents reacted against progressive movements that they blamed for destabilizing the society. Smith describes this as a politics of "revanchism," which in New York took the form of middle-class residents seeking to exact revenge on the socially marginal, whom they blamed as the source of decline and instability in their neighborhoods:

> This revanchist antiurbanism represents a reaction against the supposed "theft" of the city, a desperate defense of a challenged phalanx of privileges, cloaked in the populist language of civic morality, family values and neighborhood security. More than anything the revanchist city expresses a race/class/gender terror felt by middle- and ruling-class whites who are suddenly stuck in place by a ravaged property market, the threat and reality of unemployment, the decimation of social services, and the emergence of minority and immigrant groups, as well as women, as powerful urban actors. It portends a vicious reaction against minorities, the working class, homeless people, the unemployed, women, gays and lesbians, immigrants.[13]

Smith argues that the recession of 1989–1993 led to an increase in crime and disorder. Upper- and middle-class whites resented this "loss of the city," which they blamed on poor minorities and the homeless. In liberal communities like the Lower East Side and the Upper West Side in Manhattan, a process of revanchism emerged in which middle-class residents criminalized minorities and the poor by calling for increased policing. Rudolph Giuliani responded to these calls by cutting back on social welfare programs and criminalizing the homeless and disorderly.

Smith explains the backlash against homeless people in the late

1980s by analyzing the immediate economic context of recession and gentrification and describes the role of racism and the desire for economic gain in driving some aspects of the backlash. To be a minority person in this period was to be marked as a potential source of crime, disorder, and incivility who must be controlled by an intensified use of the police. This is a populist analysis rooted in changes in the urban economy.

The reshaping of the city's economy and neighborhoods was as much the result of global as of regional economic forces. Gordon Macleod labels this economic restructuring and political backlash "neoliberalizing urbanism." He links the city's growing economic and social polarization to the uneven development inherent in neoliberal entrepreneurial economic development strategies favoring concentrated capital at the expense of the poor and middle classes. Macleod focuses on the ways in which downtown urban development creates social polarization, which leads to a large underclass, who in turn must be socially and spatially restricted from the newly developed spaces. Closed-circuit video-surveillance systems, antihomeless laws, and gated communities are elite responses to a social crisis, which they themselves created.[14]

David Harvey points out that this process of neoliberal economic development leads inexorably to social, economic, and political instability as wages and living conditions become polarized between the heavily subsidized sectors and the growing underclass of underpaid, underemployed, and jobless. He argues that it is this destabilization that breeds neoconservative politics as a strategy of managing this new level of disorder, difficulty, and destabilization. This is carried out by intensified criminal justice policies, such as mass incarceration and more aggressive policing, as well as punitive social welfare policies that blame the victim in the name of tough love measures based on an ethos of personal moral responsibility.[15]

In his analysis of the Lower East Side in the 1980s and 1990s, William Sites notes that city government was not just a victim of this process but also actively supported it through zoning and tax incentive structures favoring not only neighborhood gentrification but, more important, the transition from a manufacturing economy to one based on finance, corporate headquarters, and real estate. He calls this use of the state to redistribute resources away from social equality toward these wealthier sectors a "primitive globalization" akin to the idea of primitive accumulation in which the state, through confiscatory policies, helps concentrate capital in private hands in order to facilitate large-scale industrial investment.[16]

Each of these theorists is attempting to explain the complex interaction of political, economic, and cultural change. Some do this at a very local level, whereas other provide a more global perspective. The neoconservative theorists show how crime and disorder changed the urban culture, which brought populist calls for more punitive social policies. Urban political economists and critical criminologists describe how global and local economic changes created cultural crises that politicians and elites exploited to strengthen social control over the socially and economically marginal. All these competing urban and criminological analyses of the rise of revanchist politics and punitive policing agree that a dramatic urban transformation has been under way since the 1980s. The expanding urban underclass of the homeless and socially marginal and the reaction against them in the form of new laws and policing practices represent more than just a change in urban policing. Rather, they are a symptom of a broad shift in urban politics in response to the urban cultural and economic crisis. Neoconservatives contend that this crisis is the result of the moral deregulation of the 1960s in which liberals allowed and, in some cases, encouraged the destabilizing political demands and cultural practices of the disenfranchised in the form of welfare dependency, anomic individualism, and criminality. They also criticize liberalism for sacrificing the stability of middle-class white neighborhoods to pursue the racial integration of schools and housing. That is, liberalism becomes a stand-in for the notion of centralized governmental authority acting at the expense of the law-abiding, hardworking middle class.

In many ways, this is an accurate though partial critique of urban liberalism's tendency to rely on centralized expertise at the expense of popular participation and its commitment to the rhetoric of social tolerance, though without providing enough social stability to make this tolerance acceptable to the middle classes. Urban liberal policies have often callously disregarded the needs of poor and middle-class communities in their efforts to engineer the urban landscape in a way that is, in theory, designed to benefit exactly those communities. Accordingly, what is lacking in this analysis is any consideration of the economic imperatives driving this process.

The more economic arguments also are in many ways a critique of liberalism. Leftist urbanists and criminologists maintain that liberal economic policies are at the root of the urban crisis and the rise of the new punitiveness. The entrepreneurial pursuit of centralized corporate economic development strategies therefore are responsible for the rise of the new urban underclass that has destabilized urban neighborhoods and public spaces. Place-based competition for increasingly mobile flows of investment capital have forced liberals to mortgage their commitment to greater social and economic equality, creating what Don Mitchell calls the "postjustice" city.[17] It is this process of social and economic polarization that gave rise to the repressive policing of homeless and disorderly people in order to maintain the stability of its new entrepreneurial spaces. Neoliberalizing urbanism is a single process of the entrepreneurial subsidizing of corporate risk, social and economic polarization, and repressive control mechanisms. What this approach lacks is an analysis of the rejection of liberalism by middle-class and poor communities in favor of more repressive social policies. The "postjustice" city thus is a response to middle-class dissension as much as it is a strategy of elites to maintain their control of core commercial spaces.

What is needed is a critique of urban liberalism in the neoliberal period that incorporates elements of the analyses of both the neoconservatives and the left. The failure of urban liberalism as a governing strategy is the result of the defection of both elites and the middle classes. Any analysis of its downfall, therefore, must look at its failings from both perspectives. This necessitates a dialectical analysis of the contradictions underlying urban liberalism and how they came to the breaking point in the form of the urban crisis of the 1980s and 1990s. This combination of global and local analysis is what Michael Burawoy calls a "global ethnography" because it encourages us to look at complex local events as being situated in a larger political and economic context and not just as a reflection of it.[18] Decisions by communities, local governments, and economic actors make a difference in how neoliberalism is expressed in local spaces. To emphasize its contingent character, Aihwa Ong labels this "neoliberalism as exception," reflecting the specificity of local politics and values shaping economic, political, and cultural strategies in a globalizing world.[19]

My investigation of quality-of-life politics in New York focuses on the ways in which local actors pursued and were limited by their strategies in the context of neoliberalism. Urban liberal politicians, neighborhood leaders, and government bureaucrats all attempted to react to the changing pressures of global neoliberalism in different ways. Consequently, I explain the failures of the previous model of urban liberalism to address these pressures and how a new model emerged out of its contradictions.

Three primary contradictions in urban liberalism contributed to and accelerated the urban crisis that led to the rise of quality-of-life politics. First, while urban liberals were willing to spend billions of dollars subsidizing corporate economic development, they treated homelessness and disorder as social problems to be solved by poorly funded social programs rather than as symptoms of their own misguided economic development strategies. Second, while they supported the concept of community empowerment, their economic and social policies were designed and administered by centralized bureaucratic experts, with almost no meaningful input by the community. Third, even though they supported calls for social tolerance of diversity, urban liberals did little to create economic opportunities for diverse groups to coexist in a socially stable way.

The rest of this book is organized around three themes. The first is a theoretical and empirical investigation of urban liberalism and its contradictions. The second looks at the ways in which political leaders, economic elites, and local communities regarded these contradictions. The third theme is a description of the new quality-of-life approach that replaced urban liberalism. These themes run throughout the chapters of this book. Chapter 2 describes the quality-of-life-based urban politics by reviewing its philosophical and rhetorical roots. Chapter 3 looks in more detail at urban liberalism and its central contradictions. Chapter 4 traces the rise of disorder and homelessness in New York City and how, in general terms, urban liberal administrations dealt with it. Chapter 5 explores the first contradiction of urban liberalism by analyzing economic development strategies in New York City leading up to the crisis of the late 1990s. Chapter 6 discusses how the second contradiction played itself out in the form of urban policing. I show how the centralized expertise of the police department throughout the 1980s failed to deal effectively with the growing disorder crisis and how this contributed to the quality-of-life backlash. Chapter 7 looks at the third contradiction by describing the rise of mass homelessness and the inability of urban liberals to reduce either the amount of homelessness or its impact on the daily life of urban residents. I continue this discussion by demonstrating how the quality-of-life political backlash emerged out of neighborhood frustrations at the inability of urban liberalism to address the disorder. In the conclusion, I consider the dilemmas faced by urban liberals and some of the theoretical and practical alternatives to both the urban liberal and quality-of-life approaches to urban governance.

2

Defining the Quality-of-Life Paradigm

In 1993 Rudolph Giuliani ran for mayor of New York City on a platform of improving the city's quality of life. Citing a study by James Q. Wilson and George Kelling, he claimed that the solution to the city's disorder problem was to get tough on the minor incivilities dominating everyday life in the city.[1] His targets included squeegee men, homeless encampments, and aggressive panhandlers. By 1998, quality of life had become the dominant theme of the Giuliani administration, and it was used to frame almost every important political issue from education reform to sanitation and, in the process, redefined the notion of livability in the city:

> Quality of life is a process, not a destination. It's a way of living, not a goal. . . . Fundamentally, it means believing once again in our ability constantly to improve the City. . . . Quality of life is about focusing on the things that make a difference in the everyday life of all New Yorkers in order to restore this spirit of optimism. . . . If people don't see improvements in their individual lives, if they have to put up with incivility and disrespect for their rights every day, they will remain basically pessimistic about the future of the City, even if overall crime is dramatically down. But if a sense of tangible improvement reaches millions of lives, and millions of people understand that the City cares about their annoyances and is working hard to protect their rights, then more and more people begin to feel the true optimism of the City, and the City is moving in the right direction. We begin to feel that together, we all have a stake in the City. This is what the idea of a civil society is all about.[2]

This broad use of the term *quality of life*, however, leaves the exact nature of the term and its usage unclear. Only a careful review of the ideas underpinning its use and the practices associated with it will make its true nature apparent.

Quality of life is, in essence, a new paradigm of urban social control. A paradigm should be understood as a set of practices and conceptualizations, in this case defining social policy as the control of social disorder in public urban spaces. This paradigm is a coherent way of thinking about a wide array of social problems, as it indicates both a social theory of the roots of social problems and the form that solutions to the problem should take. That is, it points to a set of concrete social practices to be carried out in specific places under specific conditions.

"Quality of life" represents a desire by urban residents to be free from the dirt, disorder, and incivilities that were widespread in the 1980s and 1990s. At its best, it holds out this possibility for all urban residents. In practice, however, quality of life created a stark division between residents' reasonable desires to be free of fear and harassment and the belief that the way to achieve this is by systematically removing anyone perceived to be a potential source of these problems. The primary victims of this process have been homeless people and other marginalized people living in public spaces.

The Development of the Quality-of-Life Paradigm

The social policies associated with traditional urban liberalism are quite different from the quality-of-life approach seen in the neoconservative administrations of Mayors Rudolph Giuliani, Frank Jordan (of San Francisco) , Bret Schundler (of Jersey City), and Richard Riordan (of Los Angeles). Their positions were to reject the central role of the state as a force for both social reform and planning and the culture of tolerance. Instead, they relied on market principles through the privatization of public spaces and services and an overall shrinkage of government. In addition to privatization, they supported, at least rhetorically, greater community and business control of the delivery of government services and of planning at the expense of expert planners. They also criticized the centralized and universal orientation of urban liberalism as elitist in regard to the immediate local needs of residents and businesses. They were unwilling to make long-term investments in social programs in the hope that they would reduce deviance, arguing instead for short-term

punitive measures to restore order. Finally, they sharply limited tolerance of overt signs of disorderly and disruptive behavior.

Possibly the most dramatic shift was the mayors' rejection of therapeutic models of personal rehabilitation for both criminal justice and
welfare policy. Rather than focusing on the rehabilitation of "deviant"
individuals through the treatment of mental health and substance abuse,
training in life skills, and management of social work cases, they decided that individual behavior should be modified by punitive strategies
that kept people in line through the threat of economic or legal penalties or that physically removed people from locations where their behavior was disruptive. Rather than developing methods of reintegrating
"deviants" back into society, they wanted to exclude them.

This development can be most clearly seen in the area of criminal justice. Neoconservatives rejected the idea that criminals could be rehabilitated through therapeutic efforts. Instead, they argued that some people
are fundamentally evil and that it thus was impossible for them to develop into "productive members of society." So if the project of rehabilitation were foreclosed, these people had to be removed from society or
else constantly monitored to ensure their compliance with the legal order. Their noncompliance, furthermore, could lead to penal incapacita-
tion and, in extremis, the death penalty. A similar shift occurred in welfare policy, in which strategies to improve conditions for the poor
through transfer payments were replaced by negative reinforcement and
incarceration and reliance on market forces to create individual economic opportunity.[3]

The last element of this transition was the rejection of civil liber-
tarianism in favor of communitarianism. The "permissiveness" of civil
libertarians was blamed for a wide variety of urban social ills. Allowing individuals to act outside the bounds of "community standards" of
proper behavior, it was argued, opened the door to a general decline in
moral standards and destabilized local communities. The freedom of individuals was trumped by the desire of communities for stability, homo-
geneity, and social order.

The results of the paradigm shift have been paradoxical, leading to
both "community control" and larger police forces and both volun-
tarism and criminalization. Mayor Giuliani campaigned on a platform
reducing the role of government in favor of the private sector. The two
areas of government that were expanded were tax incentives for corporate expansion and huge increases in the police budget. In 1998 the

New York Police Department (NYPD) reached a record high of more than forty thousand officers, and police overtime expenses grew significantly. Finally, rather than reducing social services bureaucracies, the emphasis of these agencies slowly shifted from providing services to policing those receiving benefits.

The effect on the homeless has been a broad criminalization of their everyday lives. Increasing demands are made on those in the shelter system, but without new sources of support. Shelter rules have become tighter, and the threat of eviction always is present. For those on the street, the very acts of sleeping and sitting have become crimes. Constant police harassment has driven them out of the city's central areas, thereby creating an additional hardship for the homeless by hampering outreach efforts, breaking down informal support networks, and, most important, forcing thousands of people into the courts and jails. Officials of the New York Department of Correction acknowledged that the city's jails now house more homeless people each night than do even the largest shelters. Thirty percent of inmates reported being homeless before being incarcerated in a system with a daily average of 14,000 inmates[4] at a cost of $100,000 a year per jail bed.[5] The effect on the general population of this spatial decentralization and social atomization of the homeless has been one of "out of sight, out of mind."

Origins of the Term "Quality of Life"

The term *quality of life* did not originate as a rhetorical repository for a new urban conservatism. In fact, its early usage was suffused with social optimism befitting the late 1960s when it emerged. In this period of its usage, it represented the government's hopes of solving the problems of the socially disadvantaged through programs that would directly improve their social condition. But by the late 1980s, this positive and universal outlook had been replaced by a conservative orientation favoring the needs of the middle and upper classes at the expense of the socially marginal.

"Quality of Life" as a National Idea

When President Lyndon B. Johnson launched his War on Poverty in the mid-1960s, he largely conceptualized urban problems in terms of reducing poverty. From 1964 to 1968 in most major cities, the growing concern about the conditions of poor and minority urban residents was punctuated by outbursts of rioting. This urban crisis centered the discussion of quality of life on dealing with the conditions that gave rise to these threats to the stability of urban America. As a result, political discussions of the urban crisis, including crime and disorder—such as the Kerner Commission report commissioned by President Johnson to investigate the causes of the urban riots—highlighted the need for remedial programs for minorities and the poor.[6] During the Johnson administration, the rhetorical and strategic emphasis was on using government to improve conditions for the urban disadvantaged. There was a hopeful discourse about the possibility of positive change for the worst-off in society, whom it placed at the center of the debate.

In 1965, President Johnson proposed, and Congress approved, the creation of the cabinet-level Department of Housing and Urban Development (HUD), which broadened the conceptualization of urban problems from poverty to a wide range of urban ills, including housing and community development. In a letter to Congress urging the creation of the department, Johnson discussed "quality of life" in terms of improving living conditions for the disadvantaged:

> Let us be clear about the core of this problem. The problem is people and the *quality of the lives* they lead. We want to build not just housing units but neighborhoods; not just to construct schools, but to educate children; not just to raise income, but to create beauty and end the poisoning of our environment. . . . The problems of the city are problems of housing and education. They involve increasing employment and ending poverty. They call for beauty and nature, recreation and an end to discrimination.[7] (emphasis added)

There is no mention of the needs of other groups or social classes; instead, the focus is on improving conditions for the poor.

In 1966, Congress and HUD developed the concept further in their first major initiative, the Demonstration Cities and Metropolitan Development Act of 1966. The guide for this new program was entitled *Improving the Quality of Urban Life* and states:

> The Congress hereby finds and declares that *improving the quality of urban life* is the most critical domestic problem facing the United States.

The persistence of widespread urban slums and blight, the concentration of persons of low income in older urban areas, and the unmet needs for additional housing and community facilities and services arising from the rapid expansion of our urban population have resulted in a marked deterioration in the quality of the environment and the lives of large numbers of our people while the Nation as a whole prospers.[8] (emphasis added)

The Program Guide points out that under this law, requests for funding by cities should contain plans for comprehensive programs that include the following elements:

(a) to rebuild or revitalize large slum and blighted areas; (b) to expand housing; (c) to expand job and income opportunities; (d) to reduce dependence on welfare payments; (e) to improve educational facilities and programs; (f) to combat disease and ill health; (g) to reduce the incidence of crime and delinquency; (h) to enhance recreational and cultural opportunities; (i) to establish better access between homes and jobs; and (j) in general, to improve living conditions for the people who live in these areas.[9]

These criteria clearly indicate that the program is directed at the disadvantaged and is intended to improve cities by bringing up the people at the bottom. The goal is to obtain these improvements through new scientifically created social programs rather than punitive measures. It is forward looking and expert driven, an orientation that can be clearly seen in the HUD secretary's introduction to the Program Guide:

The objective of this demonstration is to test whether we have the capacity to understand the causes of human and physical blight, and the skills and the commitment to restore quality to older neighborhoods, and hope and dignity to their people. This program requires courage: Courage to understand the basic causes of the problem, and courage to seek the solution in the neighborhood, in the city or even in the metropolitan area, as the facts may require. I have confidence in the capacity and determination of the citizens and officials of our cities and towns, and in their willingness to work together to improve the quality of urban life.[10]

In the late 1960s and early 1970s, a number of books using the term *quality of life* began appearing that addressed areas of concern different from those at HUD but consistent with the idea of focusing on the needs of those in distress. These books attempted to deal with important contemporary problems through improved understanding and a concern for the broader human condition. As an example, *Health, a Quality of Life* makes the following statement:

> The purpose of this book goes beyond the reporting of comprehensive advance made in the health sciences. . . . Issues such as automobile safety, drug use, abortion, food faddism, sex values, and the nature of human sexuality are included. Honest, straight forward presentations of these often controversial topics are designed to assist the young adult in developing points of view in these important health areas. It is further hoped that this text will mark an end to those placid, innocuous writings that pretend these issues do not exist.[11]

The Quality of Life: Nineteen Essays, by professors at Cornell University, addresses a range of social issues:

> Each was written by a distinguished member of the Cornell faculty, each addresses itself to a topic clearly affecting the quality of life, and each strives for a better understanding of a particular set of problems. . . . They have been put together in a book because, it seems to me, they speak for a university that seeks to share its thoughts *with those who also believe that knowledge about life is a condition for securing its quality.* (emphasis added)[12]

The Quality of Urban Life is a collection of twenty papers on areas such as the urban environment, planning, health, education, the arts, and urban order and calls for an investigation of the possibilities of "progress" and "improvement":

> A major purpose of this volume is to emphasize and explore the diversity of concerns which must be dealt with if we are to stop evading an assessment of what we have wrought, both intentionally and inadvertently, in building a society of cities. In saying this, the editors by no means wish to imply that the challenges to "make sense" of our

multiplicity of dilemmas should be avoided. Indeed, the concluding section of the volume contains several efforts to suggest some sensible ways in which *we might begin to reconstruct the urban order* (or disorder) to *enhance the quality of urban life.* (emphasis added)[13]

The task of this book was to explore the complex nature of urban problems in order to develop comprehensive, forward-looking solutions.

These efforts helped policymakers think of urban problems as interconnected and related to the total social, economic, and political environment. Their progressive orientation, however, was turned on its head by the next presidential administration, which moved away from a concern about the urban poor and discussed instead the "environment" in broad terms that applied to the concerns of middle-class and nonurban residents. Rhetorically, strategically, and politically, President Richard M. Nixon initiated a shift away from liberalism at the national level.

In his 1970 State of the Union message, President Nixon declared that there was no contradiction between properly managed commercial prosperity and quality of life:

> Now I realize that the argument is often made that there is a fundamental *contradiction between economic growth and the quality of life,* so that to have one we must forsake the other. The answer is not to abandon growth but to redirect it. For example, we should turn toward ending congestion and eliminate smog the same reservoir of inventive genius that created them in the first place. (emphasis added)[14]

Nixon tried to concentrate the nation's energies on dealing with the consequences of growth without challenging its economic and governmental underpinnings. In an appeal to his core Republican constituencies, he made it clear that this was not just an urban problem: "We will carry our concern with the quality of life in America to the farms as well as the suburb, to the village as well as to the city. We must create a new rural environment which will not only stem the migration to urban centers but reverse it."[15] One of the primary goals of this 1970 State of the Union message was to redirect government attention and public discourse away from the racial and urban tensions of the 1960s. But Nixon made almost no reference to the urban crisis that, except for the war in Vietnam, had dominated public policy concerns in the Johnson administration. Instead, he raised a more universal concern about pollution and environmental degradation. By focusing on the environment, he gave "quality of life" a more conservative meaning in the sense of conserving or recreating a past environmental condition. Nixon thus succeeded in both shifting the focus from the disadvantaged to the middle class and placing government in the role of preserving and recapturing the past rather than building a new future.

This theme can be seen in the use of the term by the Environmental Protection Agency (EPA), which Nixon created. The EPA issued two major reports during this period. The first was entitled *The Quality of Life Concept: A Potential New Tool for Decision-Makers,* followed shortly thereafter by *Quality of Life Indicators in U.S. Metropolitan Areas, 1970.*[16] Both these reports make an effort to develop quantitative measures of a broad collection of environmental factors that affect people's quality of daily life, including health, education, and pollution, as well as economic, political, and social conditions. This approach provided a new framework for conceptualizing social problems that was not specifically urban or focused on the disadvantaged.

"Quality of Life" in New York City

Republican John Lindsay was the first New York City mayor to regularly use the term *quality of life.* During the early 1960s, his predecessor, Mayor Robert Wagner, followed the federal pattern and discussed urban problems in terms of alleviating poverty. In 1964, Wagner initiated a major set of urban initiatives, designed to capture some of President Johnson's Great Society spending. All these programs existed under the heading of the "War against Poverty."

When Lindsay took over as mayor in 1966, he continued to use much of the same language as Wagner had. During the late 1960s, however, the social context and Lindsay's political ambitions had changed. The threat of rioting in New York City had become a major concern, and in 1969 Lindsay considered running for president. Accordingly, he began referring to the city's problems in broader terms. Thus when New York State announced budget cuts for the city, he responded by linking concerns about urban unrest to a general decline in living conditions for the entire city:

> The cost [of these budget cuts] to the city in terms of quality of life and increased tensions is incalculable. Not only does it cut deeply into some

of our most basic programs and agencies, but it does so in such a manner as to undermine many of the most important municipal improvements of the last half decade.[17]

Although Lindsay clearly mentions concern about the poor and possible social disorder, he has broadened the discussion to include all New Yorkers.

In his 1970 inauguration speech, Lindsay highlighted efforts to give neighborhoods responsibility for charting their own course because they "set the quality of life for the city."[18] He continued:

> If the Bay Ridge homeowner is uncertain of his neighborhood's future, if the Harlem mother does not know if her child is learning at school, if the Forest Hills family fears to walk the streets at night, if the Morrisania office worker cannot travel home at night in comfort or even decency, then the city is not working for its citizens.[19]

At this point, poor neighborhoods had been put on the same footing as all other neighborhoods in terms of their needs and their relationship to the overall health of the city. By 1972, the transition from concern about the disadvantaged to concern about the middle class was complete. Moreover, Lindsay introduced business interests into "quality of life." In announcing the approval of a controversial and expensive pedestrian transit mall on Madison Avenue in midtown Manhattan, Lindsay stated that "cities are beginning to redesign their core areas to favor man on foot and so have revitalized business and enhanced quality of life in downtown areas."[20]

Following the academic literature, Lindsay established *quality of life* as a term referring to generalized urban problems with an emphasis on the "environment." This environment, however, refers primarily to pollution, amenities, and aesthetics. The main cause of these problems was not racism or social inequality but a failure to deal adequately with the consequences of growth and prosperity through planning and infrastructure investment: "The principal objective of my administration has been to improve the quality of life for this city's residents. To achieve this goal required a massive overhauling of the city's services system and equally massive investment in a better physical environment."[21]

In 1974, Abraham Beame replaced Lindsay as mayor. Beame was a

Democrat who took over in a period of financial contraction that led to New York City's fiscal crisis in the mid-1970s, in which the city came close to defaulting on its debts as a result of severe budget shortfalls. To stabilize the city's finances, broad budget cuts were instituted, and a state-controlled financial control board was created to oversee the city's operation.[22] Beame consequently dropped almost all reference to the term *quality of life*, which, for Lindsay, had indicated a forward-looking orientation. Instead, he was forced to fight a backward-looking, defensive war to maintain city services: "The prospect of New York undergoing a trauma of massive layoffs, service reductions, and drastic curtailment of programs which added to the *quality of life* in this city is unthinkable to me" (emphasis added).[23] This fundamental shift from forward to backward looking shaped the use of this term for the next twenty years.

Mayor Edward Koch also was slow to take up the term *quality of life*. Although his administration, which began in 1978, continued to be saddled by the city's fiscal crisis, he tried to deal with the city's growing social problems—crime, sanitation, and homelessness—by stabilizing the city's finances and developing new programs. The effects of the fiscal crisis, however, continued to take a toll on the city. Not only were programs for the poor reduced, but basic services, on which the middle and upper classes relied, began to deteriorate as well. By 1980 the city had lost 25 percent of its overall workforce, including 50 percent of its sanitation workers, 20 percent of its police force, and 19,000 teachers.[24] Deferred maintenance became the rule for the city's infrastructure, leading by the mid-1980s to significant problems with roads and bridges, parks, and public transportation. The city closed four of its public hospitals and had to turn over the bulk of the City University of New York system to the state. Increased crime and homelessness and reduced sanitation and infrastructure upkeep gave the entire city a feeling of social and physical disorder.

Not until late 1981 did Koch start to use the term *quality of life,* and he did so as a direct response to constituencies that were beginning to lose faith in him. After Koch attempted to blame his problems on Lindsay, who responded that it was Koch who had let the city's "quality of life" decline, even though he had had to face major urban problems of his own.[25] Middle-class residents made known their opinions through a series of increasingly contentious neighborhood meetings.

At one such meeting in Queens, residents accused the mayor of ignoring "middle-class quality-of-life issues" and of having "abandoned the homeowner."[26] Finally, business groups increasingly threatened to leave the city because of "quality-of-life concerns."

In response, Koch began using the term during his reelection bid in 1981. In campaign stops, he pledged to "work in the next four years to improve the quality of life in this city."[27] In his September 1981 Mayor's Management Report, Koch added a new section called "Quality of Life Enforcement."[28] This section outlined efforts to keep streets clean, reduce canine waste and sidewalk vendors, increase enforcement against street drug dealers, give peace-officer status to school guards, enforce traffic laws, and beef up the Environmental Control Board. There was no mention of homelessness, panhandling, or other minor disorderly conduct.

By 1984, Koch had transformed his use of "quality of life" from expressing concern about overall conditions in the city to creating the basis for a series of law enforcement efforts. In what was a precursor to many of the developments in the Giuliani administration, Koch created a work camp for minor offenders, tried to clean up Times Square, and initiated a number of "quality-of-life programs" in the police department. This last consisted of new traffic and narcotics enforcement efforts, greater patrol strength, and the first stages of the Community Patrol Officer Program, which raised the number of officers walking beats and working with communities on problem-solving efforts, as opposed to confining them to 911 emergency responses.[29] This new approach indicated an awareness of the underlying principles of the "broken windows" theory but did not fully embrace its enforcement priorities. That had to wait almost another ten years.

During the next few years, Koch continued to play up his tough, enforcement-oriented approach to improving conditions in the city. Although sanitation services and police enforcement continued to be enhanced, conditions failed to improve. Instead, the advent of widespread homelessness besieged the city and further degraded social and aesthetic conditions. The term *quality of life* reemerged as the shibboleth of his enemies on the left and right. Many middle-class New Yorkers continued to complain about the loss of services and the impact of homelessness on their daily lives. At the same time, David Dinkins, then the Manhattan borough president, assailed Koch for failing to constrain the real estate boom of the mid-1980s and its environmental effects on the city:

> Is it not our responsibility, as public officials, to leave to the next generation a city of human scale and an environment that preserves the quality of life equal to that which our predecessors left us? Manhattan real estate, in particular, has become such a hot market that the sheer magnitude of the money involved appears to overwhelm any balanced value system. For overdevelopment brings with it real costs: the loss of air and light, wear and tear on urban infrastructure, pedestrian and vehicle gridlock, and the inability of sanitation and transport services to keep up with demands.[30]

This is a very different set of problems than those raised by Queens homeowners and midtown business leaders. While Koch tried to address the concerns raised by all constituencies, he was both unable to do so and not totally committed to the task. Instead, he insisted that the city's overall financial health had improved, especially in relation to the fiscal crisis that preceded him:

> When the mayor's potential challengers decry the declining quality of life here, Koch has a simple rejoinder: Things are better now than when he took office in 1978. He is running against the fiscal crisis of that era, since it provides a better benchmark for his tenure than the mounting problems of schools, subways, crack, street crime and homelessness. Even those turned off by his "acerbic" approach, Koch said, should recognize that he has "rebuilt the city of New York" and "put us back on the map as an international capital," Should anyone try to drown out that message, as happened toward the end of the Queens town meeting, Koch simply raises his voice. "The city is prosperous!" he shouted at his audience. "We have the lowest unemployment rate in 17 years! There isn't anybody who wants a job who can't get a job! You wanna [*sic*] go back to the old days?"[31]

Koch wanted to be judged on these larger economic measures rather than on the cleanliness and safety of the streets. He had been pursuing a "global cities" economic development strategy based on enhancing New York's role as a headquarters for multinational corporations and finance. New Yorkers and the liberal *New York Times,* however, were not satisfied with that approach, and Koch lost the Democratic primary to David Dinkins, who then won the 1989 general election.

During the 1989 campaign, Dinkins was aware of the currency of "quality of life" but preferred to shift the focus from the middle classes to the disadvantaged:

> Asked to speak to the concerns of the middle class, Mr. Dinkins did not present a plan for police coverage. Nor did he discuss jobs or the economy, cleaner streets, safer subways, improved management, lower taxes or tougher treatment for criminals, as the other candidates have. Instead of offering specific solutions, he offered the conclusion "that quality-of-life issues are important to all of us" and turned back the discussion to the poor.[32]

Dinkins had no choice but to acknowledge the widespread use of the term. He tried, however, to downplay it and its appeal to the middle classes and instead to focus on the needs of more disadvantaged groups.

After winning the election, Dinkins tried to back away from using the term. But he was unable to do so because it had become so central a part of the political lexicon that even a longtime liberal like Ruth Messinger, the new Manhattan borough president and Dinkins ally, convened a quality-of-life task force to address the public impact of homelessness as well as noise and sanitation problems.[33] Dinkins, however, continued to try to recast "quality of life" as a social improvement program for the poor: "Some say quality of life is best defined by spotless parks and litter-free roadways. But for me it is best exemplified by a happy, healthy baby or by a teen-ager with a diploma in hand and a sparkle in the eye."[34]

This approach pleased some of Dinkins's core urban liberal constituency, but as we will see in chapters 6 and 7, many residents, including many African Americans, felt besieged by the growing crime and disorder. Dinkins was therefore forced to address the city's growing crime and disorder directly, and he did this with two initiatives enacted in 1991. The first was his Safe Streets–Safe City Program, which provided for a dramatic increase in the number of police officers and social services paid for by a series of new, dedicated taxes.[35] The second was the forceful and high-profile eviction by the police of a homeless encampment in Tompkins Square Park. Both these measures indicated that Dinkins was attempting to respond to the calls for improving the middle class's quality of life. But these measures also continued to appeal to social programs as the true long-term solution to these problems. This emphasis on slow-moving social rehabilitation efforts, however, left Dinkins vulnerable to a quality-of-life proponent who forcefully embraced middle-class concerns about crime and disorder and disdained the efforts of social workers and government bureaucrats.

During his 1993 campaign, Rudolph Giuliani repeatedly emphasized his concern with "quality of life" as a way of distinguishing himself from Dinkins. Much of the impetus for this came from Giuliani's interactions with the neoconservative Manhattan Institute, where he regularly attended lunchtime talks preaching tough love for the homeless and those on welfare.[36] The Manhattan Institute began promoting the political concept of quality of life in 1990 as part of its free-market anti-liberal approach to urban social problems, which included support for school vouchers, workfare, and overall cuts in social spending.[37] Giuliani's campaign themes began to reflect these views and can be summed up in two of his main campaign commercials. The first contains the following quotation from Giuliani, and the second was described in detail by the *New York Times*:

Some people call this an outer borough. I call it part of the heart and soul of New York City. I've lived here in Woodside, Queens. I was born in Brooklyn, lived in Queens, went to school in the Bronx, lived in Manhattan. I've lived or gone to school in just about every part of New York City. It's a city that I love. It's a city that I see as a city of neighborhoods. We have to listen more to the people who live in these neighborhoods in New York City; we have to listen to them when they tell us about the deterioration of the school system. And we have to fight back to make the New York City public schools the best in the country again. We have to listen to them when they tell us they want *a higher quality of life, a cleaner city, a better city, a city that draws more business and has more jobs.* We have to listen to them when they tell us that the city is crushing the small businesses of New York City. I mean, after all, that's the heart and soul of the city, the small businesses. That's what we're being told by the people who live in these neighborhoods. I've been there, I've grown up there, that's where I come from, that's where my family comes from, and I've been listening to them for the last four years. And that's what they've been telling me (emphasis added).[38]

The television and radio spots, which began the day after the Democratic mayoral primary, have coincided with an emphasis by Mr. Giuliani on what his campaign calls "quality-of-life" issues. He has assailed "the disorder that is driving the city down," promising a crackdown on street drug dealers, panhandlers and menacing "squeegee men." And last week he unveiled a policy to curtail services drastically to some of the city's homeless by setting a 90-day limit on many shelter stays, in an effort to free up funds to work with the chronically homeless. The themes, Mr. Giuliani's aides say, seek to put Mayor David N. Dinkins on the defensive about the state of the city he presides over. "It takes the campaign to the record," said Mr. Giuliani's chief strategist, David Garth. *"Do you feel safer? Do you really believe that crime is down? Are you going to have to have a searchlight to walk in the streets and to step over the bodies of the homeless who need help?"* (emphasis added)[39]

The emphasis here is on the fate of both middle-class neighborhoods and businesses. The well-being of the poor and the homeless is of no concern, and the homeless are to be swept up for the benefit of the rest of the city. Giuliani's strategy of blaming the city's physical and social deterioration on Dinkins's tolerance of disorder was successful, and it also set the groundwork for a series of punitive measures that Giuliani undertook once in office.

One of the new mayor's first initiatives was the creation of "independent living plans." This proposal called for limiting to ninety days the amount of time that people could stay in city shelters, requiring homeless people to agree to a treatment regimen, and making them pay part of the cost of their shelter. This was offered as a tough love measure to force homeless people to make plans for changing their overall situation rather than being allowed to continue in their "negative" behavior pattern: "Giuliani asserted that his tougher approach, which he said shows more love and compassion for the homeless than they have ever been shown by previous administrations, would reduce the city's homeless population by giving them more options and making them more responsible for their fate."[40] This new program made clear Giuliani's desire to deal with homelessness through punitive sanctions rather than increased services.

At the same time that this policy was put in place, the mayor began to reduce support for housing and treatment programs. The most serious was the scaling back of the city's subsidy program to landlords to house homeless families:

> Three city agencies have eliminated or tightened housing placement and referral programs, lengthening waits for subsidized housing to months. And the only evening intake unit, in the Bronx, still warehouses 100 families or more a night despite the city's attempt just this week to screen the homeless through a telephone hotline.[41]

The mayor's inability to provide basic services, however, meant that he was soon forced to back away from the time limits and case management rules.

The other major quality-of-life development during the early part of this administration was in policing. Giuliani hired former Transit Police Chief William Bratton to be commissioner of the New York Police Department. Bratton had made a reputation for himself at Transit by implementing a series of "broken windows"–based policing tactics, including driving the homeless out of the system and aggressive enforcing fare-beating laws. Bratton and his top staff developed a series of new crime-fighting strategies for the NYPD, the fifth of which was known as "Reclaiming the Public Spaces of New York." This document specifically mentions the "broken windows" theory and calls for restoring order through the aggressive enforcement of minor crimes such as prostitution, graffiti, loud music, public drinking, and "the specific crime and quality-of-life problems facing each community."[42] It also called for the passage of a "quality-of-life legislative agenda" which included new laws against aggressive panhandling and panhandling near ATM machines. The latter was passed in September 1996.

Tough love from social service providers and increased enforcement by police placed homeless people in a world full of punitive sanctions. The message was loud and clear. The way to improve the quality of life of the middle and upper classes was to make the lives of homeless people untenable in public spaces. Solving homelessness was not the goal; rather, the goal was reducing the visible impact of homelessness on the rest of the city.

Ideological Underpinnings of Quality of Life

The quality-of-life paradigm did not develop all at once or come into existence fully formed. Instead, its origins can be traced through a series of academic works on urban disorder and crime, on changing conceptions of the urban crisis by local and national politicians, and on how the mass media portrayed the crisis and its solutions. Eventually, these different groups and their approaches began to cohere around a consistent set of ideas and practices that attempted to overcome the contradictions of the urban liberal paradigm.

During the 1980s, a number of academics tried to explain the rise of disorder and crime in American cities and suggested ways of reducing it. Their theories were based on the idea that public civility had declined because of a reduction in the ability of urban neighborhoods to enforce standards of behavior both formally and informally. The solution therefore was to find new mechanisms of social control centered more on the problematic behaviors and less on the structural factors contributing to the overall urban crisis.

The Broken Windows Theory

Following on the heels of the 1970s urban crisis, James Q. Wilson and George Kelling proposed the "broken windows" theory, arguing that the unchallenged presence of minor visible signs of social and physical disorder could lead to more serious crime problems. They pointed out that when someone knocks the glass out of a window and the window is quickly repaired, there is unlikely to be further vandalism. But if the window is not repaired, then it is seen as a fair target, and soon all the windows are smashed. Similarly, if a neighborhood is able to enforce behavior standards against minor disorders, more serious problems will be unlikely to develop. Conversely, if the disorders are left unchecked, the neighborhood will be viewed as unregulated, and more serious disorders will ensue, leading to higher numbers of serious crimes and a further surrendering of the public space to disorderly people.[43]

Wesley Skogan built on this latter part of the analysis, arguing that the unchecked presence of disorder was a primary cause of neighborhood decline. Communities that failed to establish a strong public moral order were likely to be besieged by crime. This high level of crime and disorder, in turn, would discourage the constant reinvestment in homes and business that communities require in order to remain vibrant. In effect, Skogan reversed the 1960s argument that unchecked poverty generates crime to maintain that unchecked crime generates poverty.[44]

This raised the issue of how community definitions of disorder are determined. Since the populations of many urban neighborhoods are diverse, the standards for proper behavior are often contested. In the situations that Skogan looked at, he noted that the prevailing views tended to be those of whites more than those of people of color, and those of homeowners more than those of renters. As it stands now, the group making this determination is the police department, which generally lacks the mechanisms and institutions for adjudicating complex cultural and moral conflicts within communities. Moreover, the police have historical biases that favor merchants and longtime homeowners as legitimate spokespeople for community standards.

George Kelling and Catherine Coles reviewed several efforts to implement broken windows policies in New York, San Francisco, Baltimore, and Seattle. They argue that where order-maintenance activities have started with good problem-solving research and are tailored to the specific dynamics of the problem, they have been successful. They point out that community concerns must be prioritized in this process, first because the earlier failure to acknowledge these concerns has contributed to suburban flight and second because communities are crucial sources of information about the nature and sources of local disorder and crime.[45]

Kelling and Cole's notion of community involvement in the examples they use raises another problem with this approach. In each of the examples—with the exception of the Baltimore neighborhood of Boyde Booth, where the community played a central role—the efforts to maintain order were initiated by government or business on behalf of the community's perceived interests. Business improvement districts in New York, Mayor Jordan's "cleanup" of San Francisco, and Seattle's restoration of its central business district all are elite-driven efforts to restore centrally located, high-property-value locations, not efforts to revitalize troubled neighborhoods where crime rates and poverty rates are high.

The case of Baltimore is especially instructive. Kelling and Coles describe two different order-maintenance initiatives there. The first involved a community working with the city to try to retake their neighborhood from drug dealing and the violent crime associated with it; the second was a business-led effort to reduce the presence of homeless people in the central business district. The residents of the Boyde Booth neighborhood were faced with a major crime problem more than a minor disorder problem. Their response was to increase drug treatment services, to "target-harden" the neighborhood by boarding up abandoned buildings and fencing off escape routes, and to have the police target their enforcement of drug-dealing laws. The result was a decrease in drug dealing and violent crime and an increase in community drug treatment resources: a clear case of a successful community–police anticrime effort. The focus was on dealing with ongoing serious crime much more than on campaigning against disorderly behavior.

There can be no question that widespread drug dealing makes neighborhoods more dangerous and less stable economically and socially. This case, however, bears little resemblance to the order-maintenance initiatives undertaken in downtown Baltimore and the other cities discussed in Kelling and Cole's book. In each of these cases, they concentrate on unsightly and menacing behavior that is dealt with through new punitive measures that reduce the civil liberties of a specific segment of society. Removing the homeless by restricting access to and activities allowed in public parks, using the police to forcibly remove homeless people from shopping areas, and criminalizing sleeping, panhandling, and sitting on the sidewalk are very different from consistently enforcing existing laws against drug dealing and violent crime. In addition, the downtown areas of San Francisco and Seattle did not have serious crime problems, despite the prevalence of disorderly behavior.

Wilson and Kelling's first article dealt with the kinds of problems that the Boyde Booth neighborhood was facing: an increase of social disorder and crime in residential neighborhoods. At that point, homelessness was not a major source of disorder, and its relationship to the "broken windows" theory had not been established. But as homelessness increased, Kelling was repeatedly asked to help cities and police departments apply the theory to homelessness. The most important example of this is when Kelling was hired in 1989 to work with William Bratton, who was then the chief of the New York City Transit Police, to develop new rules designed to remove homeless people from the subway system. By the early 1990s, many politicians, businesses, and local residents had seen the potential of the "broken windows" theory to deal with homelessness, and Kelling was an active participant in harnessing that potential.

The "broken windows" theory has provided a powerful analysis of the rise of urban disorder and strategies to address it. This "common-sense" approach has been very appealing to people discouraged by liberalism's inability to achieve concrete reductions in public incivility. However, this theory lacks as well a political and economic context for its analysis. It does not attempt to address the changing economic realities of urban residents who were on the losing side of the growing economic polarization. In addition, little empirical evidence has been gathered to support its assertions. A major study in Chicago by sociologists Robert Sampson and Stephen Raudenbush questioned the basic connection between disorder and crime that the theory posits. They observed 23,000 streets segments in 196 neighborhoods and found that physical and social disorder were poor predictors of crime rates. Instead, the degree of poverty in a neighborhood turned out to be a much more accurate indicator of crime rates, thus reestablishing the presence of poverty as a major factor in the level of crime.[46] In the first systematic review of this theory, Bernard Harcourt confirmed these basic findings and argued that the social meaning of disorder must be understood as an empirical question specific to different social environments.[47]

Communitarianism

A central component of the new theories of order maintenance is their emphasis on community rights over individual rights as a way of restoring civility and stability to urban neighborhoods. Amitai Etzioni contends that the excessive concern with individual liberty stemming from the 1960s counterculture hampered the ability of communities to regulate themselves. He argues that in response to the growing counterculture, the process of "defining deviancy down" contributed to a greater tolerance of social disorder and an increase in welfare dependency, single-parent families, and crime that resulted in the destabilization of communities during the 1980s. Many of these communities responded by developing new, community-centered or communitarian concerns. Etzioni calls for a new, "thick social order" that highlights the interconnectedness of individuals within communities and provides a standard for judging the harmful effects of individual behavior based on shared community standards.[48]

In many ways, this new comunitarianism is also a reaction to the centralizing forces of liberalism. It is a rejection of centralized state planning, the use of scientific experts at the expense of community influence, as well as the legal rights of minorities that have been a central tenant of liberal jurisprudence. It raises the same concerns as the broken windows theory does. Who decides on the appropriate community standards? If a majority of residents in ever more local areas are given increased control, then how will the rights of minorities be protected? This move toward localism and "majoritarianism" threatens both the social diversity of urban life and the social cohesion of the city. Local neighborhoods and residents lose their sense of connection to the fate of the city as a whole, focusing instead on their neighborhood, their block, their front doorstep, without seeing how the conditions in these ever more local spaces are inextricably tied to the overall condition of the city.

Urban Neoconservatism

The most common explanation of the decline of liberalism has been offered by neoconservatives with roots in the urban liberal tradition. They argue that liberalism's fatal flaw was its inability to enforce basic standards of public civility in the face of the fractured racial politics of the post-civil-rights era. Jim Sleeper claims that liberals allowed race-based politics to divide the city and erode universal standards of civility and accountability. He champions New York's historic diversity and dynamism as its strengths. But at the same time, he points out the crucial role that social workers, teachers, and the police have played in teaching each generation of new immigrants the values of liberal capitalism. He notes, however, that this system broke down during the 1960s as a result of the political separatism of blacks and the willingness of liberal politicians to allow them to pursue this identity-based political strategy at the expense of advancing the universalizing project of liberalism.[49]

According to Sleeper, by the end of the economic expansion of the 1980s, the repercussions of this political process was a black community in disarray as a result of broken families, welfare dependency, crime, and drug abuse. The problem affected the rest of the city through crime and social disorder in the form of increased citywide crime rates, graffiti, homelessness, and a growing tax burden to finance welfare and other social programs.

By the time of the 1989 mayoral campaign . . . the boom had receded, exposing not just the perennial ethnic clashes and jockeying of elites but also a frightening disintegration of families and neighborhood institutions amid reports of soaring child abuse and abandonment. Everywhere it seemed, were the encroachments of the drug economy, of roaming packs of violent youths, and of the homeless and mentally helpless, human wreckage which no one knew how to repair.[50]

Sleeper blames much of the problem on the political extremism of some black leaders who attempted to use the legacies of racism to explain away intolerable behaviors. He points to the Central Park jogger case of 1989 in which a group of black boys were convicted (falsely, as it later turned out) of raping a white woman in the park, after which many blacks defended the boys and claimed that the event never happened. The flip side was the case of Tawana Brawley, in which the young black girl accused the police of kidnapping and raping her. In this case, some black leaders, such as Rev. Al Sharpton, rushed to echo her claims without sufficient evidence (the case was dropped on those grounds). For Sleeper, these incidents show that the black community was tolerating indefensible behaviors on the grounds that they were the result of long-standing racial antagonism. This analogy was extended to minor incivilities such as graffiti and squeegee men because society was supposedly morally paralyzed by unresolved racial conflict.

For Sleeper, the root of urban decline is not the increased impoverishment of urban minorities due to economic reorganization and government retrenchment, the ongoing problems of racial discrimination, or the decline in public schools. Instead, the problem is a lack of toughness by urban liberals to force the socially and economically marginal to play by the rules of liberal capitalism: to pursue the American dream and be civil members of the society.

This echoed the antiurban, antipoor rhetoric of conservatives at the national level. The portrayal of the poor as "welfare queens" and the Willie Horton advertisements in support of George H. W. Bush's 1988 presidential campaign mark the extremes of a tendency to describe the poor as either lazy or criminal. This rhetoric was invariably racialized. Crime and welfare became synonymous with urban minorities, even though most criminals and welfare recipients are white. Conservative discourse about homelessness was shaped by this pattern of racialization and criminalization. Homeless people were portrayed as lazy, mentally defective, or criminal.

Neoconservative urban historian Fred Siegel argues that the New Deal liberalism of the 1930s, 1940s, and 1950s was a positive development, as it gave the "truly needy" "social insurance aimed to help people caught in tragedies not of their own making."[51] A transition, however, began in the 1960s with the emergence of what Siegel calls the "riot ideology." He argues that liberals responded to the threat of riots and increased crime by creating a system of dependency for the poor and by tolerating increasing levels of social disorder. As examples of this process, he points to the explosion of welfare rolls and the tolerance of extreme Black Nationalism in the Ocean Hills–Brownsville schools conflict in New York.

Siegel blames the decline in public civility on the "moral deregulation of public space," noting that by the 1980s, the livability of urban spaces was under siege:

> What unnerved most city dwellers, however, was not crime per se but, rather, the sense of menace and disorder that pervaded day-to-day life. It was the gang of toughs exacting their daily tribute in the coin of humiliation. It was the "street tax" paid to drunk and drug-ridden panhandlers. It was the "squeegee men" shaking down motorists waiting for a light. It was the threats and hostile gestures of the mentally ill making their homes in the parks. It was the provocation of pushers and prostitutes plying their trade with impunity. It was the "trash storms," the swirling masses of garbage left by peddlers and panhandlers, and the open-air drug bazaars on city streets. These were the visible signs of cities out of control.[52]

Siegel claims that the utopian and libertarian impulses of the 1960s and 1970s had the effect of "defining deviancy down," in the words of Senator Patrick Daniel Moynihan (NY-D). The social movements of this period favored the pursuit of individual desire over communitarian impulses, resulting in a behavioral free-for-all. In particular, Siegel blames civil libertarians for their decriminalization of "victimless crimes" and the deinstitutionalization of the mentally ill. The result of these decisions by liberals was an increase in economic dependency and moral deregulation that threatened to undermine the basic social order of New York and other major cities.

In response to this crisis, Siegel champions the policies of Rudolph Giuliani, whom he credits with reversing the ill-advised liberal policies of the 1970s and 1980s following his election in 1993. He points to Giuliani's embrace of the "broken windows" theory as both a set of practices for restoring order and a social philosophy explaining the urban crisis in terms of social permissiveness rather than economic decline. Siegel contends that the way to revitalize cities is by applying tough love measures to the socially and economically marginalized.

Sleeper and Siegel continue to approve of those aspects of liberalism that attempt to universalize human experience and create a coherent and stable society in which a certain amount of diversity and competition can flourish. It is a kind of social contract in which certain ground rules must be established before the competitive aspects of capitalism and democracy can operate. It assumes that the roots of our current dilemma lie in urban liberalism's rejection of the liberalism of the New Deal and its vision of universal equal opportunity and equal responsibility in favor of a New Left liberalism of radical individual freedom and preferential treatment for those historically disenfranchised.

Conclusion

The quality-of-life paradigm is a complex set of practices and ideas about how to best handle homelessness and public disorder. It represents a dramatic shift from the policies of "urban liberalism" based on a powerful synthesis of the "broken windows" theory, communtarianism, and urban neoconservatism. As such, it united academic theorists, police reformers, community activists, business leaders, and neoconservative politicians. The media also played an important role in constructing the paradigm. Historically liberal newspapers like the *New York Times* picked up on the term *quality of life* and wielded it as a broad critique of urban liberalism. As we will see in chapter 7, neoconservative politicians responded to this dynamic and used the ideas behind the new paradigm to construct a new political coalition that was able to unseat urban liberal politicians in New York City.

With the election of Mayor Giuliani, New York was transformed from having some of the most progressive homeless policies in the country to having some of the most regressive. Instead of developing housing and social services, Giuliani became concerned with creating a series of punitive measures designed to reduce the public impact of homelessness, rather than solving the problems of homeless people.

3

Defining Urban Liberalism

I use the term *urban liberalism* to refer to the political philosophy of many postwar cities that combined entrepreneurial economic development strategies, personal rehabilitation and social work approaches to social problems, and a tolerance of social differences in the form of broad support for civil liberties. Urban liberalism is not so much a label that any particular politician consciously wears. Rather, it is a coherent set of policy tendencies that can be seen in the practices of many urban mayors from the 1960s through the 1990s. In New York City, this includes the administrations of John Lindsay (1966–73), Abraham Beame (1974–77), Edward Koch (1978–89), and David Dinkins (1990–93). In general, however, I focus on the later two administrations, since it is during this period that the full contradictions of this political philosophy emerge.

I look at urban liberalism because the new quality-of-life philosophy is a direct response to it. The economic and social policies of urban liberalism helped accelerate the urban problems associated with the decline of public order in the 1980s and then failed to address them adequately. Consequently, political actors at the neighborhood and city levels began to search for an alternative vision of urban politics that could overcome urban liberalism's contradictions and directly address the disorder facing the city in the 1990s. The issue that best exemplifies this process is homelessness, which is both a product of the contradictions of urban liberalism and a visible symptom of the inability of urban liberals to resolve the public disorder crisis that drove the backlash politics of the 1990s. This sentiment can be seen in the comments of lower Manhattan resident Richard Brookhiser, who argued in an editorial for the *New York Times* that liberal politicians and residents had failed to take seriously the rise of homelessness and disorder.

New York liberals—decent and agreeable people—do not seem to believe that their way of life merits deference or support. Their lack of self-assertion is encouraged by activists and politicians who offer long lists of other causes claiming priority. But New York liberals let themselves be distracted because they don't realize that defending civility is an urgent task. . . . It's time to clean the streets and not feel guilty about it.[1]

Although the cause of the crisis is unclear, the solution is not liberal idealism or some grand strategy to save the city by saving the world. Instead, the answer is to take concrete action to clean the streets and worry about the long-term problems after order has been restored.

Rudolph Giuliani clearly understood this desire in his successful mayoral campaign of 1993, in which he hammered away at the issue of "quality of life," which was a codeword for the problems of disorder affecting communities throughout the city. Indeed, Giuliani's entire 1993 campaign revolved around the theme that as the city became unlivable for the middle classes, liberals were coddling criminals, homeless people, and those on welfare. He made it clear that if he were elected, he would exchange the urban liberals' social tolerance for tough love, backed up by the threat of police action and other punitive sanctions against those who continued to threaten public civility.

A good example of this rhetorical strategy was Giuliani's insistence that if elected mayor he would refuse emergency shelter to anyone who failed to comply with the strict new homeless services rules, which included participation in drug treatment, job training, and housing programs. The fact that few of these services actually existed was irrelevant. Rather, the point was to communicate to the public that people were homeless by choice and that they needed punitive sanctions to change their behaviors rather than the bleeding-heart compassion of urban liberals.

The Urban Liberal Paradigm

The first element of the *urban liberal* paradigm is the belief that government planning and coordination is the key to resolving social problems. Building on the New Deal tradition, urban liberals felt that the best strategy for reducing poverty and other social problems was to rely on the power of the state. Rather than investing all their energy in social movements to change fundamental aspects of housing and labor markets, they emphasized mobilizing the state's resources to regulate these markets in order to ameliorate their most polarizing qualities. Urban liberals supported higher minimum wage laws, improved welfare state transfer payments, and broader access to health and social services.

First, in order to make government function more effectively, urban liberals felt they had to rely on experts for comprehensive planning on a wide range of subjects. They had faith in the ability of the social sciences to produce a deeper understanding of the roots, nature, and solutions of social problems than those provided by "free-market" theorists. One implication of this reliance on experts is that it creates an elitist orientation that denies the input of local groups in the formation of social policy priorities, which also undercuts their connection to a grassroots constituency.[2]

Second, urban liberals relied heavily on social programs as a way of both reducing social problems and enlarging their electoral base. They used a variety of therapeutic and social work models to transform the behaviors of "deviants" and integrate them into mainstream society. Economic and social opportunities were thus equalized through the state's intervention in the economy and social intervention through programs designed to improve people's ability to compete in the market system or to sustain themselves outside it. Those who received help (in the form of transfer payments, including AFDC, SSI, and housing subsidies) presumably would not be a source of public disorder in the form of either crime or political discord. This approach relied on investment in education and job training, as well as more specific therapeutic strategies to reduce psychological problems and substance abuse.

The key to this approach was liberals' desire to reintegrate people on the margins into the mainstream. They believed that people engaged in behaviors associated with social problems for reasons that could be determined, and remedied, by social science and behavioral experts. Accordingly, during the 1960s and 1970s, liberals favored social science theories such as labeling theory[3] and strain theory[4] to explain deviant behavior. *Labeling theory* maintains that people become deviant only after being repeatedly labeled as such by schools, courts, and other institutions. The more often that young people are told they are "no good," the more likely they are to adopt this persona and act on it. Howard Becker showed how being called an outsider became an identity adopted by such deviant subgroups as jazz musicians. Edwin Schur described how the process of criminalizing homosexuals and drug addicts helped create a deviant self-image, which tended to drive them further into the margins of society, thereby contributing to a subculture of deviance. This process strengthened people's identities as social outcasts, propelling them toward criminal careers. Schur called for the decriminalization of marginalized groups, claiming that they were committing "crimes without victims." All these approaches relied on a form of labeling theory that placed the responsibility for causing deviance on the social control practices of the state and society, which therefore should be reformed to encourage inclusiveness rather than exclusiveness.

Strain theorists argued that crime and deviance were the result of a mismatch between people's desire to participate in the mainstream of society and the opportunities actually available to do so. Robert Merton claimed that the bulk of serious deviance was the result of people using illegitimate means to achieve the same legitimate goals in life that the rest of society desired. People pursued these illegitimate means because they did not have access to legitimate means because of the inequality in educational and employment opportunities. Therefore, the solution to this kind of deviance was to use the government to create equal opportunities to encourage people to pursue legitimate means to achieve success.

Finally, urban liberalism emphasized individual social freedoms in the form of civil liberties and a tolerance for social diversity. Classical liberalism is predicated on the ideal of individual liberty in the face of a controlling state. For some groups in the post–World War II era, this desire for individual liberty in relation to the state was transformed into appealing to the state to grant group rights in the face of a hostile society and economy. The forces that galvanized this strategy were the black civil rights movement, the anti–Vietnam War movement, the women's movement, and the gay rights movement. This reliance on the state to secure inclusion into the mainstream meshed nicely with the existing liberal priorities regarding rehabilitation programs.

In the 1960s and 1970s, liberals supported a wide range of legal changes that expanded individual rights in relation to the state. These included U.S. Supreme Court rulings concerning criminal procedures such as *Mapp v. Ohio*,[5] which established the federal exclusionary rule for evidence collected in illegal searches, and *Miranda v. Arizona*,[6] which forced police to notify people of their right to remain silent and their right to have an attorney present during questioning.

The courts also limited the powers of the police to engage in order-maintenance activities. Beginning with *Shuttlesworth v. City of Birmingham*[7] in 1965, the U.S. Supreme Court began to curtail the degree of police discretion in dealing with disorderly people. The Shuttlesworth decision ruled that Birmingham's loitering law was overly vague because, in the words of the Court, "This ordinance says that a person may stand on a public sidewalk in Birmingham only at the whim of any police officer of that city."[8] In 1971, in *Coates v. City of Cincinnati*, the Court ruled that the "ordinance prohibiting three or more persons from congregating on a sidewalk and conducting themselves in a manner 'annoying to persons passing by' [was] unconstitutionally vague where violation 'may entirely depend upon whether or not a policeman is annoyed.' "[9] In 1972, the Court ruled in *Papachristou v. City of Jacksonville*[10] that Jacksonville's (Mississippi) vagrancy statute gave the police too much discretion and could be used in a discriminatory manner: "Those generally implicated by the imprecise terms of the ordinance —poor people, nonconformists, dissenters, idlers—may be required to comport themselves according to the lifestyle deemed appropriate by the Jacksonville police and the courts."[11] Finally, in 1983, the Court expanded its concern about discriminatory police discretion in *Kolender v. Lawson*.[12] Kolender was a black man living in a mostly white neighborhood in Southern California who liked to take long walks at night. He was routinely stopped, questioned, and arrested by the police for failing to produce identification. The Court ruled that "the statute lacked an explicit standard for determining how a suspect could satisfy the requirement of providing credible and reliable identification, and thereby encouraged arbitrary enforcement by police."[13] These decisions significantly expanded the rights of people to be a source of minor disorder, regardless of community or policing standards of civility.

These legal rulings also expanded individual rights at the expense of state and community standards. Of particular interest are the constraints placed on the police. These rulings limited the discretionary powers of the police in dealing with minor disorders, thus legalizing a wide variety of behaviors that might be offensive to some community standards but were viewed by the courts as deserving the tolerance of the police and the state. Many of these rulings were the product of advocacy efforts by liberal groups such as the ACLU.

Contradictions of Urban Liberalism

The politics of quality of life did not begin with the rise of homelessness. Rather, the origins of this urban middle-class backlash date back to the 1960s and 1970s, when middle-class white constituencies began to question the liberal policies that were threatening their economic and social position in concrete ways. Efforts involving racial integration, in particular, challenged people's commitment to the progressive tendencies of liberalism and pushed many into a more conservative urban politics. The rise of this backlash in New York City can be clearly seen in three events that straddled the late 1960s and early 1970s. Each one entailed a racial conflict that alienated whites from some of the core values of liberalism. The first pitted local African American residents against the mostly white teachers' union in a battle over control of local schools.[14] The second was a conflict between the New York City Housing Authority and the white Jewish residents of Forest Hills, Queens, who were opposed to the development of a large public housing project in their neighborhood.[15] The third was the resistance by the mostly Italian American residents of the Canarsie section of Brooklyn to a plan of forced busing to integrate their schools.[16]

In 1966/67, the New York City Board of Education began drawing up school decentralization plans after being pressured by state government and backed by local foundations and many community groups. In 1968 the Bundy Plan—named for McGeorge Bundy, the president of the Ford Foundation and the chairman of the Mayoral Advisory Panel on Decentralization—called for the creation of community school boards, which would have power over the budget and personnel of local schools. In 1967, despite resistance from the teachers' union, a series of pilot experiments in decentralization were approved. The most notorious of these was in the Ocean Hill–Brownsville section of Brooklyn, a mostly poor, African American neighborhood.

A conflict soon emerged between the local school board and the teachers' union. The teachers viewed the enhanced power of the local school board as a threat to their civil service protections, and in April 1968 when the board attempted to transfer some teachers and principals out of the district, the teachers went on strike, which was followed by a community lockout. The decision to transfer the teachers was made because the local community felt that the teachers and principals were actively resisting their reform efforts. The teachers, however, felt emboldened to resist the reforms because the Board of Education made it clear that it was ambivalent toward the decentralization effort, which was made evident through the lack of clear lines of authority or the availability of resources for the local community school boards. During that year there were several short, citywide teacher strikes, and in November the district was placed under a state trusteeship, effectively ending local control. This conflict created a great deal of racialized conflict in the city. Blacks felt that the school system (including the teachers' union) was both failing to provide their children with an adequate education and resisting their attempts to be more directly involved in improving the system. Whites felt that blacks' increasingly militant demands for control over the delivery of government services was threatening the stability of these systems. In addition, many whites felt that whatever gains blacks might achieve would come at their expense.

In 1972 the New York City Housing Authority announced its intent to build, as part of the federal Scatter Site housing program, a large public housing development on vacant land in the Forest Hills section of Queens. Many of the mostly Jewish residents of the neighborhood bitterly resisted the project, claiming that the introduction of low-income residents in such large numbers would destabilize their neighborhood, causing higher crime and, eventually, white flight. Like most public housing development decisions, the community was not brought into the process until the Housing Authority already had made its decision. The Scatter Site program required that public housing not be built in existing low-income neighborhoods. This meant that wherever these projects were located, a local, higher-income community had to be nearby. As a result, the Housing Authority became very defensive about the inevitable local objections to its plans.

New York City's land use procedures required that the Housing Authority receive permission for the project from the city's Board of Estimates, which at the time was made up of a representative from each of the five city boroughs and three representatives from the mayor's office.[17] This provided the semblance of a public process involving the oversight of elected officials, but in practice their decisions were generally far removed from neighborhood concerns, and once this body made a decision, it was very difficult for local residents to challenge it. Sometimes, local residents were not even aware of a possible nearby development until after the Board of Estimates had already made its decision.

Objections to the project were not limited to local residents. Many sociologists, urban planners, and even black community activists were opposed to the project's size which, they felt, would only intensify and isolate the social problems associated with low-income status. In essence, the financial pressure to build high-density developments to recoup land costs ensured the continuation of segregation and poor conditions, even in the midst of otherwise stable, middle-class communities. The lack of transparency and the high stakes for the community in regard to the project's potential destabilizing effect led to sustained neighborhood mobilization, which resulted in scaling back the size of the development and designating many of the units for elderly, rather than low-income, tenants. Despite the victory, many residents had become soured on the liberal agenda of achieving greater racial equality through social engineering.

A similar dynamic emerged in the middle-class, mostly Jewish and Italian American neighborhood of Canarsie in Brooklyn. In the early 1970s the New York City Board of Education attempted to better integrate the city's schools through busing and the reconfiguration of school boundaries, which had become highly segregated as large numbers of whites left the city and the school system after World War II. The local residents resisted the busing plan, staging demonstrations, student strikes, insurgent political campaigns, and even low-level violence reminiscent of the busing conflicts in Boston. In fact, resentment of liberal integration policies became so great in Canarsie that many local residents voted for Nixon in 1972, despite its strong historical legacy of support for the Democratic Party. The reason was that residents felt that the twin threats of residential and school integration were being forced on them by liberal planners far removed from their local concerns about property values, educational standards, and public safety. While many of them had participated in the labor and socialist movements, which historically supported integration and other progressive social policies, they resisted its implementation in their midst.[18]

These three cases show that urban liberal policies were in crisis in the late 1960s and early 1970s. Despite liberals' desire to use social engineering to improve economic and social conditions, they were unwilling to empower communities or provide adequate resources to accomplish these goals. Improving public schools through underfunded and poorly designed decentralization plans was a halfhearted response to the real need and political pressure for school reform. Building oversized public housing projects was a shortsighted response to racial and economic housing segregation that saved the city money but failed to solve the problem because the new projects themselves became sites of social and economic isolation. And busing was a cheap, short-term response to the larger structural crisis of educational segregation. As a result, few of these problems were resolved. Overall, the poor received little concrete support for their education, housing, and employment needs, which further removed them from positive government action on their behalf. Middle-class whites also came to resent government action because it threatened their already declining standards of living without giving them any real control over the fate of their neighborhoods.

Unequal Development

The first contradiction of urban liberalism is its attitude toward markets. Urban liberals regularly intervene in economic markets to help shape the direction of economic development. They provide real estate development subsidies, offer companies tax breaks to relocate or remain in their cities, and adjust taxes and zoning to encourage one economic sector over another. Accordingly, New York City spends hundreds of millions of dollars each year subsidizing various forms of economic activity in order to stimulate the overall economy. The belief is that economic growth will benefit everyone in the form of increased employment, wages, and tax revenues, according to the familiar mantra that "a rising tide lifts all boats." On the other hand, urban liberals have been reluctant to intervene in housing and labor markets in response to social problems. They regard homelessness, crime, family breakdown, and neighborhood decline as problems to be dealt with through social services. Social workers, after-school programs, and various therapeutic methods are used to try to restore those who are viewed as somehow defective, the proof of which is their needing assistance.

In chapter 5, I discuss in more detail the economic development priorities of urban liberalism. In sum, they encouraged the transformation of the economy from a manufacturing to a finance and corporate base. This in turn polarized the labor market as middle-class jobs were replaced by a small number of high-paying jobs tied to the global economy and a large number of low-paying service jobs. In addition, unemployment increased; more of the jobs at the bottom of the labor market became part time and temporary; and social services for the unemployed were cut. The result was more homeless people, drug addicts, and untreated mentally ill people, many of whom became the core of the new disorderly populations that disrupted the everyday life of residents throughout the city.

The response of urban liberals has been to treat the rise of this underclass as a social problem to be dealt with by individualized therapeutic regimes. But this strategy ignores the liberals' own role in producing these problems and the changes in the labor and housing markets. Urban liberals have relied on a small and shrinking army of social workers to deal with these pathologized individuals. But these social workers, albeit well intentioned, lack the basic resources of adequate housing, health care, and jobs to solve their clients' real problems. Instead, homeless people are shuttled back and forth from emergency shelters, short-term social programs, limited outpatient health care, and, increasingly, incarceration.

In particular, urban liberals regarded the problem of homelessness as a social services problem requiring mental health and substance abuse treatment and life skills training. The provision of jobs and housing has been largely limited to emergency shelters and welfare-to-work programs. In some instances, liberal mayors have attempted to intervene in housing markets by subsidizing housing for homeless families and individuals and even providing much needed supportive housing. But these efforts have been limited because local governments, given their current tax and incentive structures, do not have the financial resources necessary for large-scale intervention in the housing market. When David Dinkins tried to use city money to provide apartments to homeless families, the intake centers were quickly inundated by tens of thousands of homeless and underhoused poor families. The city was not prepared to provide anywhere near the amount of housing that was needed. Consequently, it had to create stringent qualifying criteria to limit access to the small amount of available housing, which meant that hundreds of thousands remained doubled up with relatives, sleeping on the streets, or cycling in and out of the shelter system.

The emergence of this contradiction in relation to the rise of homelessness and disorder can be seen in the spending priorities for homelessness services. Throughout the 1980s, the city's spending on homelessness related services was directed toward providing emergency shelter and social services. Only a small amount was spent on creating new affordable housing for those on public assistance or working for low wages. At the same time, however, billions of dollars were spent on tax incentives and direct subsidies to encourage the development of high-rent commercial buildings and luxury housing, which often displaced low-income housing and low-skilled jobs. This *unequal development* destabilized many middle-class communities through the twin problems of rampant disorder emanating from the growing underclass and gentrification pressures coming from the new, extremely wealthy, professional class.

The fundamental contradiction of this aspect of urban liberalism is that when a company or business sector has problems, the local government is often willing to intervene through the use of tax breaks, development deals, and regulatory relief, but when individuals or communities suffer unemployment, homelessness, and social disorganization, the solution is to hire social workers. Although historically, urban liberals have based their legitimacy on helping the disenfranchised and downtrodden, during the 1970s and 1980s, they often made conditions for these groups worse. They then used individualized therapeutic responses to address them while actively pursuing structural market interventions on behalf of elite interests, at a much greater cost.

Empty Empowerment

The second contradiction of urban liberalism is its support of centralized planning of social programs, on the one hand, and community and client empowerment, on the other. Beginning with the New Deal, urban liberals harnessed the state's power to address compelling social needs. In the postwar period, the emergence of large-scale urban redevelopment programs were the most dramatic example of this process. These projects were intended to deal with the problems of slum housing, racial segregation, and inadequate public facilities. Urban liberals believed that the way to improve low- and moderate-income housing, provide additional cultural resources, and create new stable neighborhoods was through central planning by professional experts in these fields.

Efforts at slum clearance, for instance, could not be left up to free-market or neighborhood-led initiatives. The market had no interest in providing low-cost housing without direct government subsidy, and local communities lacked the technical and financial resources. In addition, local communities were viewed by urban planners as a potential impediment to their projects. Slum clearance meant the sometimes temporary, but often permanent, displacement of current tenants in order to achieve a perceived greater social good. Furthermore, urban liberals were committed to achieving these greater goods even when they might contradict the interests of the existing local neighborhood.

New York's preeminent urban planner, Robert Moses, was the embodiment of this aspect of urban liberalism.[19] Moses was charged with providing public goods, which could be done only at the expense of some local areas. In order to increase the flow of goods and people into and out of the city he destroyed several different neighborhoods to create new highways and bridges. He also razed slum areas in order to create modern high-rise, low-income public-housing projects. The stability of the communities where these projects were located was of little concern, since the objectives being achieved were perceived to be of central importance to the health and progress of the city as a whole.

> When [Moses] replied to protests about the hardship caused by his road-building programs, he generally replied that succeeding generations would be grateful. It was the end that counted, not the means. "You can't make an omelet without breaking eggs. . . . When you operate in an overbuilt metropolis, you have to hack your way with a meat ax; I'm just going to keep right on building, you do the best you can to stop it."[20]

During the fiscal crisis of the mid-1970s, local government largely abandoned significant market interventions to solve social problems. This trend was exacerbated by the severe cutbacks in federal urban spending as President Richard Nixon dismantled the War on Poverty and President Ronald Reagan implemented dramatic across-the-board cuts in social spending. The legacy of centralized expert planning, however, remained in the form of elaborate social service bureaucracies that oversaw the social spending. While many social services were provided by nonprofit and community-based organizations, the choices of which agencies received funding and for what kinds of services still was highly centralized rather than community controlled.

This commitment to centralized expert planning, however, runs counter to a competing tendency of urban liberalism, which is an ethos of community empowerment. Most urban liberals supported the ideals of community involvement in land use decisions and client involvement in service delivery. Indeed, strong communities, including geographic communities as well as communities of identity, are at the heart of the urban liberal project. Urban liberals support a rights-based approach to governance in which the well-being of individuals and communities should not be drowned out by the interests of markets or the state. This can be clearly seen in the areas of class and race. Urban liberals also have been strong supporters of union movements, recognizing that workers gain economic and social well-being when they have some collective power over their conditions of work. In addition, urban liberals believe that racial equality can be achieved only by empowering minority groups. They supported the civil rights movement's struggle for the right to participate in the political process and, by extension, the right of blacks and other minority groups to have a voice in their own fate. Both labor unions and minorities have been at the core of the political coalition of urban liberals as far back as the New Deal.

This commitment to community empowerment is expressed in efforts to decentralize control over growing public bureaucracies. In 1943, New York City created Community Precinct Councils, in which the local community meets monthly with neighborhood police officials to discuss crime trends and prevention efforts. The future mayor and then Manhattan borough president, Robert Wagner, created the first Community Planning Boards in 1951, and in 1975 the city charter gave them formal status across the city. These boards are made up of local residents appointed by local politicians and focus on land use planning and the delivery of city services. In 1961, the Board of Education created Community School Districts, in which parents elected representatives to their local board. Throughout the 1960s and 1970s, numerous efforts like these to involve clients in the delivery of services such as public housing and welfare were initiated. These institutions, however, often become the source of major conflicts with government policy. In essence, urban liberals often are paralyzed in the conflict between trying to implement citywide policies for social improvement and responding to the wishes of the local communities that might be harmed by these efforts. The result is *empty empowerment,* in which communities participate in governing but have no effective power.[21] Community Precinct Councils are essentially controlled by the police; Community Boards are controlled by local politicians, who appoint their members and have no actual power, being only advisory; and the school system made efforts to give parents some control over how the schools were run, but none of them had had real power and resources, and when elected school boards asserted more control, they were disbanded and replaced by a parents' advisory council, with no concrete authority.

This orientation toward centralization and expertise is apparent in two important ways in relation to the emergence of the political backlash and the rise of quality-of-life policing. The first is that the philosophy of policing under urban liberalism was removed from local input. In chapter 6, I discuss in more detail the professional model of policing that predominated in New York until the early 1990s. This form of policing relied on a variety of specialized policing units that focused on specific types of crime such as organized crime, arson, sex crimes, and narcotics. Each of these units was centralized and thus was divorced from any kind of local community interaction. In addition, although local precincts maintained some ties to the community, they resisted calls to enforce minor nuisance crimes in favor of concentrating on serious crimes. Those police subscribing to the professional model felt that their job was to use their expertise to go after serious crime, as opposed to spending their time arresting public drunks, prostitutes, and even petty drug dealers. That is, these crimes were viewed as symptoms of larger social problems beyond the police's power to correct.

This separation of the police from the community was useful in reducing corruption and improving the technical abilities of police officers at all levels. It also instilled a clear sense of mission for the police that meshed with larger political trends in favor of decriminalizing minor crimes related to social problems. The separation came, however, with important political costs for both the police and urban liberal mayors. As social disorder grew along with the rise of widespread homelessness, the professional model of policing was ill equipped to respond to the complaints of local residents and businesses about their declining quality of life. This breakdown in support for the police was a key component of the urban backlash of the 1990s.

The second policy area in this dynamic was the provision of emergency homeless shelters. As homelessness increased throughout the 1980s, New York and many other cities were confronted by the need to provide an alternative to the streets. In part this was motivated by humanitarian concerns about the well-being of homeless people. These policies also were motivated by the need to respond to complaints about the presence of these people in public parks, subways, and sidewalks. In New York, in particular, an additional force was driving the creation of emergency shelters. In a 1981 consent decree following from *Callahan v. Carey* (1979),[22] a right to shelter was established as consistent with the New York State Constitution. As part of the consent decree, the city agreed to provide emergency shelter on demand for anyone who wanted it, which meant that the city had to find spaces to shelter thousands of people every night.

Because of the size of the problem, the most efficient way for the city to respond was to create large shelters that could accommodate hundreds of people a night. This also was cost-effective in that it reduced the overhead expenses of large shelters. Communities, however, were not happy about having these facilities located near them precisely because their large size had a dramatic impact on the local community, since the shelter's residents were generally compelled to leave the shelters during the day and therefore roamed the surrounding streets and parks. Planners often resisted local concerns and accused neighborhood activists of just displacing or obstructing development in a Not in My Back Yard (NIMBY) approach. Neighborhood residents accused the city of notifying them late in the process of opening new facilities and attempting to use the public hearing process to build consent rather than a true partnership of power sharing. The only way that communities could respond effectively was to veto projects with which they strongly disagreed. This created a paralyzing dynamic in which planners, fearing rejection, tried to avoid informing neighborhoods in advance about opening new shelters, and local communities, becoming more distrustful of the city, resisted allowing more services to be located in their neighborhoods.

Hollow Tolerance

The final contradiction of urban liberalism revolves around the tension between extending individual rights without creating true opportunities to exercise these rights. Historically, urban liberals have supported the extension of individual formal rights as a way of overcoming discrimination and enhancing economic, political, and social equality of opportunity. In the past, this has taken the form of efforts to extend rights to groups such as African Americans, gays and lesbians, and women. Often, though, this extension of rights has been largely symbolic, such as granting same-sex couples the right to form domestic partnerships and civil unions that, however, lack the same legal authority as marriage. More important, although the language opposing discrimination in employment and housing appears to establish important new rights, it has been hamstrung by inadequate enforcement. In addition, the creation of social programs designed to enhance opportunity have been poorly funded and, at times, directed to those who least need them. Finally, formal efforts to integrate schools have failed as whites have used their economic advantages to withdraw their children from the public school system or have created special merit-based enclaves within the system.

While urban liberals may have preached social tolerance and enhanced opportunity for disenfranchised groups, they have rarely made the concrete political, economic, and social investments necessary to achieve these objectives. This failure to extend formal facilities in keeping with the extension of formal rights has created a kind of *hollow tolerance,* which does not meet the needs of either disenfranchised groups or middle-class and elite groups who are asked to tolerate difference without any reasonable hope that social integration will be achieved. Both groups tend to support the extension of formal rights as long as they generate real progress for both those groups and society as a whole. It is this aspect that is the key to understanding the urban backlash. Urban residents have historically been sympathetic to the integrative aspirations of disenfranchised groups, especially when they do not radically threaten existing social standards.

In the early days of the homelessness crisis, there was a broad political willingness to tolerate the presence of homeless people and to support the creation of a few emergency shelter and social services as long as a solution to the crisis appeared to be on the horizon. But when the problem grew, residents became less open to appeals to tolerate the daily disorders they were experiencing. As we will see in chapter 7, when residents lost hope of an imminent solution to mass homelessness, their willingness to support calls for tolerance declined. In the end, they found Giuliani's program of zero tolerance more appealing because it promised to immediately end the disorder they were experiencing.

4

The Rise of Disorder

The backlash against the socially marginal in New York began with the increased social disorder of the 1970s. Squeegee men, panhandlers, and people sleeping in public spaces came to be the most visible symptoms of an urban environment that many people felt was out of control. The roots of these problems, like the roots of the homeless problem itself, were economic, political, and cultural. The greater economic polarization of the late 1970s through the early 1990s contributed to the formation of an economic underclass that was drawn into prostitution, crime, and other forms of public disorder. Culturally, the social tolerance established by the social movements of the 1960s and 1970s was abandoned as social disorders such as crime, prostitution, and graffiti increased. Politically, as the homeless problem emerged in the early and mid-1980s, urban liberalism lost public support as more and more neighborhoods and economic elites called for immediate punitive action to restore order. The paradigm of urban liberalism was no longer able to respond to either the economic or social changes under way. Urban liberalism's core principles of social tolerance, the preference for social services over market reforms, and the model of expert-driven centralized planning both failed to ameliorate social problems and alienated many important political constituencies. Instead, what developed was a contradiction between the practices and conceptualizations of the urban liberal paradigm, and the actual experiences of people in these cities.

One of the central roles of municipal government is the management of social problems, especially when they become so severe that they threaten the economy of the city, reduce the quality of life of large numbers of residents, or destabilize their neighborhoods. In the 1980s and 1990s, New York's urban liberal politicians were confronted by just such a challenge: the rise of mass homelessness and a variety of other social and physical disorders such as prostitution and graffiti. This chapter looks at some of the urban social problems confronting New York City and the strategies used by its urban liberal political leaders to address them. Urban liberals tended to view these social problems as symptoms of larger social forces at work and, as such, treated them as secondary concerns of the city government. In general, urban liberals responded to these problems in emergency terms that treated only the worst of the symptoms in response to community demands. In the process, they failed to develop long-term solutions, adequately involve the community in their problem-solving process, and called for social tolerance without effective concerted strategies for change. As chapters 5, 6, and 7 explain more fully, it was the inadequacy of these strategies that led to a broad community and business backlash against urban liberalism.

Defining Disorder

In the 1970s and 1980s, New York City faced a number of serious social problems. The fiscal crisis of the mid-1970s undermined a variety of public services and contributed to the decline in public infrastructure, the reduction in poor New Yorkers' standard of living, and the sense that the city was on the brink of collapse. The crime rate began rising in the 1970s and took another bad turn in the late 1980s and early 1990s. These problems, combined with the private sector's abandonment and disinvestment, created a sense of crisis in the city's various neighborhoods.

Few of New York's residents were exposed to these problems directly. Even though many were victims of crime or were burned out of their buildings, the majority of New Yorkers experienced these things secondhand through the news and informal communication networks. What people did see everyday, however, was the growth of disorder. Dirt, vandalism, visible homelessness, panhandling, prostitution, and graffiti all were daily indignities to be managed by city residents. They were both the physical manifestation of the city's problems and a symbol of its decline. Disorder, therefore, was at the center of people's conception of the city's health and the ability of government to get things moving in the right direction.

This concept of disorder also had problematic qualities of its own. It was brought back into vogue by the proponents of the "broken windows" theory, who argued that minor socially disruptive behavior in public spaces could have profound negative consequences for neighborhood stability. Disorder is typically divided into social and physical categories, and in either form it represents conditions that engender fear in the public to such a degree that law-abiding residents become less willing to inhabit public spaces, thus leaving them vulnerable to predators and contributing to an overall climate of social permissiveness.

Disorder must be understood as an interactive, socially embedded concept. Wesley Skogan reviewed surveys conducted between 1977 and 1983 of residents of forty urban neighborhoods. He found that the highest-ranked disorderly behaviors were public drinking, loitering youths, public drug use, noisy neighbors, panhandling, and prostitution. The most serious physical disorders were vandalism, graffiti, dilapidation and abandonment, and trash, categories of disorder that resonate with most urban residents.[1] Kelling and Coles claim that we can define something as disorderly only in relation to community responses. Therefore, if a social behavior or physical condition provokes a response of fear and withdrawal, it can be considered disorderly. But if the same behavior does not produce that response, it is not considered disorderly. For example, although public drinking is accepted in some communities, it is a source of fear in others. Similarly, the same activity at different times or in different social contexts can have very different social meanings. That is, a person panhandling on a Sunday afternoon on a busy commercial street is unlikely to produce fear and public withdrawal. But the same panhandler late at night on a residential street might produce a very different reaction from those who have to walk by him.[2]

One of the weaknesses of the disorder concept is precisely its contingent nature. Who decides which behaviors produce fear and what the consequences of that fear are? Since disorder is really a social concept rather than an objective set of behaviors or conditions, it is subject to change and disagreement. Might it be possible to reduce the negative consequences of certain behaviors by changing not the behaviors but people's social reaction to them? Graffiti or panhandlers are not themselves a threat to personal safety. They may be an annoyance or may symbolize people acting outside the boundaries of socially accepted behavior, but they are not inherently dangerous. In fact, it is exactly this notion of "socially acceptable behavior" that is most troubling about the concept of disorder and the broken windows theory: the implication that neighborhood stability is achieved through moral conformity. This approach tends to ignore the importance of economic investment and the quality of government services in the process of neighborhood improvement and decline.

This is essentially how social problems become quality-of-life problems. When minor nuisances become widespread and interfere with the everyday activities of a broad segment of the population, they become quality-of-life issues, and it is at this point that they take on a greater political salience. Isolated litter or the occasional panhandler does not engender a crisis of confidence in municipal governance, but daily interactions with prostitutes, squeegee men, and homeless encampments do bring these problems to the fore. Consequently, the framing of these phenomena as disorder and quality-of-life problems changes them qualitatively from difficulties for the poor and disadvantaged to difficulties for the rest of the society who are inconvenienced by them.

This qualitative change thus placed an extra burden on urban liberals. Their approaches to what had been perceived as nuisances were not capable of addressing these issues now that they had become quality-of-life problems. Moreover, urban liberals tended to deal with these problems in an incomplete and contradictory manner. Rhetorically, they acknowledged that quality-of-life problems were an expression of larger social and economic forces, but practically, they continued to pursue economic development policies that only exacerbated these conditions. At the same time, they claimed that the residents' concerns were important to proper governance, but they continued to rely on centralized bureaucratic experts to develop social policy with little meaningful input by local communities. Finally, urban liberals preached the values of social tolerance while undermining both the civil liberties of the homeless and poor and the legitimate social needs of residents besieged with social disorders.

I now consider three major social problems at the center of the quality-of-life backlash: homelessness, prostitution, and graffiti. In each case, urban liberalism was unable to develop a meaningful solution for either those who were the source of the problem or the rest of society. Indeed, in some cases the urban liberal approach actually made the conditions worse for both groups, leading to a broad disenchantment with a tolerant, social services model of dealing with social problems that extended beyond these problems to areas such as welfare reform, education policy, and housing.

Homelessness

New York has always had people who on a given night have no home. In the nineteenth century, local police stations housed hundreds of people each night and operated soup kitchens as well. For much of the twentieth century, the infamous Bowery was the city's skid row, the center of a small population of street alcoholics and the very poor who lived in shelters and single room occupancy (SRO) hotels. The number of these people ebbed and flowed within a narrow band along with economic conditions, with the major exception of the Great Depression during which numerous unemployed people's shantytowns or Hoovervilles (named for President Herbert Hoover) were constructed in many parts of the city. The city also opened a men's shelter in upstate Orange County called Camp LaGuardia, which housed hundreds of men during this period and continued as a kind of voluntary alcohol detox facility through the rest of the century.[3]

In the postwar period, the homeless again became concentrated in the Bowery, where social services also congregated, pursuing various strategies to ameliorate the situation. In 1961, one of the most ambitious of these was the Manhattan Bowery Project, created by the Vera Institute of Justice, whose aim was to reduce the number of street inebriates by offering them voluntary shelter and treatment as an alternative to repetitive short-term incarceration. But this program was limited and could not handle the thousands of people in need of assistance. Throughout the 1960s the city handed out around one thousand vouchers each day for people to stay in small cubicles in the Bowery. This number remained fairly constant, though increased in the winter months. Those receiving vouchers ("ticketmen"), along with those participating in social programs and those able to pay minimal housing costs on their own, made up the marginally housed, with the Bowery and SRO hotels around the city representing the residences of last resort for New York's poor.[4] Overall, this was a largely stable system that contained the social problems of public drunkenness, homelessness, and extreme poverty in isolated areas with some social services oversight and involvement.

As the social services systems in the Bowery became better organized in the form of growing professionalization and the rise of community-based, nonprofit organizations replacing religious charities as the dominant nongovernmental players, housing advocates began condemning the poor quality of the city's SRO hotels, demanding that the conditions in which the very poor lived be improved. This was seen as an achievable goal because of the relative stability of the number of people living in these often wretched conditions and the availability of federal urban redevelopment and block grant funds. These advocates began to call for scaling back the SROs and their replacement with better-quality affordable housing. Ironically, just as the dramatic growth in homelessness was beginning, this opened the door politically to the destruction of very low cost housing.

In 1976, with the quickening pace of economic changes, deinstitutionalization, and the decriminalization of public intoxication, the presence of homeless people outside the Bowery began to increase noticeably from midtown to the Upper West Side. The city's initial response was to hand out more SRO vouchers, and when they started to run out, the city opened emergency homeless shelters. But by 1979, this system was unable to meet the requests for shelter, and the conditions in the few existing shelters were deteriorating under the strain. As a result, Robert Hayes, a private attorney working under the auspices of the Legal Aid Society, filed suit in 1979 (*Callahan v. Carey*)[5] to force the city to provide additional beds in the Bowery and improve conditions. Over the next two years, the population of homeless people expanded in number and location, prompting the city to settle Hayes's suit by signing a consent decree guaranteeing a shelter bed on demand, first to single men in 1981, then to single women in 1983, and finally to families in 1986.

The Hayes agreement created an entitlement for homeless people. The city—with financial support from the federal and state governments—had to provide at least emergency shelter to anyone who requested it. Although this became an expensive burden for the city, it did little either to reduce the level of homelessness or to entice the most disorderly people off the streets. In turn, this meant that the city had to spend much of its social service fund for a program that was failing to meet either of the homelessness program's objectives. At this early juncture, the city had to decide whether to treat homelessness as a short-term economic problem to be dealt with by emergency social services or as an expression of a structural defect in the housing and labor markets and social services systems. Even though the latter approach was more comprehensive, it also would have been politically and financially much more difficult to carry out.

Another result of the Hayes consent decree was that New York had to find places to locate homeless shelters. The Koch administration conceptualized the homeless problem as a temporary emergency that would be alleviated once the recession of the early 1980s gave way to a new cycle of growth. Accordingly, not until the final months of Koch's administration did it engage in long-term planning or develop complex mechanisms for getting people off the streets, out of the shelters, and into permanent housing. It also did not build up a relationship with the neighborhoods affected by homelessness to develop cooperative strategies for reducing the impact of the problem and sharing in the burdens associated with solving the problem. Instead, the Koch administration consistently alienated local communities by forcing shelters into their communities without their input.

In 1981 the Community Services Society estimated that although the homeless population had grown to 36,000, there were only 3,200 shelter beds.[6] Koch's response was to call for the construction of numerous large shelters in armories that would accommodate hundreds of people. In response, through their community boards, local communities called for the creation of smaller, neighborhood-based shelters. Several boards actually drew up specific requests for shelters in their communities to give the people sleeping on their sidewalks a place to go.[7] But these communities resisted the imposition of large facilities which, they believed, would cause a decline in neighborhood conditions. The Koch administration, however, continued with its project and accused the neighborhoods of NIMBYism.

As the demand for shelters grew, the city negotiated an agreement with the courts that would allow them to set up emergency shelters with twenty-four hours' notice, bypassing existing land-use-planning rules in order to meet the need. What started as an emergency measure became standard procedure as the administration continued to open only large armory shelters as its negotiations with communities broke down. The results, according to Robert Hayes, were devastating: "This kind of crisis management undermines the work we do with communities. We've been going through [East New York] looking for possible sites and to have one rammed down their throat overnight on court order makes it difficult."[8] This practice of locating shelters in communities in the middle of the night without community involvement generated tremendous ill will and was typical of a situation in which the desire for quick, centralized decision making outweighed the rhetoric of community involvement.

Through the early and middle 1980s, the Koch administration continued to locate shelters on an emergency basis. By 1985, Koch had won his third term in office with a coalition consisting of community-based service providers benefiting from the end of the 1970s fiscal crisis, municipal workers with whom Koch had made favorable contract deals, and private developers. At this stage, Koch had a positive outlook toward government problem solving and inclusive social programs, and a moderate tolerance of social diversity. But all these were about to change under the pressure of the growing homelessness problem.

During 1985, conditions on the streets became much worse, and complaints about homeless people increased, with the number of homeless people using the shelter system rising from 7,500 in 1982 to 21,000 in 1985. Additional shelter space did little either to improve conditions or to reduce complaints. Consequently, Koch embarked on a new, two-part campaign to clear the streets. The first part was to create a cold weather emergency plan authorizing the police to take people to a homeless shelter against their will if the temperature fell below 5° F.[9] The second program brought psychiatrists into major transportation hubs, such as Grand Central Terminal, Penn Station and the Port Authority Bus Terminal, and on the streets to hospitalize homeless people forcibly if they appeared to be unable to take care of themselves. According to Mayor Koch, "We believe that anyone who chooses to be out on the streets in the cold when we offer that person an opportunity to go to a shelter, that person is not competent."[10] The Coalition for the Homeless argued that the new policy "demonstrated the inadequacy of the city's shelter system. If the system were more humane, the police would not be needed to bring the homeless people in."[11]

In 1987, Koch attempted to expand the policy. A greater range of people were to be classified as being unable to care for themselves, and the period of involuntary confinement was to be extended. It quickly became clear, however, that the city did not have the capacity to handle a new influx of psychiatric patients. The shortage of services that had contributed to the increase in the number of people living on the streets also prevented their involuntary commitment. By the end of the year, though, the state came up with money for fifty additional beds so that the program could continue on a limited basis.

This expanded policy created stiff opposition from homeless people, advocates, service providers, and civil liberties attorneys. Homeless advocate Robert Hayes argued that the solution to the homeless problem was not forced hospitalization but more housing and adequate voluntary services. New York Civil Liberties Union attorney Norman Siegel contended:

> The real obstacle to mental health care for the homeless is the serious shortage of beds for psychiatric patients caused by a lack of community mental health programs in New York City. Whenever government proposes to remove citizens from the streets and confine them involuntarily in a mental hospital, fundamental civil liberties are at stake. . . . The courts have repeatedly made clear, government does not have the power to hospitalize harmless people who are capable of meeting their basic survival needs, even if they appear to be disheveled or their standard of living is considered low.[12]

The conflict over the policy came to a head in November 1987 when the first person picked up under the new policy sued, with the assistance of the New York Civil Liberties Union (NYCLU), the city for release. Joyce Brown was drug addicted, unemployed, mentally ill, and living on the streets. But she had survived several winters on the street and was able to argue convincingly in court that she was capable of taking care of herself. The decision to forcibly hospitalize her came directly from the mayor, who spoke to her during an outreach trip and was stunned to learn that she might not meet the criteria for confinement. Koch had contended that the very decision to stay outside in the winter was evidence enough of severe mental defect. Within days, a court ruled that Miss Brown could not be held, striking a blow to the mayor's new plan. The feeling persisted in the mayor's office, however, that the city should continue to try to remove homeless people from the streets forcibly as both a humanitarian gesture and a way to address complaints about the deteriorating quality of life.

Civil libertarians and advocates continued to oppose this policy throughout the Koch administration. Some psychiatrists and civil libertarians even teamed up to condemn the mayor's policy as one of "out of sight, out of mind" and accused some doctors of responding to "political imperatives."[13] They pointed out that the program did not change the fact that the city did not have adequate mental health facilities to deal with the true need for housing and support services. These groups increasingly came to embrace the policies of the then Manhattan borough president, David Dinkins, who argued against involuntary treatment and shelter and in favor of more comprehensive service plans.

Although this approach was not an example of social tolerance, it still was a hollow effort. The city never provided the services to fully implement these measures, and so the effort quickly faded away. It was another example of trying to deal with a complex structural failure by means of a short-term emergency solution. The fact that Koch adopted a tougher rhetoric is offset by the fact that he clearly felt the need to couch the policy in terms of saving people from freezing to death rather than as an attempt to clear the streets of undesirables.

The mayor's next major policy initiative was the creation of twenty new large, armory-style shelters as a way to meet the increasing demand. The proposal called for the creation of fifteen family shelters for one hundred families each and five adult shelters with a capacity of two hundred each. The mayor called for the shelters to be distributed across the five boroughs, with the consultation of local borough presidents in an attempt to mollify local resistance.

This policy, however, was opposed by local communities and by the borough presidents of Queens, Brooklyn, and the Bronx. These three borough presidents argued that the mayor's continued reliance on giant armory shelters was not doing anything to solve homelessness and was adversely affecting the quality of life of the communities in which they were located. Instead, they called for "a long-range solution that would enable the homeless to break the welfare cycle. And we can do this without negatively effecting existing communities."[14] They proposed creating permanent housing through the rehabilitation of abandoned city-owned buildings and the creation of dispersed low-density clusters of new construction. Even Robert Hayes, the force behind the creation of shelters, began arguing that they were the wrong way to go and that the city should shut down the system.[15]

Although Dinkins supported the shelter plan, he did so because he felt that there was an immediate need for shelter and that the outer boroughs needed to share the burden. He also made it clear, however, that long-term solutions were needed that focused on the creation of permanent housing and comprehensive service delivery systems. In March 1987, Dinkins issued a major report entitled "A Shelter Is Not a Home," in which he emphasized the development of a comprehensive strategy for dealing with homeless families. The plan called for the creation of permanent and long-term transitional housing and a system of support services to prevent and end homelessness. It criticized the Koch administration's reliance on shelters and its overall "crisis" footing: "The City administration must recognize that its proposal [for more shelters] represents an expensive form of planned obsolescence. The continual infusion of capital dollars into creating emergency housing which cannot be adapted for secondary permanent housing is short sighted."[16] A consensus was forming among service providers and political leaders that the large-scale, short-term emergency shelter system was doing nothing to improve conditions in neighborhoods or reduce the homeless population.

By 1988, the mayor's approach was coming unraveled. Court challenges and a lack of facilities kept down the number of forced hospitalizations, and the shelter plan was moving ahead very slowly. Koch's initial attempts to use the police to control homeless people also were being rejected. In February of that year, the state courts struck down the antiloitering law, and in general, other nuisance crime laws were not being enforced (as discussed in detail in chapter 6). According to the *New York Times,* "Mayor Koch has ruled out using the criminal laws, the courts and the police to deal with the homeless except in extreme situations. 'There are other priorities in this town.' "[17]

Koch's approach to homelessness pushed the boundaries of urban liberalism. He still believed that concerted government action was required. But he increasingly turned to punitive measures to control the homeless problems, though without fully implementing them or describing them in punitive terms. Although he felt frustrated at the inability to reduce the problem using an emergency approach, he was unable to move away completely from a primarily social services orientation. And while he also was willing to alienate civil libertarians in responding to more communitarian concerns about declining public conditions, these efforts were halfhearted and largely rhetorical. By the mayoral election of 1989, however, Koch had created a "get tough" persona in response to growing public frustration. As a result, New Yorkers had to decide whether to continue the move away from urban liberalism or to reembrace its fundamental tenets.

The service provider community had turned against emergency and punitive measures to deal with homelessness, and groups that opposed Koch's various policy initiatives began looking for a new candidate to support. That new candidate was David Dinkins, who campaigned on a platform of developing a comprehensive array of temporary, transitional, and permanent housing and support services. Dinkins also was committed to the idea that government could mobilize to solve social problems. He was a lifelong political insider committed to the social programs of the Great Society. Furthermore, with his roots in the civil rights movement and his admiration for New York's "beautiful mosaic," Dinkins clearly was a supporter of social tolerance and civil rights.

Dinkins defeated Koch in the primary. An analysis of the results indicated that homelessness was the voters' third most frequently mentioned concern and that those who considered it a major issue voted heavily for Dinkins. In the general election of 1989, Dinkins faced former federal prosecutor and neoconservative Republican candidate Rudolph Giuliani. Giuliani focused on his ability to fight crime, which also was a big issue at the time. In the end, those voters who felt that crime was the most important issue voted for Giuliani and those who felt that homelessness was a major issue voted for Dinkins. The election was very close, with Dinkins winning by fewer than fifty thousand votes. The margin of difference was white independent voters, to whom the policy emphasis was the same as for the general electorate. For Dinkins to hold on to these voters, he had to show progress on homelessness or risk losing them to Giuliani, and he intended to do that by drawing up plans to solve the problem that included the rehabilitation and construction of low-cost housing, enhancing social services, and encouraging social tolerance.[18]

One of Dinkins's initial efforts was the continuation of Mayor Koch's $5 billion, twelve-year housing plan. Dinkins committed the city to spending $2.1 billion over the next four years to construct 63,000 new apartments.[19] Dinkins also pledged to make these units more affordable to homeless people than the Koch administration had done. Dinkins's goal was to dramatically reduce the use of emergency shelters and hotels and to get people into permanent housing, a priority supported by homeless advocates and the liberal constituencies who had supported his election. In addition, the mayor was developing a wide array of social services, including drug treatment and mental health services to help people remain in their existing housing.

This sense of possible improvement was short-lived, however. Later that year, the city faced a serious financial crisis, and consequently the

city was beset by additional demands for services but had fewer resources to provide them. By the end of 1989, the city had almost eliminated the use of hotels for homeless families. Instead, about two thousand families were housed in a handful of shelters and numerous transitional apartments. But by late 1991, 4,700 families and 7,000 single
adults were staying in the shelter system, and the numbers were continuing to grow. At the same time, the rhetoric of the media and neighborhood activists against the homeless and the disorder associated with
them was worsening. Owing to the great demand, Dinkins's efforts to
lure the homeless off the street through improved shelters and affordable housing had not worked, and the public's frustration was growing.

In response, Dinkins commissioned Andrew Cuomo to head a panel
to restructure the homeless services system. In January 1992, the panel
called for the development of twenty-one "day assessment" shelters that
would function as multiservice intake facilities and provide specialized
services to accommodate the needs determined at the centers. The panel
also called for these services and city homeless shelters to be run by
nonprofits. Most important, the plan called for the development of permanent housing to take precedence over the construction of additional
shelters. One example of the system's misplaced priorities was that the
city spent $18,000 a year to keep one drug addict in a "dangerous, drug
infested armory shelter" when in-patient drug treatment could be provided at the same cost.[20]

Dinkins initially resisted this plan because it challenged his existing
strategy of dramatically increasing the number of small scatter-site shelters as a way of moving people off the street. But he agreed to study the
plan and make recommendations over the next two years, thereby de-
laying its implementation until after the 1993 mayoral election. Then
in September 1992, Dinkins announced that he would implement most
of the panel's recommendations, a major victory for those calling for
structural reform. The city was now saying that it would embark on a
"unified policy" to increase the amount of permanent housing and the
number of substance abuse, mental health, and vocational services and
to bring in nonprofit organizations to do much of the work.[21] Many
homeless advocates and the *New York Times* applauded the plan.[22]

At the same time, however, the number of homeless families continued to rise, doubling over the previous year while city revenues remained depressed.[23] As a result, by January 1993, Dinkins was forced
to scale back the services part of the plan and focus instead on perma-

nent housing. He also changed the recipients of the housing to include many nonhomeless, working-poor families as a way of increasing the stability of the housing locations. Dinkins also continued to be troubled by resistance to shelters and services by communities throughout the city: "I have been particularly put out by the efforts of some on the City Council to say 'You must get out of hotels,' and the same people explain how they can't have any facilities in their neighborhoods. I've had it."[24]

Dinkins was now caught between supporting a more comprehensive structural program and not having the financial resources or political support to implement it. This conflict was aggravated by the fact that the numbers of homeless people both in the shelter system and out on the streets was continuing to rise. This left the mayor vulnerable to the criticisms that either his policies were flawed or he was incapable of implementing them. In fact, as the next chapter shows, it was the economic pressures of urban liberal economic development strategies started under Koch and continued under Dinkins that made these policies impossible to implement. The city's seemingly permanent fiscal crisis meant that without a major reordering of its tax policies, no large-scale municipal government intervention in housing markets would be possible, and welfare payments and other social services would continue to be rolled back just as wages and job opportunities for low-skilled workers were declining. Nonetheless, Dinkins never made these changes or even offered them as a possible solution. As a result, he was vulnerable to charges that urban liberalism was an inadequate social services approach that failed to involve communities or address the disorder overrunning the city. This was exactly the argument made by his Republican challenger in the fall election, Rudolph Giuliani.

Giuliani asserted that the mayor had "tried hard and failed" to reduce the homelessness problem and had created additional public bureaucracies rather than bringing in nonprofits to run homeless services.[25] He argued that the city should get out of the housing business and allow the free market to provide housing. In addition, he called for restricting shelter access to ninety days for many homeless people as a way of forcing them into the private employment and housing markets. He claimed that by tying so many services to homeless status, the shelter system was benefiting people who were not making an effort, instead of the working poor.[26] Giuliani made no claims about the ability of government programs to solve these problems. Instead, he contended that in many ways homeless services were exacerbating the problem by allowing people to remain dependent rather than being forced to take whatever minimal employment was available. To the extent that services were necessary, they should be short term and under community or private-sector control. Finally, he appealed to people's frustrations over declining social conditions by saying that it was socially acceptable to want to see public disorder and those responsible forcibly removed, whether or not long-term solutions to their problems had been found.

The differences were now set between the liberal advocates of government-provided permanent housing and comprehensive social services, and the neoconservatives calling for punitive measures to force people to return to market mechanisms. In addition, Giuliani made it clear that the real problem was not homelessness but restoring the neighborhoods' "quality of life." Giuliani's main rhetorical initiative did not mention shelters or permanent housing but, instead, the elimination of "squeegee men," who demanded money from motorists for cleaning their car windows while they were stopped in traffic. Relying on the "broken windows" theory, he argued that the key to restoring public order was not providing additional services for the poor and mentally ill but aggressively cracking down on illegal and disruptive public behavior and that by doing so, civility would be restored to public spaces.

It was the issue of "quality of life" that undid Mayor Dinkins. A *New York Times*/WCBS-TV poll taken less than a month before the election showed that 62 percent of New Yorkers felt that the "quality of life in New York" had gotten worse and that only 9 percent felt it had gotten better. These results were higher than those saying that either the economy or race relations had declined. The poll also showed that 63 percent of New Yorkers felt the city should "get tougher with homeless who make a nuisance of themselves," compared with 55 percent before the 1989 election.[27] In the end, Giuliani won election by a slim margin, made up largely of white independent voters. This swing constituency abandoned Dinkins and his liberal efforts to reduce the homeless problem and its impact on communities and instead embraced a punitive approach to restoring order to communities.

Prostitution

New York's prostitution problem goes back to its founding, when the Dutch East India Company encouraged the presence of prostitutes as a palliative for its mostly male workforce. During the Revolutionary War, New York was turned into a garrison city for the British, and prostitutes were in great demand. At the beginning of the twentieth century, great moral crusades were held against the "social evil" and "white slavery."[28] By World War I, open prostitution was on the decline, and streetwalkers were limited to a handful of areas.[29] This remained the case until the 1960s when the public impact of prostitution began to change along with public attitudes toward it.

In the late 1960s, the sexual revolution was increasing both the demand for prostitution and the public acceptance of it. Most people still opposed it, but their opposition increasingly took the form of rehabilitation measures rather than criminalization. Advocacy groups and public officials began calling for a decriminalization of prostitution or, at least, a reorganization of the criminal justice system: "Many policemen, judges and other city officials are becoming increasingly dismayed by what Supreme Court Justice John M. Murtagh calls the 'utter futility' of the traditional law-enforcement approach to prostitution."[30] Not surprisingly, those most vocally in favor of punitive enforcement measures were small businesses located near zones of prostitution. Despite their complaints and occasional police sweeps, the move toward treating prostitution as a social rather than criminal problem proceeded. Local judges began to throw out prostitution cases resulting from sweeps.[31] Mayor John Lindsay, while being careful not to condone illegal behavior, made it clear that he supported therapeutic rather than punitive approaches. Responding to this change in attitude, the state legislature reduced the penalty for prostitution from up to a year in jail to a maximum of fifteen days and a $250 fine.

Over the next two years, the number of prostitutes rose in the city's central areas, including midtown Manhattan and Times Square. These are largely nonresidential areas and the people raising objections to the problem were mostly business owners, including many quite powerful hotel owners. In this period, the effect of prostitution on residential neighborhoods was limited to the lower-income communities adjacent to these areas. The power of the business owners, however, was sufficient to have the penalties increased in 1969 to a maximum of ninety days in jail.[32] These stricter penalties did not succeed in greatly reducing either the supply or the demand for prostitution. They were, however, successful in reducing its public presence and impact, at least in the short run.

During the next several years, the controversy over prostitution remained unresolved as women's groups and legal reformers continued to argue against the criminalization of women who were already being "victimized by society" and as local business owners and residents directly affected by the trade called for more police sweeps. More than anything else, though, it was the continued demand that kept prostitution thriving on the western edges of midtown. During this period, the number of pornographic stores and movie houses grew rapidly in the Times Square area, creating a focal point for the sex trade. Periodic police sweeps seemed to have little long-term effect. Also at this time, prostitution began to expand into outlying areas, including the Jamaica section of Queens and the Fort Greene and Boerum Hill sections of Brooklyn.

By the mid-1970s a new détente had been reached on the question of prostitution. Because of the growing liberalization of views about sexual activity, the police increasingly took no action against indoor prostitution such as massage parlors and agencies for call girls. However, since organized constituencies decried the impact of streetwalking on local areas, police tried to keep it contained as much as possible, given the high demand. What emerged was a game of cat and mouse between the police and the prostitutes. One result of this new pattern was that the social divisions between streetwalkers and call girls grew. Increasingly, streetwalkers were women in the most desperate condition. They were more likely to be poor, nonwhite, drug addicted, and under the control of a pimp. As economic times worsened, more women in this situation appeared on the streets.

One result of the new approach was the growth of the pornography business. During the mid-1970s, adult bookstores and strip clubs spread to many parts of the city, including high-income areas near the Upper East Side. Although these businesses were a moral affront to some local residents, they were rarely a source of serious crime or social disorder because the business transactions and sexual activity took place indoors. Some residents continued to oppose these establishments, but growing social tolerance and sympathetic court rulings made it difficult to attack them head-on.[33] As competition with the indoor businesses grew stronger, street prostitutes often had to work longer hours and be more aggressive. But during tough economic times, even the indoor outposts of the sex industry became magnets for streetwalkers hoping to siphon off part of their trade.

By 1976, the growth in the street trade was stimulating political mobilization in some of the communities most affected. The historically liberal Upper West Side became one of the most vocal neighborhoods demanding greater penalties and police enforcement. In response, Democratic State Senator Manfred Ohrenstein, who had supported the legalization of prostitution in the past, introduced a new measure to increase the penalties significantly. According to the director of the New York Civil Liberties Union, Ira Glasser, "This is basically the same bill as the ones he refused to introduce in the past. . . . [Ohrenstein] is feeling the heat of the community. He wants to get the unseemly stuff off the streets."[34]

In the early 1980s, street prostitution continued expanding into residential areas, becoming a major public issue in Long Island City in Queens, in Boerum Hill in Brooklyn, and on Park Avenue South in Manhattan. This increase in activity reached a peak with the economic downturn of the early 1980s. Then, as the economy improved in New York during the rest of the decade, prostitution waned. By that point, however, there was widespread political mobilization against street prostitution. Many neighborhoods throughout the city felt besieged. This feeling, combined with the growing number of crimes and loss of confidence in government's ability to solve social problems, shaped people's views about the viability of public space and the stability of their neighborhoods before the homeless crisis. More and more, liberal New Yorkers were abandoning abstract principles of social tolerance when confronted by the new realities of public disorder and instead demanding a fuller commitment to the law enforcement approach. In many ways, this was a precursor to the broader backlash of the late 1980s.

Prostitution represents a fundamental dilemma for urban liberals. On the one hand, they want to respond to community complaints, but on the other, they are committed to a civil liberties orientation that respects enhanced sexual freedoms and views the sex industry as a primarily victimless crime. The result of this conflict is another form of hollow tolerance. Politicians respond to community complaints through periodic crackdowns, but no real comprehensive enforcement effort is ever put in place. The police are never forced to make this an enforcement priority, and the courts are reluctant to treat prostitution as a serious crime. On the flip side, this is a hollow approach because nothing is ever done on the services side, either. Real alternatives for sex workers are never considered, and enforcement of laws against abusive pimps is largely nonexistent. The result is a no-win situation in which residents and merchants grow more and more frustrated about the failed policies of either halfhearted social services or halfhearted law enforcement approaches.

In contrast, the Giuliani administration treated prostitution as a serious issue and devoted considerable resources to reduce its public impact. Police Commissioner William Bratton created "Operation Losing Proposition," which stepped up undercover operations against prostitution throughout the city and allowed the police to seize the vehicles of people arrested for soliciting prostitutes. In addition, the Giuliani administration targeted the legal sex clubs and adult book and video stores in many parts of the city, especially in Times Square. It created new zoning regulations that forced many businesses to close, thus breaking up informal "red light" zones where street prostitution was common. The overall result was a broad criminalization of prostitution, which forced most of the trade indoors, where it now operates through semilegal escort services and sexually suggestive advertisements in a variety of free newspapers such as the *Village Voice* and *New York Press*. While the services of sex workers are still widely available, their impact on communities and public spaces has been effectively reduced through punitive enforcement measures that forced the trade indoors.

Graffiti

During the 1960s, youth vandalism emerged as a major issue in New York. For many people, vandalism in the form of graffiti, "tagging," and the destruction of property was symbolic of the overall declining conditions in the city. The increase in these acts represented to many people the fact that young people were no longer under the supervision and control of their parents or the larger society and thus were a threat to the social order and personal security. For many people, this was especially threatening because of its racial overtones. Graffiti, in particular, was associated with poor, nonwhite, young males, who also were associated with the city's growing crime rate.

Graffiti and vandalism have a spatial as well as a social dimension. They are located primarily where young people have easy access to public places such as schools and public transportation. Their presence indicates that an area is unregulated and out of control and, therefore, potentially dangerous. Following Jane Jacobs, it suggests that no one is watching; neither the police nor the public have control over the space, so anything might happen there.[35] While this effect may not always hold, despite the claims of the "broken windows" theory, it does highlight why graffiti has become a telling sign of the decline of public spaces and social relations and a rallying point for the neoconservative backlash.

By 1970, vandalism in the bus and subway systems was costing the Metropolitan Transit Authority (MTA) $2.6 million a year.[36] In 1971, spray paint began to be used widely, raising the level and visibility of the damage being done. This was also the year that the practice now called *tagging* was started, in which people write their names on walls in a stylized form. This early tagging was located initially in the Washington Heights and Harlem neighborhoods and took the form of names followed by street numbers (for example, Taki 183).[37] Within a year, however, the practice had become widespread in the transit system and on many public buildings, prompting calls for new punitive measures by Mayor Lindsay and the city council.

Despite the higher penalties in the early 1970s, the practice of graffiti became even more widespread and complex. Graffiti writers began to produce murals on entire subway cars or the sides of buildings. Graffiti also spread beyond the confines of poor communities, affecting even the wealthy bastion of the Upper East Side. By far the most troubling aspect of the graffiti problem, however, was its growth in the subway system where, by the mid-1970s, it was endemic. Combined with the rising crime rates, graffiti lent an air of danger to the subways that ultimately affected ridership levels. This aesthetic assault was increasingly viewed as a threat to the foundations of urban civility. As one Staten Island resident wrote in a letter to the *New York Times*:

> Graffiti are an offense against public space. Subway walls belong to the people—to all the people. Public space is a necessity in urban civilization, especially for those that do not have much private space. . . . *Without decent public space, urban life is intolerable.* . . . If [graffiti scrawlers] succeed in making the city's public spaces unattractive to a majority of residents, New York will become a backwater. (emphasis added)[38]

Throughout the 1970s, a number of measures were taken to try to stem the tide, though none of them were adequately funded or sufficiently broad in scope. These ranged from new police enforcement tactics, laws that restricted teen access to paint and markers, tougher criminal penalties, community service programs utilizing both offenders and other youth in the abatement of graffiti, youth art programs designed to divert the desire for artistic expression into more suitable channels, and cleanup efforts ranging from neighborhood volunteer outings to million-dollar city and Transit Authority efforts. None of these initiatives, however, was successful in reducing the problem.

At the same time, because of federal budget cuts and the local fiscal crisis, programs for youth and spending on transit maintenance were significantly scaled back. In the mid- to late 1960s, summer youth employment programs had been a mainstay of the urban war on poverty. But by the early 1970s, the Nixon administration's agenda of rolling back urban social programs was well under way, and youth employment, training, and recreational programs were severely affected. The city tried to pick up some of the difference but was unable to do so. This left tens of thousands of young people, who had previously been employed in the summer, with nothing constructive to do. This no doubt contributed to the youth subculture that emerged out of the south Bronx and parts of Brooklyn that fueled the graffiti problem.

The city's fiscal crisis, combined with decreases in state and federal funding for mass transit, made it very difficult for the Metropolitan Transit Authority (MTA) to adequately maintain the subway trains or stations. As a result, conditions in both deteriorated throughout the 1970s. Trains and stations were not regularly cleaned, painted, or repaired, and the system acquired a decrepit appearance symbolizing another aspect of the growing vandalism problem: an unregulated space left to disorderly forces. By the early 1980s, public confidence in the subway as a safe public space was badly shaken, and ridership fell.

In 1984 Governor Mario Cuomo, desperate to reverse the situation, brought new leadership into the Transit Authority to try to clean things up on several fronts. A major investment in infrastructure was combined with a new approach to graffiti control. After a decade of failed enforcement strategy involving guard dogs, razor wire, and specialized police units, a solution emerged in the form of the Clean Car Program. This program involved a massive infusion of funds into cleaning whole subway trains at once and keeping them clean despite repeated attacks.

Once a car had gone through the program, it was kept clean by pulling it from service as soon as any graffiti appeared until it was cleaned up and then was sent back into service. This same approach was also successful on some government buildings in Manhattan, but it was very expensive.

The victory over graffiti in the subways was won primarily through a massive infusion of new resources into the system in the form of new cars and enhanced maintenance. Young people have continued to mark trains and stations with a variety of forms of graffiti after this innovation, but the constant maintenance, including daily station visits by painters, has kept the visible signs of it in check. This kind of approach was not possible in the city's streets, however. No new massive infusion of cash was available, and the extent of the problem was too great to make a real difference.

During this crisis, the Koch and Dinkins administrations concentrated on enforcement and cleanup efforts. In 1989, the Dinkins administration attempted to enhance youth services as part of his family- and child-oriented approach to social services. It created a new Department of Youth Services (DYS) to coordinate after-school and summer jobs programs, which had been severely affected by previous budget cuts. By 1990, the budget for this agency was $34.5 million.[39] Even this effort, however, was a drop in the bucket, given the one million school-age children in the city, about half of whom lived near or below the poverty line. In fact, the city that year spent more money on cleaning up graffiti ($42 million) than it did on the DYS.[40] Even for a family-oriented mayor, cleanup and enforcement won out over prevention.

The widespread presence of graffiti represented not only a superficial aesthetic defacement or even a general sign of disorder. It also was a visible symbol of the presence of young people of color acting outside the law with relative impunity, clearly indicating to many residents that the city, and thus their neighborhoods, was headed in the wrong direction. With the economic uncertainty and government cutbacks of the 1980s, neighborhoods struggled either to cash in on pockets of gentrification or to be cast out into the wilderness of inner-city decline and abandonment. When prostitution and crime became part of this volatile mixture, neighborhoods throughout the city felt besieged. The urban liberal strategies of halfhearted enforcement and limited cleanup efforts did little to reduce the problem. New approaches to fight graffiti had to be found.

The Giuliani administration made graffiti a major issue for law enforcement. In 1996 the NYPD issued its graffiti control report entitled "Combat Graffiti: Reclaiming the Public Spaces."[41] The report emphasized the criminal nature of graffiti and, consistent with the broken windows theory, elevated its importance to the city's stability. As a sign of the issue's seriousness, the city announced that people reporting graffiti in progress should dial 911 and that if the report resulted in an arrest, the caller would be eligible for a $500 reward. The department also created a new graffiti task force made up of officers from the housing, transit, and patrol bureaus, which created a graffiti database of known "taggers" and their distinctive styles for use in identifying their work throughout the city. Graffiti was thus transformed from a minor form of vandalism and youthful mischief into a significant crime engaging substantial police department resources.

Conclusion

This chapter looked at New York's disorder crisis and the failure of urban liberals to respond to it adequately. Homelessness, prostitution, and graffiti became more than minor nuisances; they became both real impediments to daily life and symbols of the city's growing incivility and instability. Urban liberals were unable to adjust to this new political reality and continued to rely on short-term emergency social services, centralized expert planning divorced from community input, and empty pleas for social tolerance to address residents' deteriorating quality of life. Consequently, they created a political space for neoconservative responses that took quality-of-life concerns seriously, both rhetorically and practically in the form of concrete measures to clear the streets of disorder.

Urban liberals were unable to respond to these problems more effectively, in part because of the budget constraints they faced. The next chapter explores how they contributed to this fiscal crisis that hindered their ability to fully fund social programs. It also explains how their increasing orientation toward the neoliberal free market and structural adjustment policies undercut their desire to intervene more directly in failed housing and employment markets on behalf of the homeless and unemployed.

5

Globalization and the Urban Crisis

Urban liberalism not only failed to deal adequately with the problems of homelessness and disorder; it also directly contributed to these problems. While federal funding cuts to cities, the deinstitutionalization of mentally ill people without offering them community-based care, and additional funding cuts at the state level were important factors in the deterioration of urban public spaces, local urban liberal administrations took concrete steps that exacerbated these problems rather than relieving them. By relying on an economic development program that favored finance, real estate, and corporate headquarters at the expense of manufacturing, and by cutting social services and failing to prop up the bottom of the labor and housing markets, they allowed the homelessness and disorder problem to spiral out of control.

New York Mayor Edward Koch responded to the homelessness crisis of the 1980s by using city money to build thousands of units of low-income housing to try to alleviate the pressure on the city's overflowing shelter system. He was praised for his plan to spend $5 billion over ten years to build housing, beginning in 1987.[1] A closer inspection, however, reveals two major problems with this strategy. First, only 10 percent of the units over the life of the program were affordable enough for homeless people,[2] and second, in the decade leading up to this point, Koch supported real estate development tax incentives that resulted in the loss of more than 100,000 units of low-cost SRO housing, at a cost of up to $238 million a year in lost taxes.[3] In effect, he and Mayor Dinkins were spending $350 million a year to treat some of the symptoms of a subsidy to real estate developers costing $300 million a year. The net result was billions of dollars spent to house a small percentage of people made homeless by Koch's own economic development policies.

At the center of this failure of urban liberalism was its reliance on a

"global cities" model of economic development, which attempted to locate New York at the center of increasingly mobile international capital
through a variety of tax and zoning incentives that encouraged high-
rent commercial and housing construction in Manhattan and parts of
Queens and Brooklyn. While urban liberals were largely successful in
this endeavor, it had profoundly negative consequences for the poor, as
they were excluded from housing and labor markets by the resulting polarization of wages and the loss of affordable housing. The cost of these
tax subsidies aggravated the problem by bankrupting local government
to the degree that they were unable to provide basic social and medical
services to the homeless, drug-addicted, and mentally ill people undermining the civility of public spaces around the city. This was a form of
"primitive globalization" that redistributed wealth from the middle and
working classes to the corporate, finance, and real estate sectors.[4] The
result was a growth in homelessness, petty crime, and a host of low-
level urban disorders such as graffiti, panhandling, and street drug dealing that in turn created the conditions for a punitive neoconservative
political backlash.

The Urban Economic Crisis

After World War II, American cities underwent dramatic transforma-
tions. Whereas the Sun Belt cities from Los Angeles to Atlanta grew
rapidly, cities in the northern tier from San Francisco to New York City
experienced periods of deep crisis as they lost millions of manufacturing
jobs to the American and global South. These cities either went into decline (for example, Cleveland, Baltimore, and Detroit) or remade themselves to better compete in the postindustrial American economy (for
example, New York, Boston, Chicago, and San Francisco). This process
of reinvention, however, was not without costs. The new approaches to
economic development in the context of emerging neoliberalism at both
the global and local levels have created significant economic and social
polarization and instability.

In this chapter I describe the economic development approaches undertaken by business elites and local government in New York in response to the changing national and international economic conditions.
New York used a variety of entrepreneurial methods to pursue a global
cities strategy of growth designed to tap into the flows of capital and in-

formation. The result of this strategy was a polarization of labor and housing markets and cuts in social services that led to a crisis in public civility that the city was unable to handle effectively, thereby opening the door to the conservative political backlash of the 1990s. Several factors contributed to differing degrees to the crisis in northern American cities in the 1970s, including deindustrialization, white flight, and disinvestment by the federal and state governments, which led to massive job and population losses and municipal fiscal crisis.

During the 1970s and 1980s, manufacturers moved thousands of plants out of the industrial Northeast and Midwest in an effort to cut costs and increase profits. Greater competition from overseas, along with federal policies that shifted defense production south and west, were major contributing factors in this process. As a result, urban areas lost millions of decent-paying, low-skilled jobs. Nationally, more than 38 million jobs were lost in the 1970s in manufacturing and related employment.[5]

The postwar period also was a time of white flight in the American North, when millions of mostly white middle- and upper-class urban residents left the central cities for the surrounding suburbs. Federally subsidized highway construction and home mortgage guarantees helped accelerate this process. Consequently, the populations of these cities became poorer and less white as those with the fewest resources were left behind to compete for a dwindling number of low-skill jobs. At the same time, the demand for social services increased as the tax base shrank from the flight of both manufacturers and many middle-class and wealthy taxpayers.

Structural Adjustment

In the 1960s, the administrations of both Presidents John F. Kennedy and Lyndon B. Johnson attempted to help those cities suffering the twin problems of population and job loss, by means of various antipoverty and urban redevelopment programs. Although these efforts, under the banner of the War on Poverty, helped stabilize some areas, they did little to reverse the overall trend and were not sustainable given the budgetary pressures of the expanding war in Vietnam. By the early 1970s, this process was reversed by President Richard M. Nixon's administration, whose suburban and rural base had no interest in helping the urban poor.

The result has been a period of structural fiscal crisis for many post-industrial American cities. The pressures of declining industry, population loss, and federal social services budget cuts have undermined the cities' ability to pay for the rising demands of the growing poor populations left behind. As a result, local budgets were cut just when the demand for services was increasing, causing support for public parks, welfare, housing, and other public services to be cut back. We can think of this as a problem of structural adjustment, not unlike that in developing countries. In those cases, pressure from the World Bank, International Monetary Fund, and other global lenders have forced national governments to cut back domestic spending in order to both subsidize development and pay back lenders. In addition, this process often includes privatization schemes designed to enhance the efficiency of service delivery. Often, however, these projects further polarize access to services, as the costs of obtaining them go up to compensate new foreign investors. In the process, services such as health care, public transportation, and education are reduced while fees are raised.

Cuts by the federal and state governments in two main areas in the 1970s and 1980s played a significant role in undermining the stability of local governments such as New York City's. At the state level, the deinstitutionalization of the mentally ill taxed a wide variety of urban social programs, including low-cost housing and health care services. The combined state and federal cuts to welfare worsened the polarization of incomes in urban areas and threatened the economic stability of millions of urban families. In addition, federal housing assistance to the poor failed to meet the increased needs of the growing number of low- and very low income households.

Even though deinstitutionalization began in the 1950s, its effects on urban budgets and social conditions were not felt until the late 1970s and the 1980s.[6] During the 1950s and early 1960s, the number of people housed in state mental institutions was slightly reduced as a result of pressure from patients' rights groups. Most of those who were released were people who could function fairly well and were able to live independently with the assistance of some of the new psychiatric drugs becoming available at the time. During the 1960s, the increasing effectiveness and affordability of these drugs, the high cost of running the hospitals, and the growing social outrage over the terrible conditions in many of these institutions led to additional releases and fewer intakes. By the 1970s, cost cutting became the principal factor driving deinstitutionalization, as tens of thousands were released onto America's streets with few or no support services. While many of those released in the early waves were able to maintain their stability on federal disability payments and, in some cases, employment, the later groups had worse problems that required ongoing medical oversight to ensure their ability to live in the community.

In the 1970s and 1980s as the hospitals were being closed, New York Governor Mario Cuomo reached an agreement with advocates for the mentally ill that a share of the savings of closing down state mental hospitals would be passed on to local communities to provide support services for the deinstitutionalized, both those released and those denied admission. Since community-based and pharmacological care is much less expensive, this seemed like a win-win situation. Unfortunately, as the state's fiscal crisis continued in the 1980s, these community care funds never materialized, and New York City and other municipalities were left to make up the difference. In 1953 there were 93,000 people in New York State mental hospitals; by 1987 the number was 20,000; and in 2005 the number had declined to 4,500.[7] In 1988 alone, New York City admitted 18,500 homeless people into hospitals for emergency psychiatric care, up from 1,000 in 1976.[8] By 1990 the city estimated there were 15,000 homeless mentally ill people in the city,[9] and by the 1990s more than 15 percent of people in the city's jail system were seriously mentally ill.[10] By 2004, the cost of incarcerating people in Rikers Island was estimated at $100,000 a year.[11] Similarly, the cost of emergency room admissions, short-term inpatient hospitalization, and shelter beds was much higher than that for state hospital beds, and the expense came out of local rather than state budgets, costing the city millions of dollars a year.

State and federal cuts to welfare programs also greatly damaged the economic condition of low-income New Yorkers, for which the city government had to pay. In the 1970s and 1980s, Aid to Families with Dependent Children (AFDC) was the primary federal welfare program, and by the early 1990s, it served five million families a year, with the program's costs shared by the federal and state governments.[12] Nationally, the median AFDC benefit fell by 42 percent between 1970 and 1991.[13] Benefits in New York fell 40 percent during this same period, and by 1991 New York City's AFDC benefit for a family of three was $577 a month, and the fair-market median rent for a two-bedroom apartment was $610 a month.[14] Similarly, Supplemental Security Income

(SSI) for those with disabilities failed to keep pace with inflation, especially the cost of housing. As a result, local government was forced to deal with a growing population of unemployed women with children whose welfare payments were unable to pay for their basic housing needs. This meant higher local costs for supplemental rent vouchers, homeless shelter beds, and foster care services for children separated from parents who were unable to provide for them.

One final issue bears noting. Many homeless advocates have pointed to cuts in federal spending on low-cost housing during the 1990s as a major factor contributing to homelessness and the cities' fiscal crisis. Measuring the changes in federal spending on housing is complicated. Federal outlays for low-cost housing were dramatically cut in the 1980s under the administrations of Presidents Ronald Reagan and George H. W. Bush. Overall, if the rate of annual expenditures had continued during the 1980s, more than two million additional low-income families would have been housed under federal programs.[15] Christopher Jencks points out that actual spending on low-cost housing during this period increased slightly, however.[16] While this is true, it masks the fact that the need for low-cost housing was actually dramatically expanding while new outlays to meet these demands were being cut back.

Fordism and Post-Fordism

Before the 1970s, most northern cities had a strong Democratic Party that worked closely with economic elites and labor leaders in a corporatist coalition that provided stability in labor markets and the tax base. This coalition worked to create a level playing field that managed competition within economic sectors and encouraged manufacturing-led economic development. This "Fordist" model of economic development emphasized high wages and unionization in return for labor peace and increased productivity.[17] High wages allowed for robust consumer spending, which in turn stimulated local-consumption-based economic activity. In addition, generous worker benefits, unemployment insurance, and at least minimal welfare payments allowed even the least-paid workers to participate in consumption. This Keynesian demand-led model of economic stimulus was at the center of postwar American prosperity.

By the early 1970s, though, the Fordist model began to experience difficulties. One of its features was reducing competition as government, labor, and capital attempted to manage the economy. As a result, productivity and innovation began to decline just as international competition from reindustrialized Japan and Western Europe increased. In response, a new, post-Fordist model of development emerged, which relied on the greater mobility of capital and products to decentralize production.[18] Corporations thus became flexible producers by outsourcing more of their work through contractors. Rather than being top-to-bottom producers, they hired consultants to perform design tasks, boutique bankers to manage capital, and small, flexible manufacturers to provide parts and assemble them in plants around the world.

Substantially cheaper shipping by sea and air, improved communication, and easier international capital flows made the relocation of manufacturing to the global South much more cost-effective. Corporations then began to view themselves as global rather than local or national entities, with allegiances to a global community of shareholders rather than to a local or even a national community. Corporations used this newfound flexibility to undermine their previously stable relationships with their workers and local governments. They now had greater leverage to force employees to accept wage and benefit cuts or risk losing their jobs to cheaper and more flexible independent contractors. Cities also had to renegotiate their relationships with manufacturers in order to stay competitive. Tax incentives and fewer regulations thus became the coin of the realm in attracting and retaining manufacturing.

This new politics of urban competition highlighted the importance of place in the economic process. Economic elites became divided between those who were tied to a specific place and those who were free to relocate. Local place-based elites, such as newspapers, real estate owners, and tourism-oriented firms, had a stake in boosting the local economy, whereas manufacturers and corporate headquarters could demand subsidies and regulatory considerations or else leave town. In response, a new urban politics developed that pitted capital against local places.[19] These new political coalitions were made up of local unions and fixed-asset firms pursuing economic growth through international competition for increasingly mobile manufacturing jobs and corporate headquarters.

Entrepreneurial Cities

One of the central characteristics of this new politics is that the cities began to assume a more entrepreneurial quality.[20] Rather than pursuing largely internal growth strategies in the form of enhancing the stability of local firms, the cities had to compete directly with one another to attract capital. These new "entrepreneurial cities" had to establish strong local booster coalitions or "growth machines" in order to mobilize enough local resources to compete effectively.[21] This required close public-private cooperation between local governments and place-based elites, the strongest incentives being a process of speculative risk absorption in which "the public sector assumes the risk and the private sector takes the benefits."[22] These entrepreneurial cities redirected local government resources from the provision of social services into tax abatements and subsidies. Convention centers, sports arena, and industrial parks are examples of the types of speculative developments underwritten by local governments.

Embedded in this approach are the concepts of governmentality and regime theory. Governmentality argues that state policy cannot be understood as the narrow result of legislative and executive action but instead is a process of interaction between government and other powerful political actors.[23] Regime theory challenges both elite and pluralist theories of the state by arguing that economic development strategies are not the result solely of either elite interests or a competition among competing interest groups. Instead, they are strategic partnerships among shifting coalitions of economic elites and government actors based on competing visions of larger economic forces and how to respond to them.[24] This allows us to look more carefully at how political problems and strategies are defined through public discourses. Knowledge of an entrepreneurial city's strategies are not limited to official government actions but can be found in an array of public and private actions and statements. Reports, studies, commissions, and other public and private accountings of a city's problems and its strategies for addressing them are a central source of information in tracking its political and economic direction. These documents and practices show that different cities approached their problems in different ways, with differing consequences.

The Global Cities Strategy

Not all cities used the same entrepreneurial strategies to exploit different comparative advantages. Seattle and Los Angeles capitalized on their position on the Pacific Rim by expanding their sea and air ports to handle the growing trade with Asia. Boston built on its educational infrastructure by promoting high-tech firms, regional banking, and corporate headquarters. New York and San Francisco chose a strategy coordinating global movements of capital and housing corporate headquarters. This *global cities* approach to economic development emphasized the development of commercial office space, business services, and communications infrastructure at the expense of manufacturing and the transportation of physical goods.[25]

Competing for manufacturing made less sense with the global bidding down of wages, environmental regulations, and taxes. As the global flows of capital and information became more dynamic, those cities that became hubs for the coordination of these flows were in a strong position to tap into the wealth they created. This process was not without its own bidding process, however. In order to attract corporate headquarters and financial institutions, the cities felt they had to subsidize commercial office space development and create tax incentives for corporate payrolls. This was offset at least in part by the sometimes fantastic profits generated by these firms, along with the growth in the business services they required. These services, however, created two tiers of employment. The very small, higher-paying tier includes design, advertising, and accounting services, while the much larger lower tier is made up of low-skilled jobs such as clerical, janitorial, and food services, contributing to a polarization of wages.

Another central feature of this strategy was a reformulation of the welfare state. Northern cities were experiencing a series of baseline external pressures stemming from the loss of tax revenue from deindustrialization and suburbanization. They also suffered from the loss of federal revenues in the antiurban backlash of the 1970s.[26] The result was the fiscal crises of the mid-1970s, which ushered in a "permanent crisis" in the funding of social services. The global cities strategy melded well with this development. In order to attract international capital, global cities had to adopt fiscal strategies consistent with the ideology of structural adjustment, which called for a hollowing out of the welfare state in favor of market mechanisms to provide such basic needs as housing, health care, and higher education.

This free-market approach led local governments to reduce their spending on social services and use that money to stimulate the finance, insurance, and real estate (FIRE) sectors of the economy, which were central to the global cities strategy. The irony of this supposedly "free-market" approach is that government was still an active participant in the economy. Rather than coordinating manufacturing, regulating wages, and providing basic social services, local governments were using entrepreneurial methods to stimulate the privileged FIRE sectors of the economy at the expense of all else.

These global cities experienced tremendous economic growth for those at the center of the flows of capital and information, but those providing low-skilled services saw a decline in their economic condition relative to the wages available in manufacturing before the transition. Both labor and housing markets became polarized, with a small but significant segment of the population being excluded from both. As a result, many urban neighborhoods became unstable because of either gentrification or economic decline and abandonment. In addition, public spaces throughout these cities became gathering places for the newly dispossessed. Homeless people, unemployed youth, and others excluded from regular participation in housing and labor markets became an omnipresent visible statement about the condition of the losers in the new global economy.

New York City

The economic polarization of the 1980s affected New York more than any other American city. It already was a major financial center and had the largest concentration of corporate headquarters and associated business services in the United States. The city government also was squarely in favor of supporting the growth of the service and corporate sector and the decline of manufacturing. The Lindsay (1966–74) and Koch (1978–90) administrations devised numerous tax incentives that pushed manufacturing out of the city (especially Manhattan) and encouraged high-rent commercial and housing development even when demand was sluggish.

In 1968, the Regional Plan Association (RPA), a nonprofit planning group funded by major corporations, released its second regional plan[27] (the first was issued in 1929), which called for a dramatic vertical and horizontal expansion of the downtown and midtown central business districts. This plan envisioned a reduction in government support for manufacturing and an increase in support for building high-rise offices. The RPA plan was based on the assumption that along with global population increases, New York would see a rise in population and employment. To encourage this, the city needed to use its limited amount of land as efficiently as possible through a concentration of use. This meant replacing low-density and low-rent manufacturing with high-density office and residential space.

The Lindsay administration adopted many of the RPA's recommendations in its Plan for New York City 1969.[28] These included the westward expansion of midtown, a new Second Avenue subway line, and the enlargement of the downtown financial district through the construction of the World Trade Center and Battery Park City. But rather than counterbalancing office expansion and manufacturing, Mayor Lindsay tried to support the development of both manufacturing and commercial office space. This was to be done by relocating manufacturing to the outer boroughs to make room for more high-rise buildings. Despite pledges to increase manufacturing, however, this relocation policy ended up substantially reducing the city's manufacturing sector. Shortly after the plan was released, New York City's economy took a nosedive, postponing the implementation of many of its recommendations. Nonetheless, the city's program of expanding its corporate and financial sectors became the blueprint for the restructuring of its economy in the following decades.

The 1970s Fiscal Crisis

During the 1970s, the new fiscal realities of reduced federal support and declining tax revenues due to the loss of population and jobs brought New York City's government to its knees. President Gerald R. Ford's administration refused to support the city's efforts to renegotiate its debts with the help of a federal bailout, so the city was required to turn over its fiscal management to a group of business leaders acting to secure the stability of the city's debt on behalf of bondholders. The result was that the financiers were able to impose their analysis of what caused the crisis and how to solve it.[29] They blamed the city's problems on too many social services for the poor, high wages for city workers, and not enough services for the wealthy and middle classes, whose flight from the city had shrunk the city's revenue base. This analysis became one of the major weapons available to conservatives over the next generation. They attempted to debate municipal policy within this framework, rather than exploring the local and federal policies that had helped create the broader economic context responsible for the crisis.

As a result, social services were cut significantly during this period. Welfare payments failed to keep pace with the cost of living; tuition was imposed at the City University of New York, and many social services benefiting everyone from poor children to seniors were scaled back. In addition, city jobs were cut and salaries lowered, creating pressure on the middle classes as well as the poor. In addition to agreeing to substantial cutbacks, municipal unions agreed to invest a considerable part of their pension funds in municipal bonds, thus bailing out private bondholders and providing a disincentive for future wage demands.[30]

Even though the city appeared to be completely without resources, in the mid- to late 1970s, the Koch administration developed and expanded a number of tax-incentive programs to try to stimulate real estate development. The hope was that a boom in high-rise offices and luxury housing would stimulate the economy by creating profits for real estate developers—a precursor to the Reagan "trickle-down" economics of the 1980s. These programs, including the Industrial and Commercial Incentives Program, the Industrial Development Agency, and sections J-51, 421a, and 421b of the municipal tax code, drove up land prices in much of Manhattan by providing tax incentives and zoning changes, which forced out lower-value uses such as manufacturing and low-income housing.

The Entrepreneurial 1980s

As the local real estate market began to improve in the late 1970s, these incentives remained in place, generating windfall profits for developers and creating a subsidy-driven inducement for building office space in a period when demand could easily be met by the existing supply. The result was a glut of new high-rent commercial office buildings, a loss of manufacturing jobs and low-income housing, and a continuing loss of tax revenues. As a member of Community Board 5, west of midtown, stated in 1979, "The city is giving away too much; we're still in a poverty state of mind when these builders are going to make a bundle off of new buildings in midtown."[31]

Rather than responding to these complaints about oversubsidizing development, the Koch administration enhanced the subsidies. Koch was motivated to do this for two reasons. First, he wanted to ensure a flow of campaign funds for his mayoral races in 1981, 1985, and 1989 and for his run for governor in 1982. The largest category of contributors for these campaigns was real estate companies.[32] Second, Koch felt that corporate growth was the key to the city's economic development. His agenda of controlling spending and supporting private development was consistent with that of major business interests, as represented by the New York City Partnership, which came to be a major supporter of the mayor.[33] This is the period in which the global cities economic development strategy emerged.

In addition, urban liberal mayoral administrations from Beam to Dinkins lowered corporate taxes. From 1974 to 1994 the city's general corporate tax fell from 10.1 percent to 8.85 percent. This tax generates more than 5 percent of the city's tax revenue and raises almost $1 billion a year. A cut of 1 percent thus is equal to around $100 million a year. Even during the fiscal crisis of the 1970s and the economic recession of the early 1990s, these corporate taxes were either cut or frozen. In 1992, Dinkins announced a four-year freeze of the tax, even though the city was in the process of cutting many city services.[34]

By the early 1980s the city's economic development policies took on a more global focus. In 1981, reports were issued by the Twentieth Century Fund and the state of New York calling for a global vision that would place New York at the center of an emerging world economy.[35] These reports argued that in order to capture the position of global leader, the city had to expand its supply of office space. In 1982, the city enacted the Midtown Development Plan, which promised additional subsidies to developers of office space on the west side of midtown. This plan, along with development subsidies for the financial district and existing market and luxury housing subsidies, created a tax loss of more than $1 billion a year by 1988.[36]

This process continued under the Dinkins administration, which encouraged the continued reliance on and expansion of corporate- and finance-based development through zoning changes and tax subsidies that cost the city billions of dollars and further hurt the middle class and the poor. Dinkins's global cities orientation can be clearly seen in his planning department's planning and zoning report of 1993, which calls for a continuation of the global cities strategy:

The City's best prospect for expanding opportunity and combating poverty is to maintain its position as a global leader in finance and advanced business services, communications, and the arts—the industries that drive the city's economy. The global cities of opportunity in the next century will be those that dominate international finance, trade, and culture, just as New York prospered by serving those roles nationally during the last century.[37]

In this economic development paradigm, even the laudable goal of combating poverty was relocated. The report also recommended zoning policies that would allow almost unlimited office building construction in lower and midtown Manhattan as well as downtown Brooklyn and Long Island City in Queens.

In addition, the Dinkins administration continued to rely on a variety of tax incentive programs to encourage corporate- and finance-related development. From 1990 to 1993, the Industrial Development Agency authorized several hundred million dollars in subsidies to major corporations and finance firms to stay in New York City. The nine largest deals totaled $350 million, the biggest going to Prudential Securities in 1992, which received $123 million in sales, energy, and property tax subsidies to keep its corporate headquarters and five thousand jobs in New York City. In 2000, however, it closed most of its investment-banking operations and laid off six hundred employees.[38]

Employment

During this period, patterns of employment dramatically changed as well. Partly as a result of the city's economic development policy and partly as a result of changes in corporate employment practices, a polarization of income ensued. New York's real estate subsidies and zoning changes encouraged the trend of replacing manufacturing with commercial office space (and high-income housing). This meant that fewer middle-class manufacturing jobs were available for the city's large blue-collar population. Between 1969 and 1980, the city lost more than 330,000 of its 825,000 manufacturing jobs. Some of these jobs moved to suburban areas where some workers were able to follow them. Racial exclusion in housing and employment, however, meant that for many New Yorkers, these jobs were permanently lost. Moreover, the jobs that remained paid lower wages relative to the national average.[39]

By the 1990s this trend was exacerbated by the widespread resurgence of sweatshop conditions in the garment industry.

White-collar employment was being transformed as well. As corporations were restructured in the late 1970s and 1980s, they increased the number of very high paying executive positions and reduced the number of middle managers. They also raised the number of low-paying service jobs. Companies that provided business services to these larger corporations soon followed suit, the result being dramatic wage polarization. During this period, those in the top 20 percent income group saw huge increases in wages and investment income, while those the bottom 20 percent actually earned less income.[40] In addition, underemployment worsened as more jobs became part time and/or contingent.

Finally, unemployment itself was a major problem in New York throughout the 1970s and early 1980s, when the city's unemployment rate—around 9 percent—was well above the national average. The result was a growing population of people who were unemployed, underemployed, or working for poverty-level wages. By 1987, 25 percent of the city's residents were living in poverty, up from 15 percent in 1969,[41] and the economic growth of the early 1980s was having little effect on those at the bottom. According to the New York State Department of Social Services,

> The beginning of the economic recovery in the state has not been accompanied until very recently by even a slowing of the growth in welfare case loads. While economic indicators rose, so did poverty. The reasons appear to be related to a broad shift in the nature of the state's labor market (from low skilled to higher skilled jobs that more often exclude the poor), and the depth of the recession, which left many people in an extreme state of hardship and dependence that takes a long time to reverse.[42]

For those on welfare, the situation was even worse. As inflation grew and benefit levels remained steady, the 1970s saw a major decline in the value of welfare payments. During the 1980s, political support for welfare programs dropped as well, and some benefits were cut and eligibility tightened. As a result, 1990 welfare payments were worth only 63 percent of what they had been in 1970. At the same time, housing costs were rising, and federal subsidies were being cut back. By 1988, only 28 percent of AFDC recipients were receiving housing assistance. In 1990, the market rent for a two-bedroom apartment was $593—more than twice the AFDC shelter grant and 112 percent of the total AFDC grant —leaving welfare recipients little room to maneuver in a tight housing market.

This process of polarization continued during the 1990s as the Dinkins administration continued to look to Wall Street and its incredibly high salaries to form the backbone of the city's economy. By 2000 the average wage for finance and securities workers was almost $250,000. But these high incomes did not produce the desired trickle-down effect. In both 1990 and 2000, New York State had the widest gap between the rich and the poor and the second widest gap between the rich and those in the middle-income brackets. By 2000, the richest 20 percent of New York City households were making seventeen times as much as the poorest 20 percent, compared with a difference of ten times nationally, and the difference between the rich and middle-income groups, relative to national averages, grew as well.[43] One expression of this polarizing process was that during the 1990s, poverty levels in New York rose from 19.3 percent to 21.2 percent, and they declined nationally from 13.1 percent to 12.4 percent. In fact, wages for all but the rich fell or remained stagnant compared with those of the 1980s.[44]

What happened during the 1980s and 1990s was that jobs in real estate, finance, insurance, and corporate management shrank modestly in number and grew dramatically in compensation, whereas the number of middle-income jobs dropped precipitously, and the number of low-income jobs rose. From 1989 to 1999, New York City lost 68,000 middle-wage jobs (−3.7%) and gained 52,000 low-wage jobs (+6.4%).[45] These new low-wage jobs paid less than $30,000 a year, compared with the middle-wage jobs, which paid $30,000 to $60,000. The main explanation for this shift is that while most other large cities gained or maintained manufacturing employment in the 1980s and 1990s, New York City lost 30 percent of its manufacturing jobs.[46] These jobs were not replaced by high-paying finance jobs, but instead by low- and very low wage service jobs.

Housing

The polarization of the labor market created a growing group of wealthy executives who could afford luxury housing and a growing underclass that had trouble affording any housing. This gap was widened even further by changes in the housing market that reduced the supply of low-income housing. These changes were precipitated by three developments: local tax policies designed to encourage luxury housing and commercial development, a reduction in federal and local support for low-income housing, and a decline in the availability of low-income housing as a result of real estate disinvestment and abandonment associated with the "white flight" of the 1970s.

During the 1970s, New York lost much of its low-income housing stock. By the late 1960s, the postwar suburbanization had turned into "white flight," leading to a wave of abandonment and arson through the 1970s and 1980s as landlords lost interest in reinvesting in areas that were becoming nonwhite and lower income, such as East New York and the Lower East Side. In addition, tax subsidies encouraged the conversion of low-cost single room occupancy (SRO) hotels and boarding houses into high-rent housing and tourist hotels. As a result, by 1984 the city had lost 358,000 low-income housing units[47] even while both the number of poor households increased and wages dropped relative to inflation and the cost of housing.[48] Accordingly, large numbers of poor New Yorkers were priced out of the housing market.

The Koch administration's basic philosophy was to help housing markets move in the direction in which they already were moving. Through a series of public-private partnerships and various subsidy programs, the city encouraged the gentrification process that was eliminating low-cost housing. During the Koch administration, hundreds of millions of dollars a year were spent on tax abatements for housing construction and rehabilitation that benefited very few low-income New Yorkers. The J-51 program, created in 1955, saw a dramatic expansion under Koch. This program was originally designed to encourage the upgrading of rental properties by giving landlords a twelve-year exemption from increases in the assessed value of their property and a twenty-year abatement of their property taxes up to 90 percent of the costs of construction for major rehabilitation. In the 1970s, this program was expanded to include commercial space and hotel conversions in order to encourage development in the city, given its poor economic condition through much of the 1970s. In 1977 the program cost the city about $11 million a year.

By the 1980s, even though New York City's overall economy was improving, the level of subsidies actually expanded. By 1984, The city was losing $117 million in tax revenues from the program.[49] Most of this money was being spent in wealthy neighborhoods where little in the way of subsidies was needed, and very few of the units were affordable to the poor.[50] According to New York City Council President Carol Bellamy, "J-51 is used primarily by property owners in prosperous neighborhoods and almost never by those in marginal or badly deteriorated areas. . . . Intentionally or not, the City is subsidizing investment in luxury and speculative housing markets."[51] New York City Comptroller Harrison Goldin similarly criticized the program, calling for the city to "reduce benefits in areas where the free market is likeliest to operate unassisted so that the City's resources can be targeted at housing less easily provided by the private market."[52]

Because the J-51 incentives were given primarily to developers in midtown and downtown Manhattan, the buildings most affected were the SRO hotels that housed poor single people, who were the most marginally housed. In addition to the units lost directly from J-51 conversions, more units were lost through illegal conversions. According to City Council President Carol Bellamy, between 1970 and 1984, New York lost 80 percent of its SRO housing, or 108,500 units.[53] Overall, the city's 200,000 SRO units in 1955, when J-51 was created, fell to 40,000 units in 1995, 10,000 of which were newly rehabilitated, nonprofit-run SROs.[54]

A study conducted by Winston Smith in 1993 indicated that the J-51 program had not been cost-effective and that it had actually increased homelessness and decreased tax revenues. Indeed, in 1991 the program cost the city $207 million in lost tax revenue.[55] In 1993, Mayor Dinkins persuaded the city council to extend the program even further. City Council Member Ronnie Eldridge criticized the move as a tax break for a small number of developers, who were planning to build anyway, and Manhattan Borough President Ruth Messinger complained that the program encouraged development in already overcrowded Manhattan rather than in the outer boroughs where housing was needed and there were more available spaces.[56]

Another program that involved substantial government housing subsidies was the 421-a/421-b program, which encouraged the construction of new housing in response to the neighborhood abandonment of the 1960s. Similar to the J-51 program, there were no requirements that the units be affordable or built in distressed neighborhoods. In 1984, despite new restrictions of its use in central Manhattan, the program cost the city $70 million, and by 1991, the cost had grown to $197 million.[57] Together, the two programs cost the city $405 million in 1991, and almost all this money went toward the construction or rehabilitation of market-rate housing.[58]

The Koch administration's development strategies contributed to a real estate boom at the high end of the market. As wage polarization increased in the early 1980s, housing developers chased this high-end market, building an additional 212,000 middle- and upper-income units between 1970 and 1984.[59] This pushed up the cost of land so high that housing developers could not afford to build low-cost housing without significant government subsidies. But most of these low-cost housing subsidies had been scaled back or eliminated during the 1970s and 1980s.

In 1971, Nixon placed a moratorium on federal housing programs as part of his efforts to roll back the Johnson administration's War on Poverty. President Jimmy Carter's administration enacted some increases, but these were quickly undone in the 1980s by the Reagan administration, which cut back new funding and new construction support. New York's fiscal crisis of the mid-1970s then made it impossible for the city government to pick up the slack, given its overall fiscal commitment to global cities-oriented taxes and incentive measures, including almost half a billion dollars in market-rate housing subsidies. As a result, the demand for low-income housing far outstripped the supply. From 1980 to 2000, median rents in New York City increased at nearly twice the rate of inflation, while median incomes were stagnant and incomes for the poorest fifth of New Yorkers fell.[60] In 1983, the city's housing authority estimated that 10 percent of its units contained families "doubling up."[61] By 1987, an estimated 100,000 people were living "doubled up"; 200,000 people were on waiting lists for public housing; and the city's overall housing vacancy rate was down to 2 percent.[62]

In 1985 the Koch administration's capital budget for housing was only $25 million, spread out among a variety of rehabilitation and new construction programs.[63] The next year, in response to the burgeoning homelessness crisis, Koch announced the creation of a ten-year, $5 billion housing capital plan. In the early stages of the program, the majority of the new city money, about $150 million in year 1 and $350 million in year 2, went to middle-income housing, and not a single unit was provided for single homeless adults.[64] After extensive criticism by Manhattan Borough President David Dinkins and others, Koch put more emphasis on low-income housing.[65] When Dinkins became mayor in 1990, he continued the program, as did Mayor Rudolph Giuliani after him, though at much lower levels. In the end, the city created only ninety-five thousand units affordable to low-income or formally homeless individuals over a thirteen-year period.[66] By the early 1990s after two peak years of spending, this effort appeared to play some role in reducing the number of homeless people in shelters and on the streets.[67] By the middle of the Dinkins administration, however, spending on the program dropped off and was cut even further by Giuliani.

Throughout both the Koch and Dinkins administrations, the city continued to spend hundreds of millions of dollars on J-51 and 421-a subsidies with no affordability requirements. Together, Koch and Dinkins spent $3.3 billion on housing, about 60 percent of which went to those who were homeless or had low incomes.[68] During that same period, the city spent about $2.5 billion on J-51, 421-a, and 421-b to subsidize market-rate housing.[69] While all these programs led to the creation of more housing, there was a huge difference in their effectiveness in dealing with the wage and housing polarization problem. The spending on the J-51 and 421 programs did nothing to bring up the bottom of the housing market and in many ways helped drive up land costs, since everyone was competing in the same real estate market. This meant that the city used half its housing money to drive up land prices. As these market-rate subsidies grew during the late 1980s and early 1990s, they also played a role in undermining the city's finances, contributing to Dinkins's need to scale back affordable housing efforts.

In addition, J-51 incentives and market forces were continuing to reduce the amount of low-income housing, compounding the crisis. From 1991 to 1993, New York City lost an additional 10,000 of its SRO units.[70] Then, as more units became available, the effect was not to reduce the number of homeless people but to raise it, as tens of thousands of marginally housed families flooded the shelter system in hopes of moving out of their overcrowded and substandard housing. The mayor's director of homelessness, Nancy Wackenstein, quickly realized that a modest housing program would not be able to address the extent of the city's lack of very low cost housing: "I thought that if you just provided 8,000 units of permanent housing for a couple of years, you'd address the problem. I failed to understand that the universe of potential homeless families is very large. There are probably 200,000 ill housed welfare families in the city."[71] As the number of people in low-wage work and on welfare rose because of the changing structure of labor markets, the mismatch between the availability of very low cost housing and the need for it grew more pronounced. By the late 1990s, there was a shortfall of more than half a million low-cost apartments that would be affordable to people earning less than 50 percent of the median income.[72] The 20,000 people sleeping in the shelters on any given night was just the tip of the iceberg. Hundreds of thousands of New Yorkers were unable to find adequate housing, and the building of shelters and a few thousand units of housing was just a drop in the bucket. This meant that those with the most resources in this vulnerable population were able to negotiate the shelter system, relatives, and other tenuous housing arrangements, while those with more serious problems, including the mentally ill and substance users, were swelling the ranks of the more visible homeless sleeping on the city's sidewalks, park benches, and subway trains.

During the 1970s and early 1980s, the city government was unable or unwilling to invest substantially in low-income housing and yet spent billions to subsidize market-rent housing. The result was that homelessness continued to be a major problem throughout the city and that middle-class communities felt threatened by both the financial pressure of gentrification and the social pressure of increased homelessness in their midst. By the time the Dinkins administration began its housing programs in the early 1990s, the problem of low-cost housing shortages was so great that the city had no hope of keeping up with demand. The more housing that became available, the more people who were in overcrowded and substandard housing were waiting for the new apartments, meanwhile filling up homeless shelters and intake facilities. This was a market failure that could not be solved with small-scale incentives and subsidies.

Conclusion

One of the central features of urban liberalism is its commitment to entrepreneurial economic development strategies that use significant amounts of government resources to intervene in real estate markets, reduce taxes, and change government regulations. This commitment stems in large part from the fact that these politicians rely on the financial support of economic elites to maintain their political power. Although many of these elites occasionally give more heavily to conservative urban politicians, they also are a major source of campaign contributions to liberals. People in real estate and business tied to local enterprises such as utilities, tourism, and those doing business directly with local government make up the core financial contributors of urban liberal politicians in New York and across the country. In addition, the number of global corporations has risen and diversified their financial giving at all levels as a way of encouraging Democrats to adopt neoliberal economic policies, as seen in the support of President Bill Clinton's administration for the North American Free Trade Agreement (NAFTA) and the World Trade Organization (WTO) and the support of urban mayors for global cities-based economic development initiatives. This reliance on growth boosters and global corporations for political viability has consistently driven urban liberals toward economic development strategies that disproportionately aid these groups, often at the expense of the poor and middle classes.

The effect of this process has been to destabilize low-income employment and housing markets. Mass homelessness has become the most visible expression of a process in which incomes and government benefits are falling at the same time that housing costs at the bottom of the market are escalating and the supply is dwindling. Growing inequality in the private sector, combined with structural adjustment in the public sector, has resulted in the emergence of large underclasses that threaten the civility of public spaces in the form of crime, homelessness, prostitution, and other forms of disorder that lowered the quality of daily life for all New Yorkers.

This problem, as we shall see in the next chapter, had the effect of driving the middle classes to the right in demanding that city government respond to these disorders through ever more repressive means. The police, in particular, were called on to address the disorder problem, and when urban liberal politicians and their police departments did not respond effectively to these demands, they were replaced by neoconservative political and police leaders who did.

6

The Transformation of Policing

This chapter explores how the inability of the New York Police Department (NYPD) to adequately address the disorder problems of the 1980s and 1990s gave rise to efforts by business and community groups to pressure them to adopt quality-of-life-oriented policing methods. During this period, the NYPD pursued a *law enforcement* model of policing, which emphasizes a quick response to 911 calls, gives priority to fighting major crimes, and relies heavily on centrally controlled and specialized units. In addition, it considers disorder and, to some degree, crime to be symptoms of larger social problems outside its control. This approach turned out to have many of the same contradictions as the city's homelessness policies, in that it paid little attention to community concerns, relied on centralized expertise, was underfunded, and tolerated disorder despite its deleterious effects on the city's neighborhoods and public spaces.

This new quality-of-life approach to policing did not just represent an increase in the number of police or a greater aggressiveness in existing methods; instead, it consisted of new police practices and new ideas about the best way for cities to deal with homeless and disorderly people. Because these people's activities are either legal or only marginally criminal, this new approach had to return police to their nineteenth-century roots of order maintenance rather than its twentieth-century orientation toward the legal system. While developing these new policing practices and philosophies, they thus laid a large part of the foundation for the new *quality-of-life* paradigm.

Many policing scholars have noted that changes in the style of policing are uncommon and difficult to achieve.[1] The conventional wisdom is that the rise of quality-of-life policing in New York City was a direct result of the election of Rudolph Giuliani and that his election was motivated in large part by the rise in serious crime. This chapter argues, however, that neither of these is an accurate assessment of what happened. First, although crime was a factor in people's discontent with David Dinkins and the Democratic Party, it was the larger issue of disorder that played the central role in bringing down his administration. Second, while Giuliani accelerated and institutionalized quality-of-life policing, he did not initiate support for it either within the NYPD or among residents. This chapter shows that instead, support for quality-of-life policing grew out of discontent with the NYPD's lack of ability and willingness to address low-level disorder problems associated with the crisis of homelessness and that before Giuliani's coming to office, many communities as well as police executives had already begun to implement and support broken-windows-based policing initiatives.

Community actors in New York City in the 1980s and 1990s undermined the legitimacy of the NYPD in relation to crime and disorder. They did this by effectively articulating an alternative approach to responding to the emergent homelessness and disorder problem that coincided with important debates going on within police departments and the scholarly literature. In addition, political actors such as David Dinkins changed the allocation of policing resources and the police's philosophy and tactics. The combination of these different ways of influencing police innovation created a powerful force for change. No truly public institution can withstand that level of crisis without making some concrete adjustments. Although the extent and duration of those changes may depend on the level of the crisis, it is clear that major changes were under way within the NYPD in response to these pressures before the arrival of Giuliani and Bratton and that the primary motivation for this challenge was the growth of widespread disorder, not increases in serious crime.[2]

The Roles of Giuliani and Bratton

In 1993, Rudolph Giuliani was elected mayor on a tough-on-crime platform that made specific references to the need to deal more aggressively with the problems of public disorder. In addition to general statements about the need for more law enforcement, Giuliani also argued that the form of law enforcement needed to change. Both these goals were consistent with the "broken windows" theory of policing and neighborhood development. The broken windows theory argues that if left unchecked, low-level crime and disorder can lead to a climate of lawlessness, which in turn can result in higher levels of serious crime and economic downturn for local communities. The solution is greater police attention to these minor crimes and disorders as a way of restoring a sense of safety and order, which in turn allows residents to reassert control over their neighborhoods.

Upon taking office, Giuliani hired William Bratton to be his police commissioner. Bratton had made a reputation for himself by reducing crime in the subways as chief of the New York Transit Police in the late 1980s. Bratton also was a proponent of the broken windows theory and had worked closely with George Kelling, one of the theory's authors, while chief of the transit police. Bratton quickly began to implement a series of new policing measures that were consistent with the theory. At the end of his first year, serious crime had fallen by more than 10 percent, and by 1998 a pattern of crime reduction had emerged that continues to this day.

By the mid-1990s, it was clear that the NYPD had undergone a significant transformation, and Giuliani and Bratton were eager to take full, and sometimes competing, credit for it.[3] Giuliani's successful 1997 reelection campaign was largely organized around this issue, and Bratton became an international policing phenomenon, appearing in numerous magazines and eventually coauthoring a number of management texts.[4] Most of the academic praise for Bratton has focused on his management skills in getting the NYPD to retool itself around crime reduction as an operational priority, through the use of a computerized mapping system called Compstat.[5] This system of real-time crime mapping allows top police executives to quickly hold local precinct commanders accountable for increases in crime. In addition, these accountability sessions serve as a kind of think tank for developing innovative policing tactics, many of which are based on the "broken windows" theory and its emphasis on maintaining order.

What has emerged is a historical narrative that credits Giuliani with the political sense to emphasize crime reduction through order maintenance by hiring Bratton and crediting him with the ability to push the police to adopt this new approach as its own. The reality, however, is that neighborhood and business groups pressured the police to adopt order maintenance policing initiatives well before Giuliani took office.

The Law Enforcement Style of Policing

In his landmark book on different methods of policing, James Q. Wilson uses the term *style* to indicate a Weberian ideal type.[6] While he never specifically defines what he means by a style of policing, a close reading of his work suggests that it is clearly more than just a set of policies or practices, or even a conscious or intentional arrangement. Instead, a style of policing is a logically consistent set of strategies and tactics that fit the particular police department's institutional mission. The *service style* of policing, for example, can be said to coalesce around the strategies of enforcing the law without alienating local residents. Tactics include a heavy reliance on warnings when encountering minor traffic and other violations, quick and courteous responses to calls for assistance—whether or not they are strictly crime related—and a punitive orientation toward outsiders and "known troublemakers."

Before the 1990s, New York's policing style could be characterized as law enforcement policing because of its emphasis on its connection to the larger criminal justice system and its reliance on expertise and specialization in the fighting of serious crime. *Law enforcement policing* is an outgrowth of the professional model of policing that developed in the middle of the twentieth century, which required police departments to become experts in the science and technology of crime fighting.[7] Education and training standards were enhanced, crime labs were established, and specialized units became more common. The *professional style* stressed fighting serious crime and discounted the importance of maintaining order. Its growth was aided by the development of police cars with radios and, later, 911 dispatch systems, which allowed the police to respond more quickly to calls for service but left them little time for foot patrol and other forms of flexible deployment.

The 1967 report by the President's Commission on Law Enforcement and Administration of Justice built on the professionalization process by encouraging the coordination of various parts of the criminal justice system, with the police conceptualized as the gateway of an integrated system.[8] The result was that police administrators increasingly looked to the rest of the criminal justice system for guidance rather than to political leaders and community sentiment. Since the criminal justice system placed a priority on felony convictions, the police focused on fighting serious crime and became less interested in maintaining order.

Similar pressure to move away from order maintenance was placed on the police by academics, the courts, and public opinion. During the 1960s, social scientists and policymakers argued that the roots of criminality were social and economic, stemming from racism and economic deprivation. Edwin Schur's *Crime without Victims* led the movement to redefine deviance as a social problem and not a crime problem.[9] The outcome of this movement was an attempt to decriminalize, in both the legislatures and the courts, many kinds of minor crimes, such as prostitution, public intoxication, and loitering. Criminologists and police officials increasingly believed that the police could have little impact on minor crimes which, they argued, stemmed from larger social forces like poverty and racism. Similarly, the 1967 Presidential Commission, made up of academics and law enforcement administrators, argued that "the ability of the police to act against crime is limited. The police did not create and cannot resolve the social conditions that stimulate crime."[10]

In addition, the courts were beginning to strike down a number of law enforcement tools that had been used in the pursuit of public order. Debra Livingston points out that before the 1960s, the courts allowed police a great deal of discretion in their use of vagrancy, loitering, breaches of peace, and other public order statutes because they generally were used only against marginal groups who had no political power to resist their abuses.[11] As the civil rights movement took shape in the 1960s, however, these statutes were more often challenged, and federal courts began to review their appalling misuse. In 1972 a series of lower court rulings against order-maintenance laws came to a head when the U.S. Supreme Court ruled in *Papachristou v. City of Jacksonville* (Mississippi),[12] that Jacksonville's vagrancy ordinance was unconstitutional, opening the door to the elimination of similar laws across the country and a number of similar court rulings.[13] Faced with changing laws, court decisions, and public opinion, the police changed their own attitudes and tactics. Many police administrators themselves came to accept these views and removed the aggressive policing of minor crimes as a priority.

The case of antiprostitution law enforcement in New York illustrates how departments responded to the changing attitudes toward "victimless crimes" and order-maintenance policing. In September 1967, the state legislature voted to dramatically reduce the punishment of prostitutes from a maximum jail term of one year to fifteen days. The legislature argued that "prostitution is a social problem rather than a criminal problem" and that "a harsh penalty failed to act as a deterrent."[14] An

NYC Department of Corrections official expressed the frustration felt by law enforcement officials: "When you see the same women coming back month after month, week after week, often arrested only hours after they were released from prison, you wonder just what the whole process is accomplishing."[15] This frustration could have been channeled in several different directions. One alternative could have been to increase the penalties. However, the prevailing sentiment at the time was toward liberalization and treatment, not incarceration—the opposite of the mood twenty years later.

Judges' feelings about the problem were similar. In the mid-1960s, conviction rates for prostitution were between 70 and 80 percent, but by 1967 they had fallen to 40 to 50 percent. According to the *New York Times,* "The gradual reduction in sentences is probably due chiefly to a growing belief among judges that prison does not deter prostitutes."[16] In 1967, local prosecutors and judges also began throwing out prostitution cases based on loitering and disorderly conduct laws, claiming that their definition of criminal behavior was overly broad.[17] By the 1980s, the NYPD considered prostitution a low-priority issue. Fred Siegel provides an account that captures this sentiment:

> While responding to complaints from a Brooklyn residential neighborhood overwhelmed by street prostitution, a police captain explained that if his men were too forceful in removing pushers and the prostitutes from the streets, they themselves would be subject to arrest and a possible suit for a civil rights violation. An active or perhaps overly active cop, the captain explained, could destroy his career.[18]

As a result, overall enforcement was reduced, and prostitution was allowed to continue on a modest scale in several parts of the city.

In the late 1970s and early 1980s, the law enforcement style of policing began to run into difficulties as it was confronted by the emergence of homelessness and other visible forms of disorder. The most common early complaints were "aggressive panhandling"; people sleeping on sidewalks, in subway trains, and other public spaces; sanitation problems; and the so-called squeegee men who tried to obtain money for cleaning the car windows of motorists stuck in traffic. These all were problems that had been of little concern to the police in the preceding decade, and the NYPD was not prepared to take this on as a major policing issue. Instead, they tended to refer to this disorder as being the result of social problems outside their control or to point out that they were stretched to capacity dealing with serious crimes and 911 calls for emergency assistance. It was in this context that the new quality-of-life style of policing that would more directly address disorder issues began to be formed.

Defining the Quality-of-Life Style

The strategies and tactics of the quality-of-life style of policing are very different from those of the law enforcement style. Several recent works have evaluated this new approach's claims of success.[19] Although these studies have challenged the effectiveness of the new quality-of-life policing, there is no question that a new style has emerged that has had a significant effect on the way that the police and citizens interact. None of these, works, however, seriously examines how this new style of policing emerged.

The primary strategic orientations of *quality-of-life* policing are tied to the broken windows theory and problem-oriented policing.[20] Accordingly, the police believe that the strategic and sustained targeting of disorders and minor quality-of-life violations are key to preventing more serious crimes and that rather than just reacting to calls for service, the police should actively use crime-fighting tactics based on identified crime patterns. These strategies are then implemented through the use of a variety of tactics including *stop and frisk, zero tolerance, civil enforcement, flexible deployment,* and the *creation of new laws, rules, and regulations.*

Some police scholars have confused the categories of strategy and tactics. The promotion of zero-tolerance policing as a broad strategy of policing in parts of the United States and the United Kingdom, for instance, applies a tactical label to what is often really the quality-of-life style.[21] Conversely, some police practices have been labeled *problem-oriented* policing when they really are just zero-tolerance tactics used in the service of an ongoing legalistic or professional style of policing. A *tactic* is a series of specific crime-fighting practices, whereas a *strategy* is a broader philosophy of crime fighting based on an analysis of the causes of crime and the mechanisms of crime control. Tactics are therefore used in the service of a crime-fighting strategy, and many tactics can be used with different strategies. A style of policing is differentiated from a tactic by its institutional character. A police department is more than just a series of crime-fighting procedures. It is a public institution with a mission and set of values, which tend to be formed into a coherent whole that can be defined as a style of policing.

Some studies have directly addressed the quality-of-life style. For example, Katz, Webb, and Schaefer tested the effectiveness of the quality-of-life style of policing. While they never systematically define this style of policing, they do offer some philosophical and tactical criteria. Philosophically they tie it to the "broken windows" theory and its emphasis on maintaining order. The tactics on which they focus primarily involve the zero-tolerance enforcement of "order-maintenance laws and zoning ordinances." They do not deal with the problem-oriented policing philosophy or the tactics of *stop and frisk, creation of new laws,* or *flexible deployment*.[22] Golub, Johnson, Taylor, and Eterno also evaluate the quality-of-life style of policing without adequately defining it. They do, however, discuss the centrality of the "broken windows" theory but offer no descriptions of actual police practices. Instead, they review a variety of offenses that they associate with this style, such as fare beating, smoking marijuana in public, and littering. In their study, they ask the people arrested for these types of crime whether they felt that the police had been targeting this type of behavior.[23] This adds very little to our understanding of the actual police practices that make up quality-of-life policing and therefore make it difficult to assess the value, effectiveness, or origin of this style of policing.

Core Tactics of Quality-of-life Policing

Zero-tolerance is a tactic that assigns officers to a specific trouble spot and asks them to aggressively enforce the law for the purpose of establishing a new standard of behavior.[24] Bratton did this effectively when he was head of the New York Transit Police.[25] He asked officers to stop every person jumping the turnstiles at a particular location and to ticket them after checking them for weapons and outstanding warrants.[26] Similar efforts were used to disrupt panhandling in Seattle and to target parking and alcohol violations in Washington, D.C.[27] In Seattle, the aggressive enforcement of a new law against sitting on the sidewalk was used to displace from the downtown area both homeless people and others deemed to be disorderly.

Another tactic associated with quality-of-life policing is *stop and frisk*. Again, there is nothing new or unique about the use of this tactic. In the case of quality-of-life policing, it was used to disrupt patterns of weapons possession and low-level drug dealing in high-crime neighborhoods.[28] Officers in New York City were told to use any pretext to stop young men on the streets who they believed might be carrying illegal drugs or weapons and to search them. The legalities of the search were sometimes questionable, but consistent with the "broken windows" theory, the emphasis was on establishing a new standard of behavior rather than making arrests that would necessarily end in successful prosecutions.

One of the tactics developed in conjunction with community- and problem-oriented policing and regularly used in quality-of-life policing is *civil enforcement*. This tactic involves developing a cooperative relationship between the police and other city agencies, especially city attorneys' offices, to enforce a variety of city codes and regulations. This can include closing down businesses associated with drugs and other crime because of violations of liquor licenses, building codes, or noise ordinances. Civil enforcement is used especially in cases in which the alleged criminal violations are minor or do not come with penalties that get to the root of the problem. For instance, although numerous low-level drug arrests may be made at a particular location, the larger drug-dealing organization is not affected.

A related tactic is the *creation of new laws, rules, and regulations* to control ongoing crime problems. This tactic has been used largely in the service of the "broken windows" theory and its emphasis on eliminating disorderly behavior. New laws criminalizing panhandling near ATM machines, regulations against sitting on the sidewalk, and rules forbidding the blocking of subway platforms give the police new tools to regulate disorderly behavior. To create new laws, the cooperation of the mayor and other political leaders is required, but new administrative rules and regulations can often be adopted more quickly and with less public discussion by administrative agencies such as parks departments. George Kelling's recommendations for new rules in the New York subway is an example of the latter.[29]

The final tactic that constitutes quality-of-life policing is *flexible deployment*. This tactic is based on the notion that the police will never be able to reduce crime if they spend all their time reacting to 911 calls. Instead, the police need to actively address crime problems by assigning officers to details that anticipate crimes based on local intelligence or crime pattern mapping. Flexible deployment can take the form of saturating a known prostitution area that also has had high levels of other crimes, as a way of eliminating or at least displacing the problem. This tactic also has been used to target burglars by saturating one part of a neighborhood with uniformed officers while leaving an adjacent area to be covered by plainclothes officers, hoping to catch burglars in the act.

By the late 1990s, the NYPD was using most of the tactics associated with the quality-of-life style. Many specialized policing units were either broken up or placed under the command of precinct or borough commanders in the service of problem-oriented crime fighting. Zero-tolerance campaigns against everything from public drinking to graffiti and, even for a short period, jaywalking, were commonplace. Giuliani advocated the creation of numerous new laws and regulations designed to control disorderly behavior such as panhandling near ATM machines. Every precinct in the city had a reserve of officers not regularly assigned to 911 patrol duty who could be flexibly deployed to respond to emerging crime patterns. One of the most visible new strategies was the widespread use of stop and frisk, especially in crime-ridden neighborhoods. By the late 1990s, officers were making tens of thousands of such stops in an effort to go after drugs, guns, and quality-of-life crimes.[30] The practice became so widespread that it engendered a great deal of resentment from law-abiding New Yorkers who were routinely stopped based on what they felt was solely their race.

The Emergence of Quality-of-Life Policing

The following case studies show that quality-of-life policing did not arise primarily in response to serious crime. It also was not strictly a product of the Giuliani administration. Instead, it was a response to the growing disorder in the city's public spaces, which challenged existing methods of policing for being complacent and ineffective in restoring public civility. In particular, commercial elites in midtown began using quality-of-life methods in their development of the Grand Central Partnership in 1985. Neighborhood residents in the Lower East Side of Manhattan formed a number of organizations in the 1980s designed to target disorderly behavior such as street vending, drug dealing, and homeless people hanging out near shelters and living in local parks. Finally, I explain how the Dinkins administration, in the passage of Safe City, Safe Streets in 1991 and the implementation of anti-squeegee-men measures in 1993, opened the door to quality-of-life enforcement before Giuliani's and Bratton's arrival, in direct response to widespread public pressure to address the disorder problem.

Even though quality-of-life policing is at heart a neoconservative policy, many of its proponents had a long history as urban liberals. Community organizations on the Lower East Side and in Tudor City were not longtime conservatives who used homelessness to advance an ideological agenda regarding the need for more punitive policing of the homeless and disorderly; nor were they strictly parochial actors whose desire for relief from disorder and crime was co-opted by the police to further a more punitive agenda.[31] Instead, these were largely new formations whose members were driven to action by a loss of control over their community and its public spaces and who were frustrated by police inaction. These groups often relied on organizing skills developed by members of the progressive social movements of the 1960s and 1970s. As such, they were successful in pressuring the police to rethink their commitment to the law enforcement model of policing and to begin to experiment with new policing strategies based on "broken windows" and order maintenance.

Crime

Few issues have played as large a role as crime has in shaping public perceptions of New York City in the last thirty years. Images of Central Park muggers and gangs of youths on the subways evoke social breakdown and also, invariably, race. This volatile combination contributed significantly to the destabilization of both the city's neighborhoods and the city itself. As crime rose in the 1960s and 1970s, neighborhoods were transformed by the flight of those who could leave and an abandonment of public space by many of the rest.

Crime rates began to increase in the 1960s and 1970s, with the total number of FBI index crimes in New York City rising from 434,000 in 1972 to 658,000 in 1976,[32] when the first wave of crime increases peaked. The level of anxiety created by personal experience and media coverage rose dramatically during the summer of 1977, when a blackout in which looting and vandalism broke out in several neighborhoods contributed to a sense that criminals were everywhere, just waiting for an opportunity to strike. Although public confidence in the civility of the general public and the ability of the police to control disorder were shaken, they were not completely lost. And in fact, during the next few years the crime rates leveled off.

By 1981, however, crime was on the rise again and surpassed earlier levels. A survey late that year reported that 60 percent of New Yorkers said that they or someone they knew had been mugged in the last two years, and 80 percent said that the problem was worse than it was four years ago.[33] The survey also showed that public confidence in getting police help declined from 36 percent to 16 percent during the same two-year period.[34] New York was in crisis. Crime was out of control, and public confidence in the police and courts was at an all-time low. The fear of crime was now "woven into the fabric of city lives."[35]

Unlike the initial increase in violent crime, which was concentrated in poor neighborhoods, the new increase was citywide. In fact, in some periods, crime decreased or leveled off in high-crime areas but increased in middle-class neighborhoods.[36] Crime was now a concern for all New Yorkers.

From 1982 to 1985 the crime rate stabilized again, but public confidence did not recover. A 1985 poll indicated that half of New York residents viewed crime as the city's number one problem, far outpacing schools, housing, and public transportation.[37] A mood of desperation also emerged as increasing numbers of residents supported vigilante actions, such as calls for armed neighborhood patrols in Howard Beach and the Bernard Goetz shooting in 1984, in which a white man on the subway shot three black youths who aggressively asked him for money.[38]

The examples of Howard Beach and Bernard Goetz evoke the role of race in the city's growing crime problem. Roger Starr described the problem:

It is the nature of current crime in the city that is perhaps even more frightening than its high rate of incidence. As in the past, the newest arrivals in the city are those most responsible for anti-social behavior. That means, in general, the blacks and Hispanics. Together these groups are involved in about 80% of the crimes, perhaps an even higher percentage of the random street crimes. The difference in skin color, when it occurs, between the offender and their victims doubtless gives the victims a special feeling of danger.[39]

The factor of race is important to understanding the visceral reaction of many New Yorkers to the emerging homeless population, which was overwhelmingly black and Latino.[40]

In 1986, crime began to accelerate again with the infusion of crack into a burgeoning underclass of poor and homeless people. The result was a growing feeling that the city's social fabric was unraveling. Once again, the effects of the increase were not confined to historically high-crime areas. In 1986 and 1987, the murder rate in Queens increased by 25 percent a year, prompting local politicians and residents to declare that "local drug violence is threatening the very stability of what has long been considered New York City's most middle-class borough."[41] They felt that this was causing people and businesses to move away, thereby threatening the economic and social stability of the neighborhood.

While the 1970s are often considered to be the worst crime years in New York in recent memory, in fact the late 1980s and early 1990s were worse. More important, public confidence, which was shaken in the 1970s, came unglued in the 1980s. People no longer felt safe in public spaces and did not believe that the city government or the police knew what to do about the problems of crime and disorder. In addition to these individual fears, whole neighborhoods were beginning to feel that their stability was being undermined by crime. This breakdown in public confidence was taking place while homelessness was still an isolated problem. By the late 1980s, however, the crime and homelessness problems converged in many people's perceptions, creating a major crisis for neighborhoods and a powerful threat to the legitimacy of the New York City Police Department, which had been unable to bring either crime or disorder under control.

Homelessness and Disorder

As discussed in chapter 4, homelessness and public disorder emerged as major problems in New York City in the mid-1980s. Individuals, communities, businesses, and government struggled to devise strategies to reduce the impact of these social problems on the city. One of the questions confronting New York was the role of the police in this process. Over the previous generation the police had embraced the professional model of policing, which defined their mission in terms of their relation to the criminal justice system. The police viewed themselves as fighters of serious crime who used a variety of technologies and special skills to deal with the city's significant major crime problems. These strategies included forming specialized units dealing with different major crimes such as organized crime, sex crimes, and narcotics. In addition, they relied heavily on the city's 911 system to organize police responses to calls for assistance. The following case studies show how these institutional characteristics were challenged during the 1980s and 1990s by a variety of actors using different methods.

The Grand Central Partnership

One constituency that felt especially besieged by the growing problems of homelessness and disorder was property and business owners. As a result of these problems and the overall decline in city services stemming from the 1970s fiscal crisis, many businesses formed associations to tax themselves and provide their own security and sanitation services. These Business Improvement Districts (BIDs) became codified in state law in 1981, allowing a majority of business owners in an area to establish a system of forced taxation to provide enhanced services. The relative strength and effectiveness of these BIDs depended in part on the wealth of the areas being served. One of the earliest and most powerful BIDs in New York City was the Grand Central Partnership (GCP), formed by business and real estate owners in the vicinity of the Grand Central Station in midtown Manhattan. One of the first tasks of this BID was to try to address the homelessness and disorder problem by both pressuring city government in a variety of ways and using its own resources for remediation efforts. How it dealt with homelessness and disorder directly influenced the development of quality-of-life policing in New York City. The effectiveness of the BIDs in reducing these problems threatened to displace the police in their role as guardians of public order and safety. In turn, the BIDs' success forced the police to reexamine their relation to the problems of disorder and homelessness and the methods they might use to address them.

The GCP directly pressured the police and the city to take disorder more seriously. It did this in two ways. First, it engaged in a discursive shift that changed the debate about the relation of homelessness, disorder, crime, and neighborhood stability. By describing conditions in and around Grand Central Terminal (GCT) as a threat to both public safety and economic health, the GCP managed to raise the stakes of ignoring homelessness and disorder as policing issues. Stepping around homeless people was no longer an unpleasant annoyance; it now was the central problem facing midtown Manhattan and, by extension, the rest of the city. Second, the GCP threatened the police's institutional domain by providing an alternative example of how to reduce crime and restore order, by directly replacing some of the police's central functions. The GCP did this by hiring private security guards, social workers, and outreach workers. The goal was to use a carrot-and-stick approach to remove homeless people from inside the GCT and immediately surrounding blocks. This effort was a concrete example of a problem-oriented approach to reducing disorder as part of the strategy to take back control of an important public space. These efforts were very successful and provided a model for other BIDs and the city government, and William Bratton mentioned them as a source of inspiration when he took over the NYPD.

Throughout the 1980s, the homeless population in and around the Grand Central Terminal expanded, thereby depressing real estate values in the area and making the terminal an unpleasant and, at times, even dangerous destination. In July 1985, real estate developer Peter Malkin announced the formation of the Grand Central Partnership (GCP), an informal business group made up of local property owners, which became an official BID in 1988 with the hopes of bringing to bear a comprehensive solution to the homelessness problem by utilizing aggressive policing, restrictive physical barriers, and token social services. Throughout the late 1980s the Metro North Railroad had been ineffective in resolving the problem on its own. Although it undertook a series of temporary and superficial police sweeps, it was unwilling to engage in sustained punitive policing for fear of bad publicity and because of a lack of resources. The result was the continued presence of homeless people and a frustrated and demoralized police force that occasionally engaged in random acts of abusive behavior toward people living in the terminal.[42]

In 1989, the GCP created a uniformed security force of twenty-nine officers and, with Metro North and the MTA, developed rules for the terminal that provided new tools for the police and security force to drive out homeless people. The new rules banned washing clothes in restrooms; changing clothes in restrooms; giving away food; lying on floors, platforms, stairs, or landings; occupying more than one seat; and creating unreasonable noise.[43] This approach was similar to the efforts by the transit police to eliminate the presence of disorderly homeless people from the subways. In October the MTA started enforcing these rules under the banner of "Operation Enforcement." Support for this effort by the police and politicians, however, was mixed. While top officials in the MTA and the transit and MTA police supported the operation, many politicians and rank-and-file officers resisted it. The president of the Transit Police Benevolent Association, William McKechnie, opposed the operation, saying that homelessness was "a social problem, not a criminal problem" and that officers should use their time to "concentrate on fighting crime not rousting the homeless."[44] He later continued this argument, stating, "The plight of the homeless should be left to social service agencies. This is not our job. It can't work."[45] Governor Mario Cuomo intervened as well, ordering that the new rules should not be used simply to throw homeless people out of the transit system and onto the streets, where they were at risk of freezing to death. He also created a panel that included homeless advocates to monitor the implementation of the new rules.

These initial efforts at eliminating homeless people from the transit system were unsuccessful. It was at this point that the GCP became actively involved and forced reluctant liberal politicians and the police to support punitive action by threatening to displace their authority. In 1990, in response to intensive lobbying from GCP members, Governor Cuomo and Mayor Dinkins signed a contract with the GCP to provide social services, including a drop-in center and referrals to shelters and other homeless emergency services. As part of this program, the GCP began paying homeless people a stipend of $50 a week to perform outreach to other homeless people in and around the terminal. At the same time, the MTA spent millions of dollars on physical changes to make access to underground hiding places more difficult and created a MN Police Homeless Outreach Unit designed to root the homeless out of underground tunnels and other out-of-the-way locations. By 1992, the program was touted as a success for removing large numbers of people from the terminal, even though the police acknowledged that social services had "provided help for only a fraction of the people who once lived underneath Grand Central."[46] The combination of physical barriers, intensified zero-tolerance policing, and intensive outreach was very successful in improving conditions inside the terminal.

The GCP eagerly took credit for the improvement and began to expand its homeless services and broader order-maintenance efforts. In 1992, its general counsel, Andrew Mansel, drafted a new local ordinance designed to limit the presence of sidewalk vendors, some of whom were homeless. In 1993, the measure was approved by the city council and Mayor Dinkins,[47] and in the same year, the GCP began contracting out its outreach services to banks trying to keep their ATM vestibules free of homeless people. At this point, it had a $500,000 contract to provide security in the ATM vestibules of several major banks and was receiving $500,000 in grants from the U.S. Department of Housing and Urban Development.

Several residential neighborhoods near the terminal also asked the GCP for help in removing homeless encampments. One example of this was the attempt to remove an encampment adjacent to Tudor City, a middle-class housing complex on Manhattan's East Side near the United Nations.[48] The encampment had been in place for several years and resisted isolated police efforts to remove it. A member of the Tudor City Association (TCA) said that they had made repeated efforts to get the police to take action against the encampment by enforcing existing laws. Every time they met with police, they brought a lawyer with them to indicate their willingness to take legal action against the city if things did not improve.[49] This tactic was not successful, however. According to one TCA member, "The police do come in and move them out but they just go to another park in the area and come back."[50] As a result, the TCA turned to the GCP, which had been successful in removing an encampment near the Thirty-fourth Street Esplanade. The TCA paid $2,600 for a sixty-day outreach effort that was really a removal effort.[51] The GCP used low-paid homeless people connected to their drop-in center to visit the area repeatedly to try to get people living there to take advantage of housing and other services. They were successful in getting some people to leave the area, but many others refused these offers and were removed with threats of beatings.[52] While the GCP was only partially successful, the fact that a middle-class, mostly white neighborhood group put so much effort into removing an encampment sent a strong message to the city that dissatisfaction with both the police and social service providers was growing.

In three cases, the GCP initiated policing functions that were taken over by the police during the Giuliani administration. In the first, the GCP took over security for the streets surrounding Grand Central Terminal. Its primary concern was to target homeless people as a source of disorder by providing social services, high-visibility security guards, and low-visibility intimidation by homeless outreach workers. In the second case, the GCP signed contracts with banks to provide security at ATM machines by preventing panhandling and sleeping in the ATM vestibules. Third, the GCP negotiated contracts with nearby neighborhood associations to provide outreach services in homeless encampments in the area.

When William Bratton took over the transit police in 1991, he was well aware of the efforts of BIDs in general and of the Grand Central Partnership in particular. Grand Central Terminal was one of the first places he visited as chief of the transit police, to see how the GCP had been able to achieve such improvements. Although the GCP was not Bratton's first exposure to problem-oriented methods, it did serve as an important example. Bratton felt that because of the decline in city services as a result of the fiscal crisis, BIDs were crucial as both public-private partnerships and sources of innovation.[53]

East Village

In the late 1980s and early 1990s, there was a great deal of community mobilization in Manhattan's East Village around the problem of disorder in the neighborhood, including street drug dealing, street peddlers, the opening of a new homeless shelter on First Street, and conditions around the Third Street shelter. The NYPD was reluctant to take on these "social problems" because disorder control was a low priority for the department. As a result, a growing number of people began to call for police action to restore order in the park and the surrounding neighborhood and to initiate various neighborhood watch and patrol efforts. In response, the local community challenged the department's basic value orientation, demanding that it take local quality-of-life matters more seriously. Second, by forming local groups that took specific actions to fight disorder and crime, these people threatened to displace the role of the police. As a result, the police were forced to adopt new crime-fighting strategies that more directly addressed these problems.

The issue of street-level drug sales affected several areas of the community and led to the creation of a series of community groups dedicated to reducing the drug trade by becoming a visible presence on the street and pressuring the police to take action. These groups became mobilized because they felt there was a dramatic decline in the conditions of public streets and that the police and city government appeared unable or unwilling to adequately address the problem.

In 1987, residents on Thirteenth Street formed Thirteen Resolved to Evict All Dealers (THREAD), which organized block patrols to try to displace drug dealers by calling public attention to their activities. They eventually called in the Guardian Angels to supplement their patrols, supplying them with free housing (provided by a local landlord) and funds (they raised $2,500 in $5 and $10 amounts and organized forty-six buildings to support them). The Guardian Angels were formed in the 1970s as an all-volunteer organization intended to give citizens an opportunity to restore order in public spaces through organized patrols that directly confronted street criminals.[54] This was in response to a crisis in confidence in the ability of the police department to effectively fight crime and restore order on its own. In practice, the group tended to be made up of young people who were hired by local business groups to maintain order on their streets by rousting "undesirables" such as homeless people, drug dealers, and young people hanging out.

Similar efforts were undertaken by the Extra Place Neighborhood Association (EPNA), started on First Street, and by the East Villagers Against Crack (EVAC), which targeted the area between Twelfth and Seventeenth Streets and First and Fourth Avenues. These groups were motivated by the fact that previous policing tactics, such as Operation Pressure Point, appeared to be driving dealers from targeted areas farther east into their neighborhood.[55] At a THREAD rally, one local activist noted that the event

is a signal that the community will not settle for Pressure Point breaking drug dealing in one area, simply to have it moved to another. . . . If there are insufficient number of police to cover the problem, then the City must supply sufficient personnel like the CPOP [Community Police on Patrol] officers. Additionally, the City must bring the Narcotics Investigation Unit for the Borough and make a major sweep of the area to harass dealers to prevent them from settling in.[56]

There also was a lot of frustration with the police department's long-term orientation in dealing with the drug problem:

As EVAC founder John Woods admitted the next day, the only mistake in organizing the event, "was in inviting more than one politician." As

EVAC proposes an immediate, local, public action, the audience grew impatient with the politicians' often lengthy discussion of long range and international cures for their local drug problem.[57]

These politicians focused on foreign affairs and drug interdiction efforts and downplayed the role of local police enforcement. A representative from the mayor's office made the latter part explicit: "It is easy to say that, if you quadrupled the police force and arrests, it would make a difference. But history belies that would make it better."[58] The result of this movement was a greater reliance on local police as neighborhood problem solvers and an antipathy to long-term, root-causes approaches. Instead, people wanted immediate local action taken to drive out the visible presence of disorder. These groups held frequent rallies, built links with local elected officials, had frequent meetings with the police, and organized letter-writing campaigns to Mayor Koch.

In the area near the Bowery, members of BASTA (Before Another Shelter Tears Us Apart), a neighborhood association, frustrated with the growing problems associated with the homeless population and not satisfied with the police response, formed to fight the placement of shelters. The primary problems were garbage, noise, and street-level drug use and dealing. In the late 1980s, to the dismay of local activists, the police were not actively dealing with these violations. According to one BASTA member, "We were not very pleased with the police. We got impatient and walked out of a meeting with the commander who was doing a presentation on heroin in Southeast Asia's Golden Triangle *when we were concerned about our block*" (emphasis added).[59] One person recalls the police told them, "You live on 3rd Street, what do you expect? You should move!"[60] Eventually, the police performed periodic sweeps, but the community sentiment was that the police were sympathetic and gave good advice to activists but were otherwise useless in helping them regain control of the area. One action the police did take was to release statistics showing that 46 percent of crime in the precinct was in the area around the homeless shelter and that 15 percent of those arrested gave the shelter as their address.[61] But in a meeting with community residents, Police Commissioner Benjamin Ward clearly stated, "The problem is beyond the police. . . . While they continue to make arrests, *something more fundamental needed to be done*" (emphasis added).[62]

In order to press the city to take action, BASTA filed suit against the city, organized meetings with top administration and police officials, and built alliances with local elected officials. In the process, it tried to mobilize support for its cause by transforming the discourse about homelessness and crime in their community. Antonio Pagan, who then was president of the Third Street Block Association and went on to win election to the city council, explained the connection between disorder and neighborhood decline in his welcome address to a rally against the shelter: "Welcome, to the great Third Street area. Welcome to the place the City has forgotten. Welcome to the place everything goes. Welcome to fear and terror. Welcome to nowhere."[63] For the members of BASTA, the presence of homeless people was not just an eyesore but was seen as a source of crime and a major threat to the stability of their neighborhood. By couching their arguments in these terms, they were able to more effectively challenge the police's inaction.

Another problem that mobilized local residents to pressure the police on the Lower East Side was street peddlers. A series of organizing efforts began in 1986 with the formation of the groups Save Our Streets and the Second Avenue Task Force. Both attempted to pressure police to take enforcement action against the peddlers. In 1988, We Are Resolved, Peddlers Are Total Hell (WARPATH) criticized the police's seeming unwillingness or inability to consistently shut down the illegal open-air markets along Second Avenue that sold used and sometimes stolen household items. WARPATH called for a combination of social services and police enforcement, but the police bore the brunt of their criticism. A prominent Second Avenue merchant described the frustration with the police: "There is urinating in public, constant noise, and no law enforcement, I've been here for 22 years—I've lost all respect for the Ninth Precinct. The situation is appalling."[64] A local resident reported that his wife was once "attacked by a 'peddler' bearing a stick. Upon calling the Ninth Precinct, he was told that they were too busy to respond."[65] Other residents and employers noted the connection between minor disorders and serious neighborhood decline: "We're living under siege. . . . There is an appearance that anything goes here, and if you give that appearance, anything *will* go. It's an issue of people who contribute to the community versus people who take from the neighborhood. It's a confrontation in terms of lifestyles" (emphasis in original).[66] "A remedy must be instituted—and soon! It is next to impossible to keep employees at night. Because the situation is so dangerous and they experience so much harassment."[67] "The City must do something before vigilante action becomes or [*sic*] only result."[68]

What emerged was a discourse about the community's problems that placed disorder at the center and threatened to displace the role of the police. By failing to dislodge peddlers, the city was allowing the neighborhood to decline into chaos.

In 1989, the confrontation escalated as local residents dropped water balloons from rooftops onto peddlers and poured ammonia on the sidewalks in front of their buildings to drive them off. The local precinct finally responded to the growing intensity of the neighborhood's anger. Deputy Inspector Michael Julian had just been put in charge of the precinct in the wake of the Tompkins Square Park riot in 1989. Julian was chosen for this difficult assignment because he had a background in the Community Police on Patrol (CPOP) program, lived in the neighborhood, and was viewed by Commissioner Ward as someone who could communicate with any group.[69] This last point was essential because of the level of public involvement in policing issues. Julian was chosen because Ward felt that he could get a handle on the problems there and restore public confidence in the police.

Upon taking over, Julian was immediately pressured by the local business community to eliminate the peddler problem. He responded by assigning his Conditions Unit of eight officers to work on the problem, splitting the unit into two-person teams so that they could maintain coverage at all times rather than just making occasional concentrated sweeps. Julian also decided to increase the number of arrests and then follow up with warnings and a constant police presence.[70] The ultimate solution, however, was to arm these officers with a new tool. After consulting the district attorney's office, Julian determined what the legally permissible peddling locations were on St. Mark's, based on the presence of other sidewalk impediments. He then explained to local business owners his plan to use paint to mark the legally permissible locations, which were far fewer than had previously been allowed. The local businesses were so pleased with the plan that they actually donated the paint used to mark the locations.[71] Rather than having a hundred tables set up, the new painted slots were limited to a couple of dozen. This clear indication of the legal standard gave beat officers the backing they needed for consistent tough enforcement.

The local response to the problems of disorder on the Lower East Side exemplifies how widespread grassroots mobilizations in the 1980s made specific demands for changes in policing at the neighborhood level and, in turn, created a crisis within the law enforcement style of policing. The possibility that residents would take the law into their own hands undercut the authority of the police and the rule of law and threatened to displace the police as providers of law and order in the neighborhood. The people's ability to rhetorically link disorder to serious crime and neighborhood decline created a discursive framework that forced the police to act. While Captain Julian had previously been exposed to problem-oriented and "broken windows" policing methods, it was the local neighborhood that first articulated its problems and demands in this form, not the NYPD or the mayor's office. In addition, these public demands and the police department's response—all of which were consistent with the quality-of-life style which was instituted well before Giuliani was elected mayor.

Safe Streets, Safe City

Throughout Dinkins's term as mayor, crime and disorder continued to grow as public concerns. Over this period, the tenor of public discourse changed from calls for enhanced services for the homeless to demands to restore order through immediate punitive measures such as more police and the greater use of incarceration. In response, Dinkins undertook two measures: the Safe City, Safe Streets initiative and the anti-squeegee-men effort, both of which embody the central tenets of the neoconservative agenda. These efforts were not, however, couched in the reactionary language of the neoconservatives, which undermined the efforts' appeal to besieged and angry residents. Just as important, they occurred too late in his term to significantly affect public perceptions about the amount of crime and disorder. Ironically, the great crime drop of the 1990s actually began in 1992, but Dinkins was unable to capitalize on this politically because of its late occurrence and entrenched public perceptions that he was soft on crime. Bratton later pointed out that if Dinkins had started these initiatives earlier, Giuliani might not have been elected in 1993.[72]

The Safe Streets, Safe City program, which was announced in 1990 and implemented in 1991, dedicated new taxes to fund the hiring of thousands of new police officers and other criminal justice workers and created new law enforcement and prevention initiatives. This program was launched by Dinkins as an effort to reshape and expand the NYPD. Some of the core strategies it proposed contradicted quality-of-life policing, but its overall emphasis on expanding the department, enhancing flexibility, and taking a more problem-oriented approach was important to the full realization of quality-of-life policing under Giuliani and Bratton. In particular, it was the dramatic increase in officers that allowed Giuliani and Bratton to adopt many of their zero-tolerance and flexible deployment strategies on a wide scale.

In 1990, at the direction of Mayor Dinkins, Police Commissioner Lee Brown undertook a major analysis of the NYPD's staffing needs. This study called for an increase in the size of the department and a change in orientation toward the strategies of community and problem-oriented policing. The plan specifically recommended the creation of a new special operations unit that would coordinate existing community policing, anticrime, street narcotics, and conditions units. These units could then be deployed in a coordinated fashion based on the particular problems in each precinct. This represented a major change in the way that the department conceptualized the deployment of specialized units.[73] By unifying localized control rather than having separate chains of command, this new approach would "greatly enhance the ability to respond to community priorities at the precinct level by developing a flexible cadre of policing experts in each precinct."[74]

In order to implement this plan, the department needed more officers. Dinkins found a new way to fund this reorganization. In October 1990, he released his "Safe Streets, Safe City" proposal, which called for the addition of thousands of new police officers as well as more funding for corrections, courts, and a variety of prevention-oriented social programs. The plan would be paid for by a series of new dedicated taxes, including a property and payroll tax surcharge. Besides describing how the new money would be raised and spent, the plan offered new directions for the police department.

The plan's overall orientation was toward a model of *community policing,* a term with widely different interpretations. The report recommends the decentralization of policing activity, a reduced emphasis on 911 responses, an increase in flexible deployments, and a problem-solving orientation. Each precinct would have officers assigned to it who were not tied to 911 radio calls and could instead target crime patterns in the precinct. This included a mix of serious crime fighting and order maintenance: "The officers will not only fight crime in the neighborhood but will also seek to restore a sense of order in their assigned area and to enhance the quality of life for its residents."[75] All these objectives would become central features of policing under Bratton.

It is clear from this report that much of the conceptual basis for quality-of-life policing was in place in the department before Bratton's arrival. It is important to note, however, that Brown and Dinkins were not successful in implementing this plan before the election in 1993. There was significant resistance from within the department to many of the measures, and Commissioner Brown had to resign in 1992 for family reasons.[76] The most significant legacy, therefore, of Safe Streets, Safe City was the funding to hire several thousand new officers in 1993 and 1994. These new officers gave Bratton the resources he needed to implement many of his new initiatives. Without them, it might have been very difficult for him to create new flexible deployment patterns necessary for real crime problem solving. In particular, the use of large numbers of officers for quality-of-life zero-tolerance enforcement efforts would probably have been impossible under previous staffing levels. Bratton notes that Dinkins's efforts were consistent with much of his own thinking about crime fighting and that if he had been able to put the newly funded officers on the street a year earlier, Dinkins might have won reelection.[77] The Safe Streets, Safe City plan was a direct response to community pressure for significant concrete improvements in the crime and disorder problems. As such, it began the process of reorienting the NYPD toward quality-of-life policing. These changes, however, came too late to prevent the neoconservative political backlash that swept Dinkins from office in the 1993 election.

Squeegee Men

Dinkins's efforts to change policing can be seen most clearly in the 1993 campaign to rid the city of squeegee men. Ironically, this effort is most associated with the Giuliani administration, even though the Dinkins administration did the planning and implementation. Dinkins was trying to change the department's mission to emphasize the need to make the city appear safer by going after the visible disorder, through controlling homeless and socially marginal populations. Whereas these groups had earlier been seen as a minor nuisance, they now had become the rhetorical center of a nexus of crime and municipal decline. With the adoption of the squeegee men strategy, the criminalization of the disorderly was well in hand.

Squeegee men, who washed the windows of cars stopped at traffic lights at major intersections, were symbols of New York City's menacing nature in the late 1980s and early 1990s. Even though these men themselves committed very few crimes, the public identified them with the overall increase in crime and the disorder problems associated with homelessness and drug use. They thus came to represent a city out of control, a police force unable to deal with the most visible sources of disorder, and a mayor who was letting this all happen.

In 1993 Dinkins ordered Police Commissioner Raymond W. Kelly to do something about the squeegee problem, so the department initiated a pilot program in eight precincts to eliminate it. Using quality-of-life tactics, local commanders deployed community and patrol officers to make arrests and give out summons and warnings in a consistent, ongoing manner. The result of this effort was a 70 percent decline in observations of window washers over an eight-week period.[78]

A report prepared by Kelling and Julian makes it clear that by 1993, the department understood the squeegee issue as part of a larger problem of disorder and crime, and that as long as open incivility was allowed to flourish, the city would spiral into decline.[79] Their report begins with a discussion of the role of civility in making urban neighborhoods livable: "Tolerance of, indeed pleasure in, diversity and pluralism can only be achieved and maintained when people behave in minimally civil ways—and when people who have a stake in the community encourage civil behavior and discourage uncivil behavior."[80] This is very different from the kind of discourse normally present in police reports. The influence of the "broken windows" theory is clearly in place. Moreover, it emphasizes the extent to which the new approach to policing was seen as the key to creating a new experience of the city.

Procedurally, the primary innovation was the elimination of summonses in the enforcement process. Previously, people stopped by the police for squeegeeing were given a summons on the spot that ordered them to appear in court at a future date to face the charges against them. The problem was that few of those cited ever appeared in court, and because the charges were very minor, warrants squads were never interested in trying to enforce the resulting bench warrants. This was similar to the enforcement problems associated with fare beating on the subways, and the solution to that was similar. In this case, local precinct officers, rather than the centralized warrant squad, were allowed to enforce the warrants. Now the local precinct could actually take offenders into custody and hold them in the system until they appeared in court, twenty-four to forty-eight hours later. This incarceration was longer than any the judge was likely to order upon conviction, so the police were now in a position to mete out punishment on the spot rather than waiting for the reluctant judicial system. The initial use of this new method turned out to be very successful in clearing out targeted intersections and was eventually expanded to cover the entire city. By the mid-1990s this approach was used to deal with all forms of disorder, resulting in the brief incarceration of hundreds of thousands of New Yorkers in the last decade.

By late 1993, the NYPD was already using many aspects of the quality-of-life style. The very decision to treat squeegee men as a serious problem indicated a changing sense of mission and values. In addition, the central role of both broken windows and problem-oriented policing strategies is visible. The tactics used to control the problem relied on the use of flexible deployment, zero-tolerance enforcement, and the renewed use of previously ignored legal codes. This confirms that the conceptual framework of quality-of-life policing, which has always been identified with Giuliani, was well established within the NYPD before his election in 1993.

Conclusion

In many ways, Dinkins's efforts to reorient the NYPD toward quality-of-life policing represented a victory for neoconservatism in a bulwark of urban liberalism. In essence, Dinkins was trying to have it both ways. He wanted to continue his progrowth, global cities model of economic development, which was increasing inequality and undermining city finances, and at the same time pursue both a progressive agenda of providing housing and social services for the homeless and poor while stepping up punitive police interventions. In the end, he was unable to afford this entire package. So instead of cutting real estate subsidies or raising taxes to finance a more progressive agenda, Dinkins used his limited political capital to create a new tax dedicated to hiring more police. Dinkins opted to embrace the neoconservative desire to deal aggressively with the symptoms of disorder rather than a more progressive agenda of reforming housing markets and enhancing social services.

Overall, the later years of the Dinkins administration shared many of the same qualities of the early Giuliani administration. They both undertook a global cities model of economic development and pursued punitive, quality-of-life policing strategies. The primary differences were Giuliani's rhetorical rejection of Dinkins's social programs—most of which he continued to fund—and his embrace of a neoconservative political discourse that blamed the poor and disenfranchised for the city's plight. This suggests that many residents wanted not just neoconservative policing but also a neoconservative rhetoric that validated their fears, anger, and frustrations and their somewhat reluctant turn away from urban liberalism.

The preceding cases demonstrate that while Giuliani and Bratton were important to formalizing quality-of-life policing throughout the department, many of its key elements were already in place when they arrived. Moreover, most of the innovations created by Bratton were organizational rather than institutional. While he helped diffuse the quality-of-life style throughout the department, he was not the original source of the new mission, values, and core strategies. Even the Compstat system, which helped advance the spread of the quality-of-life style, was as much a mechanism of organizational innovation as one of institutional innovation.

The most important mechanisms of institutional innovation also were being used by a wide variety of actors outside the police department. In the late 1980s and early 1990s, the Grand Central Partnership and activists on the Lower East Side were undermining the legitimacy of the police department by challenging its mission, values, and core strategies, by emphasizing the need to apply a problem-oriented approach to minor disorders. Mayor Dinkins provided important political and primarily financial resources that made wide-scale quality-of-life policing possible. Finally, the 1993 campaign to eliminate squeegee men demonstrates that the NYPD's institutional dimensions had already undergone significant, if incomplete, change before Bratton and Giuliani came on the scene.

Police innovation cannot be understood as a process internal to the world of police planners, creative managers, or crusading politicians. Although all these forces are important to understanding the development of the mission, values, and core strategies of a police department, other important, external, factors are at work as well. The police, like any public institution, cannot function effectively without the support of the public. In periods of change, such as the rise of homelessness and visible disorder in the 1980s, the police often are slow to adjust their entrenched methods of carrying out the business of policing. It is only when a crisis of legitimacy emerges in combination with calls for doing things in a new way that the police respond. The depth and length of that response depend partly on the severity of the crisis and the pressure on the police from elected officials. The more effectively that community actors are able to generate this sense of crisis within the department by challenging its core values, mission, and strategies while at the same time clearly articulating possible alternatives, the more successful they will be in changing core police philosophies and practices.

7

The Community Backlash

In chapter 6, I demonstrated how the failure of the NYPD to adequately address the disorder problem led to a public backlash against it that undermined its basic legitimacy. This process began before the election of Rudolph Giuliani as mayor and led to many of the changes in the basic policing strategies in New York City. A similar crisis of legitimacy took place in regard to urban liberal politicians. In 1993, the Dinkins administration was voted out of office, in large part because of its inability to reduce the level of homelessness and moderate its effect on the everyday lives of the rest of the population. Rudolph Giuliani, who replaced him, campaigned on a platform of replacing the urban liberal social services approach with a series of "tough love" measures designed to force homeless people either to enter rehabilitation programs and shelters or to face eviction from public spaces and ultimately incarceration. Whereas the police were accused of being insensitive to community concerns about disorder, urban liberal politicians were accused of responding to the disorder crisis without the full participation of the communities and of calling for social tolerance without creating the possibilities of acting on that tolerance. This chapter considers how these two contradictions led to community backlashes against urban liberalism, which in turn helped usher in the new conservative Giuliani administration and the quality-of-life paradigm.

As discussed in chapter 3, urban liberalism relied on rehabilitative social programs coordinated by centralized experts to address social problems. As the homelessness and disorder problems intensified in the 1980s, urban liberals attempted to respond to them by creating a series of emergency social services. This approach was driven by citywide concerns about the legal requirements to shelter the homeless and the desire to ameliorate the conditions of homeless people within the constraints of the city budget, as discussed in chapter 4. This approach never directly addressed the changes in the labor and housing markets that were largely driving this crisis. In addition, local communities were given little voice in how or where these services would be provided. Shelters were often dropped into communities in the middle of the night without prior community review. Social services were provided based on the availability of cheap space and the lack of political resistance, not on the specific needs of the community.

The second problem was that urban liberal administrations had a philosophical orientation in favor of individual rights and social tolerance but did little to cultivate social tolerance and respect for rights. It is one thing for a government to insist that everyone has the negative right to education, meaning that no one can prevent someone from attending school. But it is another thing to provide the positive right to education, meaning that adequate school facilities are provided to make the attainment of education possible for all. In the case of social tolerance, the city's demand that residents tolerate the public presence of homeless people became an untenable negative right for homeless people to be free of harassment. Without putting in place mechanisms to make that social tolerance reasonably possible, however, the positive right to be free from harassment did not truly exist and thus failed to operate effectively. Once homeless and disorderly people became so numerous that they interfered with public accommodations, such as the use of parks, sidewalks, and subways and the security of private property, local residents could no longer be expected not to take action to secure these public and private goods, even if it was at the expense of the rights of homeless people to live free of intolerance, cruelty, and criminalization.

Throughout the 1980s and 1990s, many communities expressed a willingness to provide housing and social services for the extremely poor in ways that allowed them to maintain the overall stability of their communities.[1] Although in some cases, extreme forms of NIMBYism were evident, this was in fact quite rare. Rather, what most communities objected to was the imposition of services that they felt did little to address the social problems in their communities and, in some cases, actually exacerbated their problems. Similarly, while some communities consistently called for the criminalization of the disorderly, many called for compassion, charity, and substantial positive government action for years before turning to the police as the primary tool for addressing disorder. The following case studies show how three New York communities reacted to the failure of urban liberalism to involve them in the delivery of social services that would have provided the positive conditions necessary to create social tolerance.

I have chosen the cases of the mostly liberal, mixed-race Lower East Side of Manhattan, the high-rent commercial area around Grand Central Terminal, and the African American neighborhood of East New York in Brooklyn to show that the urban liberals' approach was destined to lead to political failure. The three main constituencies committed to urban liberalism in the 1980s were African Americans, public-sector workers, nonprofit social service providers, and white "clubhouse" democrats. Together, these groups supported Edward Koch and put David Dinkins in office in 1989. As homelessness, disorder, and crime increased in the early 1990s, the first three of these groups remained loyal to liberal politicians. The final group, traditional white liberals who had historically supported the Democratic Party, however, defected to the neoconservative Rudolph Giuliani. They did this because urban liberals were unwilling to address their everyday quality-of-life concerns directly, which lessened the possibility of social tolerance through either major new investments in housing, employment, and social services, or the creation of new styles of policing that targeted these quality-of-life problems. By the end of Giuliani's first term, even African Americans were muted in their support of urban liberalism, staying home in large numbers in the 1997 election, as can be seen in the East New York case.

These historically liberal community activists, combined with business groups and traditional conservatives, laid the basis for a new political coalition capable of displacing the urban liberals. This chapter describes how "club-house" democrats in the Lower East Side became increasingly estranged from urban liberalism because of its inadequate response to the quality-of-life crisis. These activists felt that the centralizing tendency of urban liberalism was resulting in the abandonment of their neighborhoods. They regarded its emphasis on limited social programs as an inadequate response that too often served to enrich and empower a handful of politically connected service providers, rather than effectively resolving neighborhood social problems. The Grand Central case demonstrates the importance of commercial elites in pressuring the city to provide a concrete alternative to a social services approach, by emphasizing the effectiveness of coercive security measures. Finally, the East New York case shows how aggressive quality-of-life policing successfully undermined African Americans' support for urban liberals, who, they felt, did not adequately respond to the needs of their community.

The East Village

In the early 1980s, the East Village was controlled politically by two camps. The first was centered on the mostly Jewish housing projects on Grand Street, the base of such political leaders as Sheldon Silver, the speaker of the New York State Assembly. This group functioned very much like a Democratic machine in which constituencies that actively supported the machine received preferential treatment in the form of social programs and government subsidies for housing and government services. The machine also groomed candidates for a range of public offices, thereby creating an integrated set of political leaders able to influence policy on the local, state, and federal levels. The machine tended to support redistributive social policies of benefit to the middle class. This was a state-centered approach based on the belief that social problems could best be addressed by government action.

The other major grouping was a coalition of social service providers and community activists made up of both white and Latino residents. These groups came of age in the 1960s and 1970s in a variety of local struggles, including those over affordable housing, police accountability, and youth services. During the 1970s, many of these groups formed nonprofit, community-based organizations in an attempt to institutionalize some of the political victories they had won. This grouping had its power base in the local community board and its relationship to government and foundation bureaucrats. These groups believed that some degree of local activism was needed in addition to government action, and they argued for increased local control of government programs and resources and the growth of the nonprofit sector. Neither group had complete control over any one sphere. In addition, conflicts were common at the community board and the ballot box.

During the 1980s, these two groups were challenged for power by newly mobilized community groups concerned about drug sales and a variety of disorders associated with homelessness. The eventual focus of this new level of community activism was the homeless encampment in

Tompkins Square Park, in the northern center of the neighborhood. By the early 1990s, these groups had transformed local politics and supported the implementation of various measures designed to control disorder in public spaces. They favored maintaining order over ongoing efforts to develop comprehensive solutions to the underlying social problems contributing to public disorder.

Four major events mobilized this new political grouping: (1) the rise of street sales of crack, (2) an increase in illegal street peddling and fencing around Second Avenue and St. Mark's Place, (3) the opposition to homeless facilities in the southwestern part of the neighborhood, and (4) the conditions in Tompkins Square Park (TSP). Next I describe each of these and discuss how the approaches used by urban liberals contributed to these mobilizations. First, they refused to work with local residents to locate homeless facilities; they failed to take measures to alleviate the worst conditions on streets and in parks; and they preached social tolerance while disregarding the actual breakdown of public civility. This failure of urban liberalism created a wedge between the social service providers, who remained loyal to Dinkins, and the traditional democratic activists, who defected—first in their support of Antonio Pagan for city council and later in their support of Rudolph Giuliani for mayor.

The first conflict revolved around the provision of homeless services in the western part of the neighborhood, which included sections of the Bowery, the historic skid row of New York. During the mid-1980s, this area housed one of the city's largest homeless shelters, on East Third Street, in which adult males were given meals, shelter, and referrals to other services. The primary effect on residents was a burgeoning crack-cocaine trade on adjacent streets where homeless people bought and sold crack, creating a market that drew in other buyers and sellers. As a result, in the mid-1980s, crime rates in the area went up 26 percent.[2] Residents also complained of noise, garbage, and human waste on their stoops and sidewalks,[3] concrete problems that affected residents in their everyday lives.

As part of Mayor Edward Koch's 1986 shelter plan, the city announced its intention to build an additional shelter on East First Street that would accommodate up to one hundred families. This generated a new coalition of local residents and merchants called BASTA (Before Another Shelter Tears Us Apart), which brought together existing groups and mobilized many people who had not been politically active previously. BASTA's members were racially mixed, and most were longtime supporters of the Democratic Party. Also joining BASTA was the Cooper Square Committee (CPC), a community-based housing and social services provider formed in 1959 to oppose a nearby urban renewal project that would have displaced low-income residents. Since then, it has been one of the neighborhood's central tenants' organizations and low-income housing and social services providers.

The relationship between Cooper Square and BASTA was tenuous. Several members of BASTA felt that even though Cooper Square had been promoting itself as a community-based organization for many years, it had never attempted to deal with the problems created by homeless people using the Third Street shelter. "We didn't trust Cooper Square to do the job or help fight [the proposed First Street shelter]. They had been around for years without addressing 3rd St."[4] The community board's support for BASTA also was weak, which one BASTA member attributed to the increasing political power of local social service providers. "Support from Community Board 3 eroded because [City Council member Miriam] Friedlander appointed new social service oriented members [to the community board]."[5] This was viewed as part of general political shift in the neighborhood's electoral base from local political clubs to nonprofit service providers. This conflict was indicative of the general tension between some community activists and local social service providers and proved to be a force in undermining political support for David Dinkins and urban liberalism in general.

The groups claimed that the area was already the site of a disproportionate share of homeless and drug treatment services and that these services had a detrimental effect on the community. A BASTA member pointed out that "according to [Human Resources Administration's] HRA's own statistics, the vast majority of the homeless are from Brooklyn and the Bronx. They have been forced into this neighborhood by HRA policy, and not any so-called tradition of refuge on the Lower East Side."[6] They also complained about the ability of the city's Human Resources Administration to run the facility, given its poor track record in resolving community complaints concerning the Third Street shelter.

People were especially angered by the process by which the city selected this and other shelter sites. The CPC had been negotiating with the city for several years about creating a mix of low-income and market-rate housing on the sight chosen for the proposed shelter in an effort to develop much needed permanent housing. The local community board had suggested five other sights for smaller shelters that were not used, and it was not consulted about the siting or size of this shelter. This lack of consultation alienated many residents from local government. One local resident described it as a "slap in the face," and another, "[an] example of the contempt the city has for our community."[7] Borough President David Dinkins also wrote a statement opposed to the shelter, asking, "What planning principles did the City Administration have in mind when it proposed to put another shelter for single adults in a community board which already shelters between 20–25 percent of the City's homeless individuals, only one block away from the central intake facility for the entire five borough system?"[8] State Senator Manfred Ohrenstein pointed out how the area's historic openness toward homeless people was being abused:

> The record of responsibility of the people of the Lower East Side has demonstrated the humanity and compassion of the community towards the homeless and helpless who sought food and shelter here. To introduce another shelter in the area would severely strain existing services in the neighborhood.[9]

In response to these complaints, the community board abandoned its previous support for new shelters and, in its advisory capacity, voted overwhelmingly against the planned shelter.

The Lower East Side was an area that had traditionally welcomed the less fortunate. It was a center of socialist activity in the early part of the twentieth century, a site of Hoovervilles during the Great Depression, and radical political activity in the 1960s and 1970s. But the city ignored this tradition of "refuge" and "openness" in its development of citywide homeless shelter plans. Rather than adjust its plans to suit what the neighborhood was eagerly willing to accept, the city tried to impose on it a shelter that was viewed negatively by almost everyone in the community. As a result, many of the moderate and even ardent supporters of the need for more services for the homeless opposed this approach and began to look at more punitive options.

Later that year, the city dropped plans to build the shelter, and local residents went on the offensive against conditions at the Third Street shelter. In 1988, this shelter had become the intake center for the entire city's shelter system. A local resident accused the city of, "dumping 2,000 homeless men into a residential neighborhood without adequate supervision or facilities. The city has created an urban free-fire zone where anything goes."[10] Community members felt that a lack of services and supervision meant that people were free to roam the streets and get into trouble instead of trying to improve their situation. A community board task force set up in 1987 recommended in 1988 that the shelter no longer be used as an intake facility but only as a shelter with support services. When the city refused, BASTA, with the support of local politicians, filed a lawsuit claiming that the city's conversion of the shelter into an intake facility did not follow proper land use procedures. Support for the lawsuit, however, was not universal.

Many groups, including those associated with Sheldon Silver, the community board, and the Cooper Square Committee, were unhappy with elements of the shelter but did not want to disrupt the shelter system or appear to oppose homeless people. These groups continued to feel an attachment to the urban liberal social services model and were reluctant to make a total break. BASTA, however, was willing to make that break. It was not tied into the social services system and was able to mobilize large numbers of residents, business owners, and real estate developers to speak out against conditions around the shelter. In September—using an Alinsky-style organizing campaign—they forced the deputy mayor, police commissioner, HRA commissioner, and local politicians to attend a "community accountability session" on the shelter, in which local officials had to answer to community complaints in a mass meeting.[11] This event helped mobilize more residents to become involved with BASTA and generated negative publicity toward the city. BASTA used progressive grassroots-organizing tactics to fight against the provision of social services, while the service providers chose to rely on their connection to the elected officials who financed their work.

By the end of the year, the city agreed to convert the facility back into a shelter and to include social services. BASTA members wanted the services because they felt that drug and mental health treatment might reduce the antisocial behaviors of the people living there. These two victories represented a partial shift in the balance of power in the neighborhood. The community board showed that its support of specific programs was limited, although it maintained its generally pro-social-services stance. The board also created a new set of neighborhood leaders tempered by the conflict. The most important of these was Antonio Pagan, the president of the Third Street Block Association, who went on to win the local city council seat. At a rally in July 1988, Pagan expressed his feelings in a greeting to those assembled:

Welcome, to the greater Third Street Area. Welcome to the place the City has forgotten. Welcome to the place [where] everything goes. Welcome to fear and terror. Welcome to nowhere.[12]

The other important leader was Howard Hemsley, who was president of the First Street Block Association and went on to serve on the community board and to provide guidance to new community organizations around Tompkins Square Park.

They and other members of BASTA had been past supporters of progressive politics. One of BASTA's cofounders is Howard Hemsley, who is African American, volunteered during Jessie Jackson's two presidential runs, and supported liberal presidential candidates as far back as Senator George McGovern.[13] The other BASTA cofounder, Antonio Pagan, is a gay Latino who had worked for a number of progressive causes in the past. As the homeless problem worsened and the existing urban liberal political leadership refused to remedy the neighborhood's declining quality of public life, these two people and several others began to look for a new politics of community activism that treated even local concerns as paramount.

The fight to oppose the First Street and Third Street shelters is an example of the several weaknesses of urban liberalism in dealing with the growing homelessness problem. First, its reliance on nonprofit social service providers as its electoral base was problematic because they had had years to reduce the impact of homelessness on the community and had failed to do so. Second, the city continued to keep the management of the homelessness problem centralized to such a degree that communities' wishes were ignored even when they made a good-faith effort to work with the city. The result was that community activists with a history of liberalism were becoming alienated from the local Democratic Party and were beginning to look for alternatives.

The second issue of concern was the presence of illegal street peddlers on both St. Mark's Place and Second Avenue. Residents and even legitimate booksellers and business owners were upset at both people illegally selling used personal possessions, stolen goods, and miscellaneous junk as well as even more legitimate sidewalk booksellers. The overall effect was of a late-night bazaar that generated noise, garbage, and people sleeping and relieving themselves in doorways. Many of the stands were also viewed as a cover for a variety of illegal activities, according to one resident's description:

The streets look great early in the morning after they have been cleaned, and they deteriorate gradually until 1 A.M. when it looks like *Night of the Living Dead*. Zombies walk through the crowds of "peddlers" ripping open garbage bag after garbage bag. It's not our outside any more. It is the scummiest block in the city.[14]

The area had a history of street peddling going back to the mid-1970s, but in the late 1980s the problem got much worse, causing local residents and merchants to form WARPATH (We Are Resolved, Peddlers Are Total Hell). Local residents and merchants attributed the escalation to the expansion of the nearby Third Street shelter, which had recently been transformed into the city's principal intake facility. Hundreds of additional homeless men were thus congregating in the area. But the city did not do much to address the problem other than to wash down the streets in the morning. Through the 1980s, local residents and merchants tried to pressure the city to improve conditions. Earlier, two organizations had been formed: Save Our Sidewalks and the Second Avenue Task Force (established by the community board). Both had been unsuccessful and had disbanded in frustration. Another local resident expressed the frustration felt by WARPATH members:

There is the appearance that anything goes here, and if you give that appearance, anything *will* go. It's an issue of people who contribute to the neighborhood versus people who take from the neighborhood. It's a confrontation in terms of lifestyles. The [political] leadership Downtown is one of benign indifference and a lack of local concern from the politicians.[15]

A quotation from another resident indicates the growing disdain for civil rights advocates and the breakdown of social tolerance:

I'm very happy that there are people out there that share my attitude towards this problem. I hope we succeed. Although the city passed recently the law forbidding the police to arrest or even to harrass [*sic*] those bums and drunkards (Civil Liberties Union forced the City to do so) I hope still something can and should be done.[16]

This issue mobilized people who were upset about the very evident deterioration of conditions in their immediate environment and the seeming inability or unwillingness of local government to take action to address it. As a result, the attitudes acquired by those involved were critical of both local politicians for failing to respond to local needs and civil libertarians who failed to acknowledge the effect of social tolerance on their neighborhood. The ideological battle lines were drawn. Any expressions of "civil rights" or "social tolerance" were equated with a public culture that was out of control. Anyone who was soft on panhandlers, drug dealers, street peddlers, or visible homeless people was contributing to the downfall of public civility. The solution was increasingly evolving into demands on the police for stepped-up enforcement activities. As I showed in chapter 6, the police's initial resistance to taking such action only served to further mobilize and radicalize these community activists.

The last and most important arena of political mobilization in the East Village was the homeless encampment in Tompkins Square Park (TSP). During the mid-1980s, a growing number of homeless people began moving into the park. What had been a daytime congregation quickly turned into an around-the-clock encampment that by 1988 numbered between 150 and 200 people. The community response to the deteriorating conditions in the park was mixed. The community board and the Friends of Tompkins Square Park supported the encampment as a way of highlighting the Koch administration's lack of support for affordable housing and social services to deal with homelessness. On the other side was a growing number of neighborhood groups made up of merchants and residents, including the Avenue A Block Association and the Tompkins Square Park Neighborhood Council, which wanted more immediate action taken to clean up the park. By 1991, however, support for removing the encampment had broadened considerably, and the park was closed for more than a year by the Dinkins administration for extensive renovations.

There were two aspects to the TSP problem. The first was the growing homeless problem, which made parts of the park unusable and contributed to the sense that the park was out of control and dangerous. The second was the presence of noisy young people each evening who used the park as a place to congregate and play music, often well into the night. It was this latter problem that became the wedge issue that in the end brought about a more substantial backlash against the homeless people living there and precipitated the closing of the park.

During 1987/88, several local groups began to organize against conditions in the park. The lead group during this early period was the Avenue A Block Association, made up of local residents, merchants, and landlords. The issue of closing the park was first raised officially in August 1987. The parks department proposed closing the park for renovation as a way of removing the encampment and the noisy young people. But this effort was rejected by the community board, which had a neighborhoodwide constituency, as well as the more immediate Friends of Tompkins Square Park group.

On August 2, the local police commander arranged a meeting with a select group of community residents from the Avenue A Block Association and the precinct community council to garner public support for enforcing a curfew in the park. This body bypassed the existing parks committee of the community board and appeared to offer a way for the police to obtain community "cover" for enforcing a curfew that they knew would be unpopular. On August 6, the police attempted to close the park at 11 P.M., based on the previously unenforced park curfew. Although the police attempted to remove only the noisy youth and not the homeless encampment, they ended up in a bloody confrontation with the young people when they resisted the eviction. Emergency assistance calls from the outnumbered police brought in hundreds of unsupervised officers, who indiscriminately beat demonstrators and passersby.

Over the next two years, there were ongoing confrontations in the park and various political venues, with the community deeply divided over the deteriorating conditions in the park and the solutions being proposed. The police's overstepping their bounds brought a stinging rebuke from the local community board and many progressive residents. Nonetheless, the new conservative groupings were gaining strength as frustration over the disorder associated with the park worsened.

In September 1988, the community board voted overwhelmingly in favor of a statement drafted by its own Tompkins Square Park Task Force, which proposed leaving the park and allowing the homeless to remain. It also called for a regular but nonpunitive presence of police and parks workers as a way to reduce disorder without evicting the encampment. This established that a significant part of the community was in favor of permitting the homeless to stay until the city could provide adequate alternatives. Over the next nine months, more conservative forces challenged this position. In addition, pressure was mounting from conservative residents and the media on Mayor Koch to take action against homeless encampments around the city. In response, on July 5 without consulting with the community board or local politicians, he ordered the police to remove the structures from the park. The result was numerous clashes in the streets with protesters and a round of protests by local political leaders and the community board, ending in a resolution restating the board's support of the homeless encampment. The move was applauded by the media and conservative political forces in the neighborhood. The *New York Times* ran an especially pointed editorial that summed up the growing conservative sentiment about the park:

> People have lost sight of the principle behind the city's decision to remove the makeshift homes: the parks belong to the people—all the people. To turn them into a shantytown is to rob the larger community of its park.
> Some neighbors say they are willing to pay that price for the sake of the homeless. That assumes the homeless have no real choices. But they do. The city runs shelters for people who have no place to live. Whatever the inadequacy of those shelters, is living semi-exposed in a park, with barely more plumbing than a campsite, really any better?[17]

What's more, not all those living in the Tompkins Square park were homeless—if the homeless are defined as poor people without the financial or mental resources to support themselves. The shanty population included radicals angered about neighborhood gentrification, drug addicts, skinheads, self-proclaimed anarchists, and people furious at the city for tearing down an abandoned building where they had been squatting. Apparently, and sadly, some people in the park were cynically using the plight of the truly homeless to further their own agendas.

> New York does lack affordable housing. New waves of affluent residents do unsettle and upset neighborhoods like the Lower East Side. Homelessness is a tormenting social problem. But to solve these problems by creating another—unusable parks—is no solution. The Parks Department, by enforcing old rules and new, is only trying to give the park back to the people it belongs to: all of them.[18]

This is the *New York Times*'s first statement in favor of punitive action to eliminate a homeless encampment, and it is clear that the particular circumstances surrounding Tompkins Square Park made it easier to make this statement at this time. The fact that the conditions in the park could be described as the result of disingenuous political disruption and not just on the presence of the truly needy lowered the tolerance for disorder. That is, this equating of Tompkins Square Park with a general sense of disorder and radical activism, and not the specific state of the homeless, made punitive backlashes more acceptable and ultimately more successful. The door was now open for a broad attack against disorder and, with it, the homeless.

At this point, rather than the backlash's being restricted to longtime supporters of law and order politics, new, more liberal community activists became involved in the effort to evict the encampment. The following letter to the editor from a member of the St. Mark's Block Association illustrates that once the condition of the park was redefined as an order problem, liberal concern for the homeless was displaced by a new communalist concern with access to social goods like the park:

I've always considered myself very liberal, but now anyone who [doesn't] support the tent city is made to feel guilty. [The anarchists] pop up in the park or at Community Board meetings and try and make us liberals, who care about the homeless but don't believe in their anarchistic agenda of allowing anything and everything, feel guilty.

The anarchists don't care if you can't sit on a park bench in Tompkins Square because every available spot reeks of urine. The anarchists don't care if you can't walk your dog in the neighborhood[']s only green place because the dog run is fil[l]ed with tents and debris. They don't care if your child can't use the playground because it is filthy. They don't care if you can't sleep at night because of the noise from the park. They don't care if you can't walk on the sidewalk because peddlers have taken up the walking space.

Most of we [sic] "bad" liberals have lived in the East Village for many years and are far from upwardly mobile. I've been here for 14 years and made under $20,000 last year. We've fought hard in the war against gentrification and we too think Mayor Koch's housing policies stink. We rallied for commercial rent control, we voted for Jesse Jackson, we oppose funding the contras and building the nuclear home port. We're pro-choice and pro–gay and lesbian rights. We want money appropriated to build housing for the homeless and for low income people. We want money for AIDS research and for health care in general.

If we lived in any other neighborhood, we "bad" liberals would be branded flaming leftists, but not in today's East Village. We even have a councilwoman who thinks tenting in the park is O.K.

I refuse to be intimidated into silence. The tents must go. Their symbolic point has been made and attempting to put them back up is not fair to the neighborhood. City parks belong to everyone, not just the loudest segment of the population.[19]

This letter captures the dual frustration with both the ineffective policies of the Koch administration and the growing weariness at having to endure the declining conditions in public spaces. Given these pressures, the community split into two camps, those supporting the homeless as a way of protesting the city's failed homeless policies and those opposing the camp because it was no solution for either the homeless or the community.

In October 1989, two public meetings were held that exemplified the new lines of conflict. On October 19, the CB3 Parks Committee met. About 150 residents spoke out against conditions in the park and called for the full enforcement of park regulations and the installation of a curfew to prevent young people from congregating and homeless people from sleeping in the park. They also suggested that the park be closed completely for renovations as a way of restoring order. Many residents expressed their feeling that the park was "out of control" and that what had been a problem with noisy youths was now a broader problem of disorder in the park being defended as help for the homeless:

If you really want to see something done for [the homeless], then get the shantytown and the big rats out of there. The media and the political people look at the homeless, but they don't see the crack-smoking, the area's car break-ins, and the filthy and unsafe conditions.[20]

We're not heartless yuppies—we're mothers with children. I can't go into the park without being harassed. The police are not enforcing the law. The place is knee-deep in excrement. What is wrong with this neighborhood?[21]

Despite these sentiments, the community board again voted not to remove the encampment or close the park. The board held to its belief that simply evicting the homeless from the park was not a solution, but a major shift was about to take place.

On November 16, the city announced that a new support services center would be opened near the park and that all tents would be removed. This plan was drawn up with the cooperation of the local city councilwoman Miriam Friedlander, whose supporters on the community board had previously opposed efforts to remove the encampment by force. For the first time she began to use the rhetorical line that "the park should be for use by everyone in the community. We're talking about the homeless, as well as the children of the community."[22]

Also during this period a new community group was formed, the Tompkins Square Park Neighborhood Coalition (TSPNC), made up of people living next to the park. Its primary purpose was to see order restored to the park. According to one of the founders, the initial motivation was not evicting the homeless but getting rid of the all night noise being caused by young people, under the cover of the park's lack of a curfew.[23] By late 1989, conditions had deteriorated to the degree that TSPNC began to actively call for the removal of the encampment:

> Before the August '88 riot, there were approximately 20 to 30 homeless people living in the park. While nobody liked that, it's a citywide problem, and nobody was too upset. But since the riot, the park has become hostage to a purported activist homeless group. The entire park has been taken over. Sanitary conditions are deplorable; in some areas there's obvious drug use. It's a quantum leap. People in the neighborhood think this is too much.[24]

The group started as a series of "bitch sessions" and grew quickly. People were drawn to it through personal contacts and flyers asking, "Are You Tired of the Homeless in Tompkins Square Park? You're Not Alone." This flyer proved very effective in bringing people out to meetings by capturing both their anger and their sense of resentment about being attacked by both radicals and liberals for expressing any disapproval of the encampment.[25]

The group attempted to express itself through the community board but soon came to feel that the political environment had become poisoned by the radicals disrupting the meetings and the board's failure to take action because of its fear of being equated with either the reactionary policies of the Reagan years or the increasingly punitive Koch administration. The group viewed the community board as being under the control of the heads of social service agencies in the neighborhood, many of whom had been appointed by Councilwoman Friedlander.[26]

As the conflict continued, the group's frustration with the neighborhood's existing political leadership grew. Its members began a letter-writing campaign targeting local officials: "We felt our community leaders were unwilling to address problems in the park, and even more disturbing, unwilling to actively solicit the feelings of people living around the park."[27] The community board's liberal leadership was more concerned about maintaining its base of power than risking the inclusion of a potentially disruptive constituency. People's frustration with this situation caused them to look for alternative leadership within the community. They called up members of BASTA who had successfully fought off the First Street shelter and had consistently spoken in favor of addressing the disorders associated with homelessness immediately rather than waiting for long-term solutions.

The TSPNC soon reached out to other groups who shared its frustration, and members created a new alliance that brought some of BASTA's experience into the TSPNC. The first major act of this new group was a community meeting in June 1990 to discuss creating a curfew for the park. More than three hundred people came to the meeting, including several people who were active in defending the encampment. Despite the heated exchanges between the two sides, members of the TSPNC were pleased that they had brought out so many people, indicating that there appeared to be a shift in the balance of local opinion about the park.

In response to this shift, the mayor ordered that Tompkins Square Park be completely closed for renovations. This was the tactic that he had been used in midtown Manhattan as part of the revitalization of Bryant Park, which had been a refuge from Times Square for drug dealers and users. In a statement that mirrored those of the conservatives, Deputy Mayor Bill Lynch announced:

> We tried a number of things and then the realization came to us that we weren't going to get people out of the park, so we had to remove them from the park. Where the debate has to be is over the quality of the facilities that we provide for the homeless and not whether they can sleep in parks or on streets or in vacant lots. This is not an acceptable policy for the homeless or for the people who have to use the parks and streets.[28]

The administration claimed that it had made significant headway in improving the availability of services for the homeless and that as a result, public encampments would no longer be tolerated. This was largely a response to communities' increasing demands to restore the "quality of life" to their neighborhoods. For the first time in a decade, it appeared that the city might be getting the upper hand on both the problems of homelessness and public order.

This action, however, came too late to prevent the consolidation of a more conservative political force in the neighborhood. In the spring of 1991, the TSPNC and the Puerto Rican/Hispanic Political Council formed the Democratic Action Club (DAC) with the purpose of running mutual member Antonio Pagan for the city council that fall. Pagan had gotten his political start as a member of the Third Street Block Association and BASTA. He was then one of the BASTA leaders brought in to be cochair of the TSPNC and was also the head of the Lower East Side Coalition for Housing Development, which used public and private grants to build subsidized housing in the neighborhood.

Three major constituencies backed Pagan. The first was the traditional Democratic Party supporters associated with BASTA, WARPATH, and TSPNC who were looking for someone who would act on their desire to see order restored to the park and to displace liberal political leaders. The second was the Puerto Ricans. Pagan, a Puerto Rican, had close ties to the mainly Puerto Rican tenants of the Baruch Houses public housing complex on the neighborhood's eastern edge. This included a close relationship with the head of the tenant association, Roberto Napoleon, who was a product of 1960s and 1970s antipoverty programs. Some in the neighborhood regarded Napoleon as a political opportunist for delivering Puerto Ricans' votes for candidates of the Silver machine in return for more funding for his social services organizations. In fact, however, in the mid-1980s, the city removed him from control of one of these agencies because of corruption.[29] The final constituency was local restaurateurs, landlords, developers, builders, and contractors hoping to expand gentrification in the neighborhood. The bulk of Pagan's campaign contributions came from this last group, with which he had worked as a housing developer.

Pagan attempted to portray himself as the candidate of both the poor and the entrepreneurial. Both working-class Puerto Ricans and the middle classes were tired of having their neighborhood held hostage by radicals, with the tacit support of the liberal political establishment under the leadership of Miriam Friedlander. Because of his support by developers, landlords, and restaurateurs, Pagan was viewed by many as a supporter of gentrification. The campaign therefore turned into a battle between gentrification and social tolerance, the difference explained in a neighborhood newspaper report:

> The most central issue [in the campaign] seems to be the contentious problem of how to deal with the encampment of homeless people in Tompkins Square Park. While Friedlander has remained sensitive to the civil liberties of the homeless there, and is sympathetic to their assertion that they have nowhere else to go, Pagan applauds the City's recent sealing of the park.[30]

A Pagan supporter added, "The park was totally taken over by anarchists. The people deserve to have passable streets and parks which can be used for parklike purposes."[31] A Friedlander supporter then responded, "[Pagan] is on the side of gentrifiers and unsympathetic to the needs of the homeless. He's been redbaiting Miriam, saying that she hasn't done anything about the homeless situation in the park, but he hasn't offered any reasonable solutions."[32]

Pagan was adept at sidestepping the accusations of gentrification and instead arguing that conditions in the neighborhood needed to be improved for everyone. His backing in the housing projects—based on ethnicity—gave credence to his claims that his interests were not crassly economic. Pagan was able to take advantage of the fact that local progressives felt forced to defend the homeless encampments for their symbolic value as a protest against Mayors Koch and Dinkins. It was a symbolic effort because the local power structure did not have the economic resources or political power to implement any policies that would manifestly improve the underlying problems of a lack of affordable housing, drug treatment, mental health services, and low-skill employment. The shortfall of this strategy is that it left residents with a sense of powerlessness in the face of the declining "quality of life."

But by defining the problem as one of public order, Pagan moved the problem into a realm that could be addressed on a parochial level. Unlike providing housing and social services, policing is local and thus is more closely controlled locally. Therefore, when the struggle over homelessness was waged at a local level, those defining the problem in a way that could be addressed at that local level had an advantage over those who could wage it only on a general, rhetorical level. Much of the transformation to punitiveness in political outlook was therefore a move from the abstract and universal to the concrete and particular.

In October, Pagan won the Democratic primary by 121 votes, ensuring a victory in the general election that November. Pagan's success came from his ability to combine the support of locally powerful economic interests and traditionally liberal—now neoconservative—neighborhood activists through his articulation of a plan for immediate local action to restore order. He succeeded in mobilizing the middle and working classes against the very poor in response to both economic uncertainty and declining neighborhood conditions. This, in essence, was the politics of the quality-of-life backlash, which proved equally successful for Giuliani two years later.

Grand Central Terminal

As discussed in chapter 6, Grand Central Terminal is a major commuter rail and subway transportation hub in midtown Manhattan. The breakdown in social conditions there led to a transformation in policing as the city and the Metro North Railroad (MN), which runs the terminal, felt pressure from local real estate owners to adopt quality-of-life-oriented policing measures. At the root of this decision was the pressure placed on the police by the Grand Central Partnership through its adoption of aggressive security measures, which threatened to displace police authority in and around the terminal. This section shows that another of the primary causes of the failure of previous efforts to eliminate the homelessness problem was a shallow and ineffective desire to avoid punitiveness, which in turn merely created enhanced anger and fear toward the homeless people living in and around the station. As a result, the Grand Central Partnership was able to transform how homeless people in public spaces were dealt with across the city using a combination of aggressive policing, restrictive rules and regulations, and superficial social services outreach designed to address immediate disorder problems rather than waiting for comprehensive solutions to emerge.

By the early 1980s, large numbers of homeless people were living in and around the station and were creating problems for commuters trying to use the station and for midtown business interests trying to maintain property values and encourage shopping and tourism. The Metro

North Railroad, which oversees the station, made numerous halfhearted attempts to keep homeless people from congregating there, but with only minor success. By early 1985, the city's homeless problem had become so great that the MN's president, Peter Stangle—citing humanitarian concerns—ordered the terminal open to them on an emergency basis, resulting in as many as 350 people sleeping there each night.[33] Both MTA administrators and the public were ambivalent. According to MTA spokesperson Susan Gilbert, "It does tend to turn Grand Central into a homeless shelter, and we don't want to do that. The homeless people should be taken to a shelter. The terminal is not the place that they should be helped and treated."[34]

The city's Human Resources Administration (HRA) responded to the problems in Grand Central by offering direct transportation to shelters three nights a week, and the Coalition for the Homeless (CFH) brought free food, medical care, legal assistance, and cleaning supplies to people living there. The coalition also pointed out that many people were afraid of the shelter system and called on the mayor to make one thousand beds available in city hospitals as an alternative. Mayor Koch, however, refused to do this, and on February 11, 1985, he announced that because of increased crime in the station, it would no longer be left open overnight, thereby sending people either into shelters or out into the night.[35]

By 1987, conditions in the terminal had again deteriorated, prompting the MN to close the terminal at night because of growing crime problems, including some injuries to passengers. Great pains were taken, however, to avoid the appearance of undo punitiveness. Officials at the MN pointed out that "force would not be used to remove those who remained" after police sweeps and social services outreach efforts and that twenty social workers would be used to assist those remaining.[36] This effort, however, was short-lived, and homeless people continued to congregate in the terminal during the day and found nighttime refuge in out-of-the-way corners of the station and adjoining platforms and tunnels. This in turn led to a series of cat-and-mouse attempts to dislodge people through periodic sweeps and police harassment. In March 1987 Mayor Koch and the MN initiated another series of efforts to sweep homeless people from the terminal. They pointed out, however, that this was not driven by a punitive orientation. Koch claimed that "there has never been a plan to arrest anybody, never. I don't want them to sleep in the terminal for compassionate reasons."[37] In an effort to distinguish between indiscriminate police action and targeted enforcement, MN President Peter Stangl added a few days later, "I consider myself a pretty strong defenders of people's rights [but] there are people who are homeless and vulnerable and people who are homeless and also have committed criminal acts."[38] Either way, the courts ruled that the police had been overzealous in their efforts to roust people using antiloitering ordinances, which were deemed unconstitutionally vague and forced the police to back off yet again.[39]

As a result, by the next summer, large numbers of people were again inhabiting the station and surrounding areas, prompting local business leaders to discuss methods of clearing the station during the day as well as the evening. In the wake of the late 1970s fiscal crisis, in 1981 New York State granted the city the right to charter local BIDs and thus the right to tax local property owners to raise funds that could be spent to provide services beyond those offered by the city. This included hiring security guards, providing extra sanitation services, and making physical improvements in sidewalks and street lighting. As its first job, the Grand Central Partnership (GCP, formed by real estate developer Peter Malkin in July 1985) was to improve the conditions in and around Grand Central Terminal.

As discussed in chapter 6, the lack of support from police and political leaders, who were reluctant to adopt such punitive measures, doomed the effort. By the winter of 1990, an estimated two thousand people were again living in the terminal and on the surrounding streets.[40] By January 1990, however, the *New York Times* was claiming that the efforts in Grand Central Terminal and the larger subway system were a failure because of resistance by the police, some public officials, and advocates for the homeless:

> It was hobbled from the start by a lack of support from public officials and criticism from the former head of the transit police union, who contended that it turned police officers into social workers. It was hamstrung by a series of lawsuits challenging the constitutionality of some of the regulations. And the transit officers themselves seemed to have little stomach for issuing warnings, writing summons, or making arrests for behavior that had been tolerated for years.[41]

At this stage of the disorder crisis, a conflict existed between, on the one hand, liberal political leaders and parts of the police establishment who were reluctant to use strong-arm tactics in the absence of a credible alternative and, on the other hand, more conservative business leaders who were intent on displacing the problem from their vicinity, regardless of the consequences for the people being ousted.

Over the next year, the GCP and MN worked together to try to bring greater pressure to bear on people living in the terminal. Accordingly, in November 1990 Governor Cuomo and Mayor Dinkins announced the creation of the Grand Central Initiative, which spent $7 million on social services and physical barriers to keep people from living in stations, tunnels, and other hidden areas of the terminal.[42] In addition, more aggressive enforcement of the new rules was undertaken by MN police and GCP security guards. Both groups used a carrot-and-stick approach in which they first offered people access to the GCP-run drop-in center a block away, which provided meals and referrals to the city shelter system. Those who refused services were routinely ticketed, arrested for minor legal violations, committed to psychiatric facilities, and, at times, threatened in order to get them to leave the station.[43]

In July 1993, on the strength of its success in the terminal, the GCP was hired by the New York Community Trust to provide outreach services around the East River Esplanade and several other locations in the midtown area. The outreach consisted of teams of formerly homeless individuals who tried to get currently homeless people to come to the GCP drop-in center. This effort was successful in moving people out of targeted areas, mostly by driving them to other nearby locations. One of these locations was the public park and plaza across from Tudor City, a residential enclave on First Avenue and East Forty-second Street.

This effort continued for six months until the trust was unable to raise additional funds. As the money ran out, the GCP solicited funds from individual communities to continue the outreach. Some communities signed short-term contracts, but frustration about the cost of services and allegations of brutality by outreach workers brought this practice to an end. At the same time, the city began to develop more comprehensive approaches to dealing with homeless encampments that proved more effective and longer lasting than the GCP's methods.

The GCP's efforts were therefore scaled back to the area immediately surrounding the terminal. By early 1994, however, evidence had mounted that some of these outreach teams were using physical intimidation and brutality as part of their work.[44] In addition, several employees filed suit against the GCP for failing to pay minimum wages.[45]

In July 1995, the Federal Department of Housing and Urban Development sustained the charges of brutality and canceled all federal funding of GCP social services.[46] In 1998, the federal courts ruled that the GCP had failed to abide by labor laws and ordered that back wages be paid to homeless workers. As a result, many services were scaled back, and the GCP lost its stature as a shining example of business-led solutions to homelessness and public disorder.

The GCP has since brought in outside evaluators to revise its homeless program and restore its image. Mayor Rudolph Giuliani, however, abandoned his blanket support for BIDs. He forced the head of the GCP, who also managed two other major midtown BIDs, to abandon his multiple roles and the $300,000 in salaries they produced. Nonetheless, the GCP continues to support order-maintenance efforts and still considers George Kelling and James Q. Wilson to be the guiding intellectual sources for its work.[47]

The growth of the GCP indicates that there was a significant crisis in the city government's ability to maintain order and provide basic social services. The homelessness crisis in Grand Central Terminal and the surrounding area forced residential and business groups to develop independently controlled and financed innovations to restore order. This desire was so powerful that many people were willing to overlook—at least initially—the illegal tactics being used to make it happen. Business leaders and residential groups were focused on getting results, which the city was unable or willing to provide. The result was gross violations of the rights of homeless people, on the one hand, and a political shift away from support for government-led therapeutic strategies to restore order, on the other. The following section explains how this process played out in the residential area of Tudor City, just blocks from Grand Central Terminal.

Tudor City

Tudor City was built as a planned community in the 1920s and early 1930s, with its own restaurants, shops, bowling alley, and park. It was intended to accommodate middle-class workers in the emerging midtown business district, allowing them to walk to work and to have access to Manhattan's cultural amenities. It was designed to be an aesthetic refuge from the surrounding city and was constructed in uniform

Tudor style. The development takes up most of four city blocks, and breaks the grid street pattern with a series of dead ends and retaining walls. At the time that it was built, the properties to the east were largely slaughterhouses and coal storage yards. To create the sense of a serene enclave, the eastward-facing sections were built atop a twenty-foot retaining wall, and eastward-facing windows were kept to a minimum (which was unfortunate because now they would face the United Nations building).

Tudor City is a mostly white middle-class area with a population of roughly three thousand. The cost of apartments has been kept down by rent stabilization and their small size. Local residents have a tradition of community activism, including a well-organized tenants' group that in the past has mobilized to protect local interests. For example, when real estate developer Harry Helmsley attempted to construct office towers in their park, residents tore down the construction fencing and sat down in front of bulldozers until a court injunction was obtained. They also have been adept at working with local politicians and community groups to resist development in the surrounding area and protect their services.

In the 1990s, these concerns about parks and aesthetic preservation were transformed into an antihomeless, propolice agenda involving the eviction of homeless people from public spaces adjacent to the neighborhood. This example, like that of the East Village, highlights the way in which a culturally tolerant and politically liberal community greatly concerned about the quality of public spaces was quickly drawn into a punitive approach toward the homeless.

In the early 1990s, around twenty homeless people began regularly camping in a small sidewalk park along one of Tudor City's east-facing walls. Their small encampment began to be a source of garbage and human waste, and residents began to express concerns about their presence in the area. From 1993 to 1996, the residents' association, the Tudor City Association (TCA), developed a number of strategies to dislodge the campers. The progression of different strategies demonstrates the failings of the liberal approach to social problems and the reason that many progressives came to support quality-of-life policies.

In early 1993, the TCA had just changed leadership. and the group had taken on the homeless encampments as a major issue. Residents complained that the presence of homeless people made them unwilling to travel in that area because of fear of crime. They accused the homeless people of being drug dealers and complained that they urinated near their buildings and created a trash problem. Eventually, sanitation at the site became a major issue as well when rats were sighted in adjoining basements and human excrement was regularly seen in the area. The TCA president continually cited this issue, noting that exterminators had to be brought in to try to get rid of the rats, which remained a concern a year after the removal of the camp. He and others also were deeply concerned about the presence of human waste. In addition to the obvious health concerns, the sanitation problems represented a strong visual sign of the breakdown of basic standards of civility and marked the park as off-limits to residents.

Fear of crime was also a common concern, with residents attributing the recent increase in the crime rate to the presence of the encampment. Local police officials agreed to regularly check on activities in the park and conducted regular walk-throughs and surveillance. Despite this, they never observed criminal behavior there and told the residents that they did not feel it was a source of crime.

In response, residents decided to learn more about the availability of services to homeless people in the region. After investigating city and nonprofit services, one member said that the TCA felt that there was no shortage of available services, including emergency shelter, food, benefits advocacy, and various treatment services. The TCA decided that homeless people needed to be told about these services and that the city should help encourage them to accept them.

The TCA decided to meet with the Department of Homeless Services and explore its options. Residents brought with them lawyers to give the impression that legal action would be taken if the city did note cooperate. However, rather than forcing the city to take on the whole burden, the residents decided, as a show of good faith, to enlist the services of outreach workers from the Grand Central Partnership. They were hired with TCA money to encourage people in the camp to voluntarily accept services and leave the area. According to the TCA's president, Harry Laughlin, "Until the City can get its act together, and can provide housing and jobs for everyone, the GCP outreach program is an answer to this problem in our area."[48] As in the East Village, residents of Tudor City were no longer willing to wait for possible long-term solutions, even when they supported them in principle. Instead, they demanded immediate action, and in this case they were willing to pay for it themselves rather than wait for a city bureaucracy that was slow to answer their demands.

Responding to reports from homeless people of brutality by GCP outreach workers, the New York Coalition for the Homeless and its volunteer offshoot, Streetwatch, challenged the GCP's efforts near Tudor City. Together these groups succeeded in preventing the use of violence by GCP outreach workers, and so the GCP was unsuccessful in removing any of the people living in the park. For its part, the GCP characterized the campers as "hard-core service-resistant" people who were more interested in doing drugs than improving their situation. After a meeting at which the GCP gave its side of the story and local campers organized by the Coalition for the Homeless gave theirs, the GCP's contract with the TCA was canceled.

With the failure of the GCP's effort, residents pressured the city to use its outreach workers to try to get the homeless people to leave the park voluntarily. The association's members understood that using the police only was no real solution: "The police do come in and move them out but they just go to another park in the area and then come back."[49] Instead, they hoped to solve the problem by getting people into services that would change their situation and get them permanently off the streets. After several months of outreach, however, the encampment remained. Residents then scheduled additional meetings with the city to discuss other strategies. An agreement was reached in which the parks department would clean the park daily, thereby forcing people to move their belongings each day. In addition, city outreach workers would continue to try to entice people into services. The Tudor City residents hoped that this combined carrot-and-stick approach would get people to leave the park by entering services that would help them. After several weeks of this, however, the homeless people refused either to accept services or leave the park voluntarily. The city would not sustain the commitment of resources, and the daily cleanups stopped.

Finally, residents had had enough. They no longer were willing to use long-term strategies to solve their problem but wanted homeless people removed from their parks immediately and permanently. In 1993, the residents adopted a tougher strategy of regular police sweeps:

> These people severely disrupt the quality of life of everyone living near these camps. We paid for outreach prior to police sweeps to show our

good intentions. Now, it's like the tough love approach at many of the treatment centers. We have to start enforcing the laws against camping. Sooner or later people will realize they need help. It doesn't help them to leave them wallowing in these conditions; dying of exposure.[50]

Another frustrated resident with a history of progressive neighborhood and labor activism said about the homeless campers:

They're terrible. The city has got to get on them. They make a mess; they urinate everywhere. These people don't want to work. They're bums. You can offer them jobs and they won't take them. You can't do anything with them. We can't have them living around here. People pay big rents to live around here. They rob you; they're dirty and filthy.[51]

The frustration had become too great. Residents were no longer willing to defer their desire for control over these public spaces.

Residents had tried using liberal strategies to solve the concerns with which many progressive neighborhoods are confronted. But these methods failed to solve their problem, and so they moved to an enforcement-oriented approach. The police came in to clear the park and to enforce the existing curfew and ban on structures (tents and shanties). By late 1995, no one was living in the park at night and few were present during the day.

During this period, a new long-term strategy was instituted as well. City Councilman Andrew Eristoff agreed to use part of his annual capital appropriations budget to renovate the park, which would allow it to be fenced off during construction. When the construction was finished, the improved facilities would encourage more use of the park by local residents, thereby making it a less attractive place for homeless people. Additional park supervision by the police and parks department workers also was used to enforce park rules and ensure that people were not allowed to establish new camps.

The Tudor City example shows how historically liberal residents became frustrated with the growth of disorder and the city's inability to respond adequately. Their attempts to create positive alternatives for people sleeping in the area were ineffective because of a lack of resources for the scale of the crisis. The conclusion they drew was that neither the city nor the GCP was able to solve the problem of homelessness and disorder in their community. As a result, they turned to more punitive measures to solve their quality-of-life problem.

East New York

The issues in East New York were quite different from those in the other examples. East New York is not located in Manhattan but is a low-income black and Latino neighborhood in Brooklyn, far from the centers of power. Even though homelessness was a cause of concern there, both the effect of homelessness and the nature of this local concern took very different shapes. None of the homeless people sleeping near Tudor City came from Tudor City. Instead they came from neighborhoods like East New York; areas that had provided housing of last resort for many individuals and families. In East New York homeless people were viewed more ambiguously, either sympathetically as former neighbors, friends, and relatives or as a threat to the already besieged neighborhood stability. This conflicted sensibility prevented community residents from expressing their hostility directly at homeless people as such, although they did connect the problems of crime and disorder. In addition, as we saw in chapter 6, serious crime was also a potent concern. The community's anger, therefore, was generally directed at the city and neighborhood politicians for their perceived mishandling of the problems of crime and disorder and their mistreatment of the community in the process. Many residents felt that local politicians built up the nonprofit social service agencies that were their base of political support rather than directly addressing the community's problems.

What was similar in East New York was the role of urban liberalism in both the community and its relationship to citywide politics. East New York was closely tied to liberal political leaders, especially David Dinkins. Political power in the community also was tied to the social service providers, which were some of the neighborhood's largest employers, and a handful of local real estate developers, whose development plans were generally tied to government housing and social programs. Power, therefore, flowed toward local officeholders with strong ties to citywide officials who supported the social services provided by neighborhood nonprofits. Accordingly, as in the Lower East Side, neighborhood dissatisfaction with how the homelessness problem was being handled was often directed to these local politicians. Unlike the Lower

East Side, no significant political opposition emerged to challenge or re-place this urban liberal quality-of-life orientation. Instead, local leaders used the lack of independent political actors and the lack of success of quality-of-life policing in reducing crime in the neighborhood as a cover for developing closer ties to the powerful Giuliani administration.

Many residents of East New York were sympathetic to the plight of homeless people and the need to address the underlying housing and employment problems that were contributing to the crisis. After the white flight of the 1960s and 1970s, the decline in low-skill employment citywide, and the residue of the 1970s fiscal crisis, East New York was in crisis. The area had lost much of its housing stock, and the economic restructuring of the 1970s and 1980s, discussed in chapter 5, had an especially profound effect on the neighborhood, resulting in high unemployment and poverty levels.

In the wake of these changes, the city added to the problem through a series of budget cuts resulting from the 1970s fiscal crisis. These cuts continued through the 1980s and into the 1990s. The *New York Times* described the effects of the fiscal crisis on the neighborhood in an article in the mid-1980s:

> East New York . . . was poor before the city's fiscal crisis, and poor it remains. But in basic ways the cutbacks have made a deep impression on the neighborhood's appearance, the texture of its political life and, perhaps most palpable of all, the expectations of many of its residents.
>
> They are changes of neglect rather than abuse, the kind of changes that come by letting parks sit unrepaired, ignoring broken street lamps, letting potential landmarks go to seed, losing programs that once provided jobs, watching buildings that once housed families remain condemned and boarded over, seeing a dream of new housing and new schools dissipate into resignation and, at times, despair.[52]

Testifying before the city council, community activist Mel Grizer de-scribed the effect of the budget cuts of the 1970s and 1980s in class terms: "When the community organizations and residents organize for a decent quality of life, they are undermined because the city government ignores the needs of its working and poor constituents."[53] Budget cuts were undermining the neighborhood's social stability, resulting in both declining physical conditions and diminished political capacity.

One specific and cruelly ironic aspect of the neighborhood's crisis was its housing shortage. The neighborhood had a large number of low-income people unable to afford housing who were surrounded by empty buildings that the city had abandoned and left to deteriorate. In response to this, a large "squatters" movement emerged in the early and mid-1980s. By 1985, the city had taken possession of more than six thousand vacant buildings (2,500 of them in East New York) that had not been renovated.[54] Squatters, organized by the Association of Community Organizations for Reform Now (ACORN), began illegally moving into these building and rehabilitating them with their own resources. The city's response was to have the squatters evicted and arrested. Many local residents began to question why the city was warehousing empty buildings while there was a growing homeless population.

It was precisely this analysis that caused many people to question Koch's and Cuomo's emergency shelter approach. An editorial from the politically leftist United Community Center summarizes the position held by many residents about the contradictions in government policies that favored business-oriented programs over housing and employment:

> Gov. Mario Cuomo's recent speeches call for the construction of temporary shelters for the homeless and tax incentives for business. Unfortunately neither proposal solves the major problems facing New York. The Governor promises "compassion for the poor" but compassion is not a substitute for adequate housing and decent jobs.
>
> Temporary shelters are not a solution to homelessness. New Yorkers need hundreds of thousands of new homes. Not only are there thousands of homeless families, living in shelters and welfare hotels, but there are over 50,000 illegal double ups in New York City public housing alone.
>
> If New York is committed to improving living conditions for its citizens, the state government should be raising money for a massive construction campaign to build more public housing. Instead, the Governor and State Legislature are cutting tax rates for businesses.[55]

In fact, the most substantial state program to help the neighborhood was a state economic zone, a type of urban enterprise zone that provided tax breaks to businesses that located in an industrial zone in the neighborhood. Unfortunately, though, this effort failed to produce many high-paying jobs for local residents.

Between 1983 and 1988, the city and state combined had created only 2,400 units of new housing, despite the growing homelessness and housing crisis.[56] This lack of action on housing and jobs thus led to antagonism when the city began to locate numerous homeless shelters in the neighborhood, often without community input. By 1988, East New York had the highest concentration of homeless shelters in the city.

Most people in the community viewed the homeless problem as a housing problem and therefore were skeptical about emergency shelters as a solution. They also objected to the shelters' negative effects on the surrounding areas. One community activist summed up the consequences of concentrated homeless shelters in a poor community:

> I'm talking about homeless people with serious substance abuse and psychiatric problems dumped without supportive services. They are merely housed, without thought to teaching them how to live in an apartment again. They're non-productive drains on the economic system and are now destroying the quality of life in this community.[57]

In 1984, the Koch administration opened a new family shelter on Forbell Avenue. No hearings or discussions were held with the community before opening the shelter because it was placed there on an emergency basis, and local residents viewed it as an additional burden on an area already suffering from numerous social problems. According to community activist Anthony Mammina, who lived near the shelter, there were many problems at the time. Relatives of people in the shelter would congregate and even sleep in cars in the area. Trash, noise, and car break-ins became a constant problem, and the city was slow to respond. Finally, after twelve weeks of picketing by local residents, new streetlights were installed; streets and sidewalks were fixed; and a greater effort was made to monitor shelter residents and their friends and families. In the opinion of Mammina and others, however, the city's Human Resources Administration regularly lied to and misled residents and reneged on agreements.[58]

This is an example of resistance to homeless shelters based on localized quality-of-life concerns similar to those seen in the Lower East Side. The difference is that the residents who were frustrated by their interaction with the city continued to support liberal politicians. Mammina and many of the people with whom he worked in the area supported David Dinkins in both 1989 and 1993. It was only well into Rudolph Giuliani's second term that Mammina and some others began to express support for the mayor who championed their quality-of-life concerns. The reason for this slow transformation was tied to the fact that he had a broader understanding of the economic roots of homelessness in East New York.

This more resistant attitude can be seen in the opposition to shelters in 1988. During this period, many community activists and neighborhood groups purposely tied their opposition to shelters to broader economic concerns and not just local and immediate quality-of-life concerns, as this article from *The Link* explains:

> Despite the fact that the central section of East New York will soon have the largest concentration of homeless shelters in New York City, Mayor Koch and local real estate interests seem determined to cram even more homeless and poor people into the neighborhood.
>
> Concentrating the homeless in East New York hurts both the homeless and the community. These shelters are not homes. They get the poor and the sick off the streets of Manhattan, but they do not change and improve people's lives. Hotel and shelter residents end up isolated from friends and families, hospitals, parks or playgrounds, Meanwhile, the already strained resources of the East New York community are further stretched.
>
> East New York needs a plan for redevelopment and rebuilding. New York City's homeless need homes not shelters. The city cannot be permitted to abandon both East New York and the homeless to a future without hope.[59]

This statement makes no mention of crime, dirt, disorder, or any of the other common quality-of-life-related concerns consistently expressed in middle-class parts of the city.

In February 1988, the local community board, controlled by the borough president and local city council member Priscilla Wooten, approved another shelter for the neighborhood. This gave the neighborhood four major shelters, housing fifteen hundred people, and two smaller shelters,[60] raising questions about why so many facilities were being located in East New York and the role of city and neighborhood politicians.

At the city level, a number of poor communities were questioning the policies governing the location of homeless shelters around the city. Neighborhoods like Harlem, the South Bronx, and East New York felt they were bearing the bulk of the burden. During the late 1980s, however, it was hard to determine the distribution of facilities exactly. The city refused to produce maps or comprehensive citywide lists of facilities. Instead, it promised to provide neighborhood data for any neighborhood concerned about locating new facilities in their area. The result of this lack of transparency caused many residents to accuse the city of outright discrimination. According to a community activist in Harlem, "People perceive [the homeless policy] as a plan on the part of the city to make our lives so miserable that we will flee and the city will be able to take our buildings."[61] The city responded by denying any intentional discrimination and instead pointing to various factors that made locating the facilities in these areas expedient. According to the head of the City Planning Commission, "The city has no deliberate policy of concentration, and the city worries a great deal about it. I believe if there is some concentration, it derives from using opportunities as you find them and putting facilities where the need is."[62]

Many homeless advocates and community activists criticized precisely this prioritizing of expediency over developing an overarching plan. In the words of the head of a South Bronx nonprofit housing developer, "We feel the thrust of being targeted for these populations. It is my firm belief that if we had a vision for the entire city and we could really put that in place, then if there is a crisis with AIDS or homeless [*sic*], we wouldn't have to overreact."[63] The irony is that while the city routinely refused community input under the guise of leaving it to the experts to deal with complex land use situations, the experts were not actually engaging in much systematic thinking about the problem. Many neighborhood community boards asked the city to involve them in developing an overall emergency shelter plan, but the city refused and instead often bypassed community land use procedures in the name of expedience.

In response, a coalition of community groups proposed a "fair share" plan to be included in the city charter. This plan would "require the planning commission to devise rules to assure that neighborhoods receive their fair share of city projects, both desired ones like playgrounds and libraries and unwanted ones like jails and drug-rehabilitation centers."[64] In November 1989 the charter revisions—including the fair share plan—were passed by local referendum, indicating the extent to which local neighborhoods felt alienated by the city's centralized and bureaucratic planning procedures.

Some East New York activists also felt frustrated with neighborhood politicians. The most prominent neighborhood politician dealing with homelessness during this period was city council member Priscilla Wooten. Several neighborhood leaders indicated that Wooten was a product of the white political club in Canarsie that had exerted a great deal of political influence in the district dating back to when the area was mostly white. In this case, the white Democratic Party regulars supported Wooten's social services orientation.

Wooten, like Friedlander in the Lower East Side, was tied politically to the local nonprofit social service providers in the neighborhood. As such, she supported plans from the city government if they involved increased spending on social services in the neighborhood, as often these services and the jobs they created were seen as beneficial. Other times, however, residents viewed these programs as ineffective or even detrimental to the community. As such, her allegiances toward the urban liberal establishment of white Democrats and social service providers created a conflict between the interests of the political establishment and those of some local residents.

One example of this conflict was the placement of shelters. One community activist argued that Wooten played a central role in pushing shelter approvals through the community board in return for political favors from citywide politicians.[65] In addition, local politicians benefited from the siting of shelters and other programs through patronage systems. Unlike city agencies, nonprofits are not subjected to civil service rules, so people can be hired and fired on the basis of political connections and allegiance. One clear example of this involved the East New York Urban Youth Corps, which participated in a number of housing development and management efforts. The executive director was very popular in the community and highly regarded by city officials and other nonprofit executives. In an effort to improve the agency's efficiency, he had increased its oversight over construction contracting and accordingly refused to allow a contractor who had performed poorly on past jobs to bid on a large new initiative. It turned out that the contractor was the head of the local political machine, and within days the executive director was fired without explanation. Several community activists pointed to this incident as an example of the intertwining of politics and patronage in the neighborhood.

The result of this dynamic of patronage and intimidation was that political opposition was slow to develop. Most community leaders develop their skills coming up through the nonprofits, which are one of the few professional political training grounds for local residents. At these nonprofits, however, skill is not the most rewarded characteristic. According to a community organizer who had worked at the youth corps. and other local nonprofits, political leaders "see talent as a threat. They don't deal with issues. They are more concerned with maintaining their personal power."[66] In the words of another longtime community activist, "Local politicians are more concerned about who speaks first at an event than the issues. They are mostly concerned with getting jobs for their cronies. The worst example is the local schools, where corruption is rampant."[67] Since these political leaders received better treatment under Dinkins than they had under Koch, it is no surprise that they remained loyal to Dinkins, despite community pressure regarding the deteriorating crime and social services situation.

Some community activists explain this lack of independent political action as being the result of neighborhood social disorganization on several levels. Historically, East New York did not have the kind of community-focused institutions that areas like Harlem and Bedford Stuyvesant had. During the civil rights movement, East New York was in transition racially, and few grassroots organizations were established that were accountable to the local African American community. One nonprofit executive described the situation:

There are no membership driven community-based organizations, except perhaps the middle class churches. In the 1960s and 1970s there were a few groups that knocked on doors and distributed newspapers, but there's none of that now. Without that there are no checks or balances in place. This allows situations like the one at the East New York Urban Youth Corp. and produces CBOs that are less than demonstrably productive.[68]

The other problem was that in the following decades, the funding for nonprofits and community organizations was focused on the provision of direct services such as housing and child care and left little room for systematic community organizing. As the same person went on to add, "If there is no funding for community mobilization, then it won't get done. I'm working as hard as I can to do the minimum to fulfill the demands of funders."[69]

The final problem was that as a poor minority community, residents were firmly allied with liberal minority politicians, and it is hard to imagine a circumstance in which a liberal African American mayor would not receive deep support. In 1989 and 1993, it was not surprising, therefore, that Dinkins won the neighborhood with more than 90 percent of the vote. This loyalty on the basis of race and historic support for minority and poor communities made it very difficult for residents to mobilize for an alternative. Giuliani, on the right, held little appeal for voters in the area, and there was no opposition from the left. At the neighborhood level, local activists such as Mel Grizer complained that whenever an opposition emerged, it was based on personal popularity or skill and not a political program that differed from those of existing politicians.

At the city level, David Dinkins represented the most progressive politics that could find broad electoral or financial support. Candidates who campaigned on dramatic changes in the housing and employment markets or in the structure of local taxation and spending were unable to get on the political map. Urban liberalism had a lock on progressive politics in part because of its connection to minority communities. As long as politics in those communities was based on support for a patronage-suffused social services system and not grassroots mobilizations, there was little possibility of a politics of systematic change to emerge.

Even though East New York residents never supported the broad quality-of-life agenda or Giuliani, they played an important part in maintaining the new paradigm. The ability of the quality-of-life approach to policing to associate itself with the dramatic reductions in crime, along with the growing dissatisfaction with urban liberalism muted criticism of the new paradigm. A community that could have been expected to be a continuous thorn in Giuliani's side was, for the most part, politically quiet through the bulk of his first term. In fact, there was so little community mobilization against the mayor that most of the neighborhood's politicians actually endorsed Giuliani in 1997 in his race against a stalwart of urban liberalism, Ruth Messinger. Messinger was the Manhattan borough president and was closely identified with defending many of the core elements of the urban liberal approach, including support for increased funding for welfare and education. She was socially tolerant, preferred rehabilitation to punitive approaches to crime, and surrounded herself with a number of well-known experts on a range of policy subjects. Her message of rolling back the new quality-of-life approach fell on deaf ears, and she was badly defeated in the election.

From the perspective of East New York, Giuliani's hold on power had become so strong, and support for Messinger was so weak, that neighborhood politicians felt it was better to try and ingratiate themselves with someone who clearly was going to win reelection than to stand with neighborhood opposition, which was passive, poorly articulated, and ambivalent about the standard-bearer of their cause. In his second term, therefore, Giuliani was able to strengthen the quality-of-life paradigm even further. He continued to cut back welfare in favor of workfare. He promoted more punitive measures toward homeless people while adding fewer units of new housing to the city than any mayor since the Great Depression. Finally, he promoted the police as the front line of his battle to restore civility to the city. It was this last part of Giuliani's program that eventually undermined his personal political power and the quality-of-life paradigm.

Conclusion

In each of the preceding examples, urban liberals failed to improve conditions for homeless people or for the neighborhoods affected by homelessness. In the Lower East Side, the turn to urban neoconservatism occurred not under Mayor Giuliani but under Mayors Koch and Dinkins. The reasons were probably that the homeless and disorder crisis in this neighborhood was more pronounced than in almost any neighborhood and that the shortfalls of urban liberalism were most apparent there. The city was unable to come to terms with even its supporters on the community board. Accordingly, the new political clubs and politicians directly challenged the social tolerance and social services orientation of urban liberals. Indeed, the transformation was so powerful that a neoconservative was elected to the city council, and Mayor Dinkins was forced to close Tompkins Square Park in 1991, despite the objections of many of his historic supporters in the neighborhood.

In midtown, the Grand Central Partnership was a product of powerful business groups' lack of faith in the city's ability to solve the major social problem associated with homelessness. They taxed themselves to create a quasi government that they could control to begin remediation efforts in their local area immediately. This created a model of local punitive action against the homeless that was successful in evicting them from the public spaces in and around Grand Central Terminal. The Giuliani administration used this model more broadly to evict encampments, such as the one at Tudor City. In fact, it was only after the city was committed to taking aggressive action against the homeless that the Tudor City encampments were successfully removed.

In East New York, urban liberalism was threatened but never completely displaced. Local residents were frustrated by the negative effects that numerous homeless shelters were having on the neighborhood. Their frustration, however, was directed mainly at neighborhood and city politicians—who made up the urban liberal establishment—and not at the homeless people themselves. In addition, Giuliani was successful in tying the quality-of-life paradigm to the reduction in crime and disorder, bringing him and the police some support in the neighborhood. As a result, political mobilization in support of urban liberal politicians like Ruth Messenger was low, allowing Giuliani to easily win a second term.

Conclusion

Neoliberal globalization has had profound effects on local spaces around the world. Rural and urban areas have been transformed by the easy flows of both capital and commodities, concentrating wealth in the hands of those who have the most control over the direction of these flows. But for those with the least control, it has meant a decline in their standards of living. Global inequality is therefore on the rise, with billions living on the margins of subsistence. While middle classes have emerged in some developing areas, they still are relatively small and vulnerable to broad economic and political forces largely beyond their control. Overall, the rich are getting richer and the poor are getting poorer, with the middle class caught in an increasingly uncertain middle ground.

In the face of this dynamic, governments have often scaled back services to the most vulnerable in the belief that this will improve their competitiveness. But this structural adjustment has only accelerated the problems of inequality and social disruption by shifting resources from the poor and middle classes to the rich. The privatization of water and electricity, cutbacks in welfare social services, and higher fees for education and health care all have had disproportionately negative effects on the poorest in a society.

While this process has created a growing underclass of people living on the margins of economic self-sufficiency, the rest of the society has been forced to invest more resources in security. This has been necessary to protect themselves from conventional crime and also from the disorderly signs of inequality in the form of beggars, homeless encampments and squatters, and the physical disorder of trash and graffiti. To deal with these problems, police forces have been enhanced, private security has been expanded, and a growing punitiveness toward the disenfranchised has emerged.

We generally associate this dynamic with third-world nations whose poverty is extreme and widespread and whose repressive apparatuses are in plain view. As Mike Davis pointed out, huge squatter camps bull-dozed in the middle of the night have come to symbolize the inequality and repression characteristic of the effects of neoliberal globalization in much of the developing world.[1] On a smaller scale, we can see these same forces at work in many parts of the developed world as well. The emergence of widespread homelessness in the United States and much of Europe, the growth of mass incarceration as a strategy of managing the unemployed and backlash movements targeting poor immigrants all are examples.

Neoliberal globalization has also been a powerful engine of in-equality and social disruption in New York City. With the decline of manufacturing and the falling pay of government-sector workers, the middle class has been put under tremendous strain. While the wealth-iest New Yorkers sit at the center of a vast system manipulating the world's wealth, millions of New Yorkers live in poverty, and hun-dreds of thousands do not have adequate shelter, nutrition, and health care.

This globalized inequality undermined the stability of New York City's social relations in the 1980s and 1990s, and the twin attacks of economic dislocation and government abandonment destroyed the frag-ile economic, social, and emotional stability of millions. The growth of homelessness, unemployment, deinstutionalization, and hopelessness gave rise to an army of the dispossessed wandering the city in search of a next meal, a next fix, a place of quiet or community. Subway stations and parks became homeless shelters, and homeless shelters became per-manent fixtures of the city's landscape.

This widespread and chronic homelessness, crime, and disorder cre-ated the sense of a city out of control. People were confronted with a concrete decline in their ability to use the city's public spaces, including, parks, sidewalks, and subways. Squeegee men, panhandlers, and home-less encampments created an obstacle course of fear and filth that had to be negotiated every day.

Residents and business owners throughout the city felt that daily life and commerce in the city were becoming unmanageable. Their faith in government had been eroded during the fiscal crisis of the 1970s when government services were scaled back. Now many believed that the city government was not only eviscerated but unresponsive. Calls for immediate assistance were met with pleas for tolerance while "long-term solutions" were enacted by bureaucratic experts. Community concerns and offers of advice were ignored. The police, in particular, argued that they were unable to and uninterested in addressing the disorder problem because of their mandate to focus on serious crime. In response, communities began to pressure the police and local politicians to take effective local action to restore order, and those who did not respond were replaced. What ensued was a new, punitive, quality-of-life approach to disorder, which focused on restoring public civility through aggressive police action.

Quality-of-life politics and policing were driven by people's reasonable desire for stability in the face of widespread disorder and government failure. Punitive policing and social policies are therefore a direct result of neoliberal globalization. Once social and economic inequality produces a broad underclass, social stability will be threatened, prompting calls for a backlash. These calls have come not just from the upper classes, the main beneficiaries of this economic arrangement. They have come also from middle-class and poor communities, since these residents crave stability and safety no less than do those in wealthier areas. This in turn creates the possibility of harnessing majority support for the quality-of-life agenda, which is exactly what Rudolph Giuliani did in 1993. He did not create the disorder crisis or the quality-of-life backlash. Instead, he gave a voice and a form to people's frustrations and promised to take decisive action in responding to them. Urban liberals were unable to deal with the problems of disorder facing the city, so people turned to Giuliani, who offered them a clear alternative.

Was the rise of quality-of-life politics and the ascendancy of Rudolph Giuliani the only possible outcome of the pressures of global economics? Could urban liberals have responded to these pressures in a way that might have interrupted the drive toward punitiveness? The answer appears to be that the only way that urban liberals could have interrupted this process was to abandon or transform some of their core political orientations, essentially ceasing to be urban liberals. In the rest of this conclusion, I review the core principles that led to the failures of urban liberalism and examine the path not taken to see whether there might have been a better approach to the challenges of globalization other than neoliberalism and punitiveness.

Urban Liberal Values

The central challenge facing urban liberals from the 1970s to the 1990s was dealing with the pressures of globalization without having them lead to disorder and a punitive backlash. Through three administrations, however, they were unable to meet this challenge. At the root of this failure were the core values of urban liberalism and their, at times, contradictory nature.

At their best, urban liberals stand for a broad project of social inclusiveness, with a variety of concrete implications. Urban liberals support ideals of rehabilitation rather than retribution in the areas of crime, substance abuse, and mental illness. Similarly, they support the ideal of full economic opportunity for all and believe that there should be an economic floor below which people should not be allowed to descend. Historically, urban liberals have also supported tolerance of minority and oppressed groups, including nonwhites, women, gays and lesbians, and immigrants. They believe in strong democratic institutions such as community empowerment in running government. Finally, they view government as a tool for achieving these values.

At the same time, however, urban liberals have invested in several core practices that contradict these values. That is, in their effort to achieve social inclusion, they have given so much authority to government that they have undermined democratic participation. They have invested power in bureaucratic expertise as an antidote to the vicissitudes of community power. They have looked to multinational corporations and local elites to develop economic opportunities, and they have failed to provide sufficient resources for government to carry out its progressive agenda. This conflict of values is manifested in three basic contradictions of the urban liberal response to globalization.

Unequal Development

The first contradiction is found in the way that urban liberals respond economically to the pressures of globalization. During the 1960s and 1970s, manufacturing in the Northeast was under pressure from competition from the American South, since the South was able to offer a lower-wage, nonunion workforce and fewer taxes and regulations. By the 1980s, this pressure was globalized as cheaper transport, easier capital, and command and control flows allowed the global South to undercut American wages and regulations more effectively. This dynamic made it clear that American cities had to tap into these flows or risk being abandoned. Urban liberals responded to this dynamic by subsidizing the companies that controlled these command and control, cultural, and financial flows. This took the form of massive subsidies to corporate headquarters, financial firms, and culture producers such as design houses, advertisers, publishing, and music and television production. At the same time, by means of zoning and tax changes, urban liberals systematically discouraged existing manufacturing.

By accelerating this transformation, urban liberals contributed directly to the economic and social polarization that began in the 1980s and continues today. The fundamental nature of a global city economy is that it is an engine not of overall growth but of inequality. Year after year, the gains on Wall Street and in the multinational corporations have failed to trickle down to individuals in the form of higher wages or to the city as a whole in the form of enhanced municipal services and fiscal stability. Instead, that money remains in the hands of a relatively small part of the population while wages for the rest of the population fail to keep pace with the rising cost of living.

Government action also contributed to the disorder crisis in two other important ways. First, subsidizing the elimination of very low cost housing in the form of SRO hotels pulled away the housing safety net just as the number of people needing this housing was increasing, owing to wage polarization and the second government action: tearing apart the financial safety net. This second action took the form of reducing the number of people on welfare and the amount of their payments. Also important to the rise of disorder was the failure to provide a mental health and substance abuse safety net. Before the 1970s, many of the city's homeless would have had access to mental health care, albeit flawed. Instead, today they wander the city's streets and subways as haunting reminders of our slowly strangling mental health system.

Urban liberals may be tempted to respond that they were hamstrung by state and federal budget cuts and their own financial constraints. While the state and federal government do share the blame for these failures, the city did not act to counter these trends but instead often helped accelerate them through its own budget cuts. Indeed, these cuts often were necessary because of the large tax subsidies for the global cities project. But the effect of this development and structural adjustment made the disorder problems worse rather than alleviating them as much as possible.

Empty Empowerment

The second contradiction involves the conflict between grassroots participation in government and reliance on expertise-driven bureaucracies. Urban liberals have been torn between the desire to empower those who need and receive social services and the expert bureaucracies that can provide centralized and rational control over government. Ideally, most urban liberals would prefer to see communities and clients developing and providing social services. This would help ensure that programs are responsive to the real needs of the relevant constituencies. It also would help build a base of political support for these programs because the recipients would feel positively connected to them and the politicians who authorized and administered them. In many ways this was the initial political impulse of President Lyndon B. Johnson's War on Poverty and continues to be an undercurrent of local democratic politics. Local politicians develop social services and then persuade the people who deliver those services—through nonprofit organizations—to support their reelection and mobilize their clients to do the same—a new kind of urban political machine politics.

The problem with this approach is that from the politicians' point of view, it proved difficult to manage effectively. The most commonly heard critique is that communities and clients have poorly articulated or contradictory demands that serve to slow down the delivery of services. Worse, in some cases this leads to corruption, as those with the loudest voices or biggest political threats obtain money for programs of dubious value. In some cases, populist mobilization can lead to extremist demands for programmatic changes that undermine the existing rights or resources of other groups, as in the case of Ocean Hill–Brownsville. Finally, many communities have been unwilling to accept programs like homeless shelters or drug treatment facilities that they believe will harm their neighborhoods. This generalized NIMBYism can make it extremely difficult to involve local communities in developing projects that have local negative effects but citywide positive ones.

These kinds of problems have been cited as justifying a smaller role for local communities and clients in developing and administering social programs beyond token advisory boards with no real power. Important decisions, especially dealing with macrolevel planning, it is argued, must be left up to "impartial experts" who can use their specialized knowledge of urban planning, sociology, or public health to determine the best course of action. In some ways, reliance on experts is a progressive development in that it tries to bring rationality and research to bear on complex social problems rather than relying on the crude politics of responding to constituencies based on their relative political power.

This seeming insurmountable tension between participatory democracy and progressive bureaucracy is not so straightforward and, in some ways, obscures much of the real problem underlying this contradiction. One of the central failings of this analysis is that it assumes good faith and best intentions on the part of political leaders toward their constituencies, a kind of consensus model of society in which government exists in order to respond to the community's needs and these communities and their needs reside on a relatively equal plain. In fact, political leaders are heavily influenced by commercial interests, which have profit, not community advancement, in mind. Indeed, the largest contributors to the political campaigns of both parties in New York City are real estate developers, followed by major corporations and finance firms. Consequently, local political leaders often resist communities' and clients' input, not because it is poorly articulated or shortsighted, but because it may challenge the politicians' political interests.

Even when local politicians are not under the sway of profit-oriented interests, they can fall prey to the influence of the nonprofit sector. In poor communities particularly, the only organized interest groups are the local nonprofit service providers. Whether controlled by local residents or tied to larger municipal or even national organizations, these groups have an interest in maintaining their funding and working closely with local elected officials to this end. In return, they provide a local structure for fund-raising and voter turnout. This close relationship makes it very hard for challengers to unseat incumbents. It also strengthens the hand of the leaders of these nonprofits in relation to the rest of the community. In addition, funding priorities by government agencies and large nonprofit foundations are central to determining their organizational priorities. Therefore, when these groups have opportunities to extend their organizations, they may look not to the community to decide on their priorities or operational mission but instead to government and nonprofit funders.

Another limitation of the current social services approach is its reliance on a "deserving poor" ethos. Social services generally are delivered based on a series of moral assessments about the recipients' worthiness. Most social services and shelters require people to be clean and sober. Welfare programs require people to work, regardless of their life situation. As a result, many people with the most severe life problems are unable to take advantage of these services and end up living outdoors with their problems on public display. In turn, their public presence exacerbates the quality-of-life backlash because of their disproportionately disorderly behavior.

The overall effect of this dynamic is that local communities and many clients of these services become alienated from government and nonprofit service providers. These agencies are sometimes viewed with suspicion and can be seen as part of a corrupt political machine under the control of local politicians. This state of affairs makes it very hard to maintain political support for a social services orientation in response to a crisis of disorder in the public sphere. From Tompkins Square Park to East New York, local residents no longer had faith in the pronouncements of government officials that they were going to sort out the problem through a social services approach.

Hollow Tolerance

The third contradiction revolves around the issue of social tolerance. Urban liberals favor the extension of social rights in the form of civil liberties protections. They also favor a generalized tolerance of social differences in the form of race, religion, ethnicity, sexuality, and the like. Having these rights on paper, however, is not the same as having the ability to become full members of society. Even though African Americans have the legal right not to be discriminated against in housing, segregation in New York City is as prevalent now as it was at any time in the twentieth century. Without economic opportunities to buy into higher-priced neighborhoods or without the enforcement of existing laws, this right is largely meaningless.

Conversely, people who are told to respect the rights of others must feel that at the end of that process, some progress toward the stabilization of social relations will emerge. If, however, they feel that tolerance is, at best, a symbolic act that may end up undermining social stability, then they will reject it. When people see that disorder is rampant and that the government has no effective plan to end it, they will reject tolerance in favor of immediate action to restore order. The only way to preach tolerance credibly is as part of a comprehensive reform in social relations. If people see homeless people being housed and given stabilizing social services, they will be more likely to tolerate the disorder of those still homeless, because they can see a real solution on the immediate horizon.

An extension of this problem is urban liberals' belief that social problems can be solved through social services rather than structural reforms of markets. Communities are told that the solution to their problems is a new homeless shelter, drug treatment facility, or after-school program. If they would just invest their energy in securing these goods, or at least not opposing them, the community would benefit. In fact, however, some of these programs make their problems worse. A new homeless intake center may actually bring more people into the neighborhood, who become a source of disorder. Even when services are of use to the community, they rarely achieve the positive goals they advertise because the problems they are trying to address are too larger and complex. No matter how well conceived or run, an after-school program cannot solve a community's crime problem. It may be a step in the right direction, but it cannot remedy all the factors contributing to high crime levels, with a high rate of poverty being the most important. By continuing to tell communities that these programs will solve their problems and then failing to deliver or even making things worse, urban liberals lose support for one of the cornerstones of their political program.

All these are hollow claims that discourage public support for long-term comprehensive solutions to the failure of labor and housing markets and the erosion of government services. If urban liberals want social tolerance, they must take concrete steps to make social integration possible. High rates of economic inequality manifest in the form of homelessness, public begging, and other types of social disorder undermine public confidence in social stability. Urban liberals must pursue economic and social programs such as affordable housing, a higher minimum wage, and adequate treatment for people with mental illness or substance abuse problems.

At the root of liberalism's contradictions are its divided loyalties. On the one hand, urban liberals and Democrats generally rely on the electoral support of working-class voters, especially racial minorities and union members. In addition, they have built electoral constituencies around the provision of government and nonprofit social services. On the other hand, a large part of the financing for urban liberal political campaigns in New York and other major cities comes from real estate interests, major corporations, and wealthy individuals. These groups expect urban liberal politicians to promote growth-oriented policies that benefit existing businesses and real estate owners. These growth coalitions, which often include organized labor, are far less concerned about the effects of their economic development policies on the most vulnerable populations. The result is major tax breaks and incentives for downtown development and a smattering of social spending in the neighborhoods.

In good times, this contradiction can be maintained. In bad times, however, the pressure from major donors to cut taxes and spending tends to win out over supporting neighborhoods, especially poor ones. The advent of neoliberal globalization created just such pressures and left urban liberals unable to respond. Instead of trying to use their limited resources to enhance low-wage salaries and expand low-cost housing, New York used them to accelerate the global cities dynamic by subsidizing corporate headquarters and finance at the expense of manufacturing. As a result, wages became polarized; low-cost housing was converted to commercial or high-rent housing; and social services were scaled back or eliminated to pay for the incentives.

Wealthy campaign contributors also demand that urban liberals rely on experts rather than populist forms of decision making. This is because they have greater influence over expert processes through the development of think tanks, like the Manhattan Institute, ad hoc symposia, and funded research projects. Expertise also has the advantage of being more predictable because its range of suggestions can be largely anticipated. Even when experts disagree with the economic designs of major developers or corporations, they do not have enough independent political power to influence policy debates. In contrast, populist processes are difficult to control and hard to predict and may result in significantly redistributive policies.

Finally, uniting both halves of the urban liberal constituency is the desire for social cohesion and integration, at least in principle. Wealthy supporters of urban liberals tend to have a socially and culturally progressive outlook. They oppose most forms of de jure discrimination and believe that in an ideal world, people of all social backgrounds should be able to form stable social relationships on an equal footing. They do not necessarily believe in equality of outcome, but they do support equality of opportunity and a floor of economic stability for everyone. Unfortunately, these supporters do not tend to support redistributive policies that might make this dream a reality. Other than token support for some forms of affirmative action—which mostly benefit elites within minority communities—they oppose efforts to guarantee improved economic status for disenfranchised groups and individuals. In principle, schools should be engines of opportunity, but in practice wealthy urban liberals hurt public education by removing their children and opposing tax increases to improve the schools. Similarly they support fair housing in principle but live in areas that are highly segregated and oppose efforts to locate low- or even moderate-income housing near them.

In order to break out of this dynamic, urban liberals need to clarify their allegiances or risk becoming either politically irrelevant or indistinguishable from urban neoconservatives. After Dinkins's election victory in 1989, Democrats lost four straight contests with Republicans. It is clear that they have been unable to show how they are going to get out of their mired position. Whereas many of their economic positions seem indistinguishable from those of the neocons, their social and cultural statements seem superficial and naive. In some cities, Democrats have managed to win election by resolving this conflict, not by embracing the poor and working classes, but instead by adopting most of the neocons' policies. San Francisco's Willie Brown is a good example of a Democratic mayor who both pursued neoliberal economic policies and repressive policies toward the poor and disorderly.

What urban liberals need to do to avoid these two outcomes is to establish a platform that clearly identifies neoliberal globalization as the source of many of the problems of urban America and calls on government to use its resources to counter its worst effects. Instead of subsidizing corporate- and finance-led development, local governments should subsidize manufacturing and other types of business that generate middle-class salaries. They also can expand and strengthen the middle class by raising government salaries rather than cutting them back. They should raise the minimum wage, expand free or employer-financed health care, and develop low-cost housing for those at the bottom of the labor market. Finally, they could create a solid floor for the standard of living of those who are unemployed, whether through economic dislocation or disability.[2]

Urban liberals should become populists. They need to develop open and transparent forms of decision making that give neighborhoods a greater voice in the delivery of services and programmatic priorities. Existing forms of neighborhood participation like community boards and precinct community councils should be given greater formal power rather than being mechanisms for manufacturing consent. Popular citywide decision-making models should be designed so that neighborhoods can resolve their competing demands on an equal footing. Bureaucratic systems and expert knowledge should not be excluded from this process but should be one part of it rather than the whole show.[3]

Social tolerance should be promoted, and along with it, the actual opportunities for achieving it should be enacted. People will be more accepting of difference when it is not equated with difficulty. Many oppose low-income housing not just because of racial prejudice or its negative effects on real estate values but because they see it as a location of entrenched difficulty; a source of crime and disorder. If residents did not have such low incomes and were integrated into employment and meaningful social services and if the housing was truly transitional and not transgenerational, then neighboring residents would be more accepting of it.

When neoliberal globalization is not regulated, it results in more public disorder, which leads in turn to demands for repressive policing. Efforts by police executives and urban liberal politicians to resist this punitive turn are doomed to fail as long as the contradictions of urban liberalism are not resolved. Pressure from business interests and residents of all economic and racial classifications will demand or at least be resigned to aggressive police action against the losers in global economic restructuring. The only way to avoid this repressive turn is to use local governmental resources to counter the worst tendencies of neoliberal globalization rather than to accelerate them. Until they do so, urban liberals will be consigned either to becoming politically irrelevant or to becoming urban neoconservatives themselves.

Notes

NOTES TO THE INTRODUCTION

1. Janet Poppendieck, *Sweet Charity? Emergency Food and the End of Entitlement* (New York: Viking, 1998).

2. Barbara Basler, "Koch Proposes Building Shelters for Homeless in all Five Boroughs," *New York Times,* October 30, 1986, A1.

3. Alan Finder, "Board Approves Plan for Shelters," *New York Times,* July 20, 1987, A1.

4. Nancy Wackstein, "Conversations: Nancy Wackstein. Memo to Democrats: Housing Won't Solve Homelessness," *New York Times,* July 12, 1992, sec. 4, p. 9.

5. Sara Rimer, "Pressed on Homeless, Subways Impose Rules," *New York Times,* October 25, 1989, B1.

6. Sara Rimer, "Ranks of Homeless Grow Despite the Millions Spent," *New York Times,* April 15, 1989, 30.

7. Celia Dugger, "Threat Only When on Crack, Homeless Man Foils System," *New York Times,* September 3, 1992, 1.

8. National Law Center on Homelessness and Poverty, "No Homeless People Allowed: A Report on Anti-Homeless Laws, Litigation and Alternatives in 49 United States Cities" (Washington, D.C.: National Law Center on Homelessness and Poverty, December 1994).

9. New York Police Department, "Police Strategy No. 5: Reclaiming the Public Spaces of New York" (New York: New York Police Department, July 6, 1994), 4.

NOTES TO CHAPTER 1

1. George Kelling and Catherine Coles, *Fixing Broken Windows: Restoring Order and Reducing Crime in Our Communities* (New York: Free Press, 1996).

2. Amiti Etzioni, *New Communitarian Thinking: Persons: Virtues, Institutions, and Communities* (Charlottesville: University of Virginia Press, 1995); Amiti Etzioni, *The New Golden Rule: Community and Morality in a Democratic Society* (New York: Basic Books, 1996).

3. Kelling and Coles, *Fixing Broken Windows*, 41.

4. Travis Hirschi, *Causes of Delinquency* (Berkeley and Los Angeles: University of California Press, 1969).

5. David Garland, *The Culture of Control: Crime and Social Order in Contemporary Society* (New York: Oxford University Press, 2001).

6. Jock Young, *The Exclusive Society: Social Exclusion, Crime and Difference in Late Modernity* (Thousand Oaks, Calif.: Sage, 1999).

7. Ibid., 66.

8. Ibid., 8–9.

9. Jonathan Rieder, *Canarsie: The Jews and Italians of Brooklyn against Liberalism* (Cambridge, Mass.: Harvard University Press, 1985).

10. Jim Sleeper, *The Closest of Strangers: Liberalism and the Politics of Race in New York* (New York: Norton, 1990); Fred Siegel, *The Future Once Happened Here: New York, D.C., L.A., and the Fate of America's Big Cities* (New York: Free Press, 1997).

11. Wayne Barrett, *Rudy! An Investigative Biography of Rudolph Giuliani* (New York: Basic Books, 2000).

12. Neil Smith, "Giuliani Time," *Social Text* 57 (1998): 1–20; Neil Smith, *The New Urban Frontier: Gentrification and Revanchist City* (New York: Routledge, 1996).

13. Smith, *The New Urban Frontier*, 211.

14. Gordon Macleod, "From Urban Entrepreneurialism to a 'Revanchist City'? On the Spatial Injustices of Glasgow's Renaissance," *Antipode* 34, no. 3 (2002): 602–24.

15. David Harvey, *A Brief History of Neoliberalism* (New York: Oxford University Press, 2005).

16. William Sites, *Remaking New York: Primitive Globalization and the Politics of Urban Community* (Minneapolis: University of Minnesota Press, 2003).

17. Don Mitchell, "Postmodern Geographical Praxis? Postmodern Impulse and the War against Homeless People in the 'Postjustice' City," in *Postmodern Geography: Theory and Praxis*, edited by Claudio Minea (Oxford: Blackwell, 2001), 57–92.

18. Michael Burawoy, "Introduction: Reaching for the Global," in *Global Ethnography: Forces, Connections, and Imaginations in a Postmodern World*, edited by Michael Burawoy et al. (Berkeley and Los Angeles: University of California Press, 2000), 1–40.

19. Aihwa Ong, *Neoliberalism as Exception: Mutations in Citizenship and Sovereignty* (Durham, N.C.: Duke University Press, 2006).

NOTES TO CHAPTER 2

1. James Q. Wilson and George Kelling, "The Police and Neighborhood Safety," *Atlantic Monthly,* March 1982, 29–38.

2. Rudolph W. Giuliani, "The Next Phase of Quality of Life: Creating a More Civil City," Archives of Rudolph W. Giuliani, 1998.

3. Joseph Davey, *The New Social Contract: America's Journey from Welfare State to Police State* (Westport, Conn.: Praeger, 1995); D. Eric Schansberg, *Poor Policy: How Government Harms the Poor* (Boulder, Colo.: Westview Press, 1996).

4. Paul von Zielbauer, "City Creates Post-Jail Plan for Inmates," *New York Times,* September 20, 2003, 1.

5. Paul von Zielbauer, "Rikers Houses Low-Level Inmates at High Expense," *New York Times,* January 16, 2004, 1.

6. U.S. Government, *The Kerner Report: The 1968 Report of the National Advisory Commission on Civil Disorders* (New York: Pantheon, 1968).

7. Lyndon Baines Johnson, *Problems and Future of the Central City and Suburbs: Message from the President of the United States Relative to the Problems and Future of the Central City and Its Suburbs: Hearings before the House Subcommittee on Housing,* 89th Cong., 1st sess., March 2, 1965.

8. U.S. Department of Housing and Urban Development, *Improving the Quality of Urban Life: Program Guide: Model Neighborhoods in Demonstration Cities,* Title I of the *Demonstration Cities and Metropolitan Development Act,* 90th Cong., 1st sess., 1966.

9. Ibid.

10. Ibid.

11. John Sinacore, *Health, a Quality of Life* (New York: Macmillan, 1968).

12. James Perkins, *Quality of Life* (Ithaca, N.Y.: Cornell University Press, 1968).

13. Henry Schmandt and Warner Bloomberg, *The Quality of Urban Life* (Beverly Hills, Calif.: Sage, 1969).

14. Robert Semple, "Nixon Stressing Quality of Life, Asks in State of Union Message for Battle to Save Environment," *New York Times,* January 23, 1970, 1.

15. Ibid.

16. U.S. Environmental Protection Agency, *The Quality of Life Concept: A Potential New Tool for Decision-Makers* (Washington, D.C.: Environmental Studies Division, U.S. Environmental Protection Agency, 1973); Liu Ben-Chieh, *Quality of Life Indicators in U.S. Metropolitan Areas, 1970: A Statistical Analysis* (New York: Praeger, 1976).

17. Martin Tolchin, "Mayor Calls State Budget 'Anti-Urban, Arbitrary,' " *New York Times,* April 3, 1969, 12.

18. Martin Tolchin, "Lindsay Sworn in for 2nd Term," *New York Times,* January 1, 1970, 1.

19. Charles Morris, *The Cost of Good Intentions: New York City and the Liberal Experiment, 1960–1975* (New York: Norton, 1980).

20. Peter Kihss, "Lindsay Announces Madison Ave. Mall Test," *New York Times,* September 17, 1972, 1.

21. John Lindsay, "Excerpts from Speech," *New York Times,* May 16, 1973, 54.

22. Eric Lichten, *Class, Power and Austerity: The New York Fiscal Crisis* (South Hadley, Mass.: Bergin & Garvey, 1986); Richard Schaffer, *Planning and Zoning in New York City: Yesterday, Today and Tomorrow* (New York: Center for Urban Policy, 1993); William Tabb, *The Long Default: New York City and the Urban Fiscal Crisis* (New York: Monthly Review Press, 1982).

23. Editorial, "Time of Reckoning Nears for a City $13 Billion in Debt," *U.S. News & World Report,* June 2, 1975, 43.

24. Tabb, *The Long Default.*

25. Eileen Darby, "Lindsay Achievements and Koch Propaganda," *New York Times,* December 16, 1980, A22.

26. Edward Gargan, "Mayor, in Flushing Listens to Concerns of the Homeowner," *New York Times,* March 11, 1981, B3.

27. Frank Lynn, "Koch Enters Bid for Re-election as 2 Party Man," *New York Times,* June 11, 1981, B1.

28. Edward Koch, *Mayor's Management Report, 1981* (New York: City of New York, 1981).

29. Edward Koch, *Mayor's Management Report, 1984* (New York: City of New York, 1984).

30. David Dinkins, "The New York We Leave the Next Generation Depends on Us," *New York Times,* February 19, 1987, A30.

31. Howard Kurtz, "New York's Koch, Unfazed by Polls, Is Spoiling for a 4th Term," *Washington Post,* December 15, 1988, A3.

32. Josh Barbanel, "Campaign Matters; the Middle Class Asks Dinkins for Solutions," *New York Times,* July 13, 1989, B1.

33. Editorial, "For New York: More Than Money," *New York Times,* April 11, 1990, 24.

34. Todd S. Purdum, "Dinkins Proposes Increases in Taxes in His First Budget," *New York Times,* May 25, 1990, A1.

35. David Dinkins, Safe Streets, Safe City: An Omnibus Criminal Justice Program for the City of New York (New York: City of New York, 1991).

36. Wayne Barrett, *Rudy! An Investigative Biography of Rudolph Giuliani* (New York: Basic Books, 2000), 245.

37. Janny Scott, "Turning Intellect into Influence Promoting Its Ideas, the

Manhattan Institute Has Nudged New York Rightward," *New York Times,* May 12, 1997, B1.

38. Todd S. Purdum, "Ad Campaign; Mr. Giuliani as a Son of the Neighborhoods," *New York Times,* August 12, 1993, B9.

39. Alison Mitchell, "Giuliani Zeroing in on Crime Issue; New Commercials Are Focusing on Fears of New Yorkers," *New York Times,* September 20, 1993, B3.

40. Nick Chiles, "Rudy to Homeless: No Treatment, No Shelter," *Newsday,* May 7, 1994, A6.

41. Rob Polner, "Policy Forces Homeless Crisis," *Newsday,* November 17, 1994, A8.

42. New York Police Department, "Police Strategy no. 5."

43. Wilson and Kelling, "The Police and Neighborhood Safety."

44. Wesley Skogan, *Disorder and Decline: Crime and the Spiral of Decay in American Neighborhoods* (New York: Free Press, 1990).

45. George Kelling and Catherine Coles, *Fixing Broken Windows: Restoring Order and Reducing Crime in Our Communities* (New York: Free Press, 1996).

46. Robert J. Sampson and Stephen Raudenbush, "Systematic Social Observation of Public Spaces: A New Look at Disorder in Urban Neighborhoods," *American Journal of Sociology* 105, no. 3 (1999): 603–51.

47. Bernard Harcourt, *Illusion of Order: The False Promise of Broken Windows Policing* (Cambridge, Mass.: Harvard University Press, 2001).

48. Amiti Etzioni, *New Communitarian Thinking: Persons: Virtues, Institutions, and Communities* (Charlottesville: University of Virginia Press, 1995); Amiti Etzioni, *The New Golden Rule: Community and Morality in a Democratic Society* (New York: Basic Books, 1996).

49. Jim Sleeper, *The Closest of Strangers: Liberalism and the Politics of Race in New York* (New York: Norton, 1990).

50. Ibid., 17.

51. Fred Siegel, *The Future Once Happened Here: New York, D.C., L.A., and the Fate of America's Big Cities* (New York: Free Press, 1997), xi.

52. Ibid., 169.

NOTES TO CHAPTER 3

1. Richard Brookhiser, "Civic Disorder and Liberal Guilt," *New York Times,* August 13, 1993, A27.

2. See Robert Hollinger, *The Dark Side of Liberalism: Elitism vs. Democracy* (Westport, Conn.: Praeger, 1996); and Oren Levine-Waldman, *Reconceiving Liberalism: Dilemmas of Contemporary Liberal Public Policy* (Pittsburgh: University of Pittsburgh Press, 1996).

3. Howard Becker, *Outsiders: Studies in the Sociology of Deviance* (New York: Free Press, 1963); Edwin Schur, *Deviant Behavior and Public Policy: Abortion, Homosexuality, Drug Addiction* (Englewood Cliffs, N.J.: Prentice-Hall, 1965).

4. Robert Merton, *Social Theory and Social Structure* (New York: Free Press, 1957).

5. *Mapp v. Ohio,* 367 U.S. 643 (1961).

6. *Miranda v. Arizona,* 384 U.S. 436 (1966).

7. *Shuttlesworth v. City of Birmingham,* 382 U.S. 87 (1969).

8. Ibid.

9. *Coates v. City of Cincinnati,* 402 U.S. 611 (1971).

10. *Papachristou v. City of Jacksonville,* 405 U.S. 156 (1972).

11. Ibid.

12. *Kolender v. Lawson,* 461 U.S. 352 (1983).

13. Ibid.

14. Maurice Berube and Marilyn Gittell, *Confrontation at Ocean Hill–Brownsville: The New York School Strikes of 1968* (New York: Praeger, 1969); Gerald E. Podair, *Blacks, Whites and the Ocean–Brownsville Crisis* (New Haven, Conn.: Yale University Press, 2002).

15. Mario Cuomo, *Forest Hills Diary* (New York: Vintage Books, 1974).

16. Jonathan Rieder, *Canarsie: The Jews and Italians of Brooklyn against Liberalism* (Cambridge, Mass.: Harvard University Press, 1985).

17. In 1989 the Board of Estimates was abolished after a state court decision that ruled that the board was unconstitutional because it gave equal weight to the different boroughs despite their significant differences in population, thus violating the principle of one person, one vote.

18. Rieder, *Canarsie.*

19. See Robert Caro, *The Power Broker: Robert Moses and the Fall of New York* (New York: Vintage Books, 1974); and Joel Schwartz, *The New York Approach: Robert Moses, Urban Liberals, and Redevelopment of the Inner City* (Columbus: Ohio State University Press, 1993).

20. Caro, *The Power Broker,* 949.

21. For a discussion of mechanisms giving communities a meaningful role in directing government services, see Archon Fung, *Empowered Participation: Reinventing Urban Democracy* (Princeton, N.J.: Princeton University Press, 2004).

22. *Callahan v. Carey,* no. 79-42582 (Sup. Ct. N.Y. County, Cot. 18, 1979).

NOTES TO CHAPTER 4

1. Wesley Skogan, *Disorder and Decline: Crime and the Spiral of Decay in American Neighborhoods* (New York: Free Press, 1990).

2. George Kelling and Catherine Coles, *Fixing Broken Windows: Restor-*

ing Order and Reducing Crime in Our Communities (New York: Free Press, 1996).

3. Brendan O'Flaherty, *Making Room: The Economics of Homelessness* (Cambridge, Mass.: Harvard University Press, 1996).

4. Ibid.

5. *Callahan v. Carey*, no. 79-42582 (Sup. Ct. N.Y. County, Cot. 18, 1979).

6. Ellen Baxter and Kim Hopper, *Private Lives/Public Spaces: Homeless Adults on the Streets of New York City* (New York: Community Service Society, 1981).

7. Robin Herman, "Attorney for Homeless Worked in Two Worlds," *New York Times*, August 30, 1981, 48.

8. Robin Herman, "Task of Finding Shelter for Homeless Confounds City," *New York Times*, October 27, 1981, B3.

9. Joyce Purnick, "Police Round Up Homeless When Cold Wave Grips City," *New York Times*, January 23, 1985, 1.

10. Barbara Basler, "Officials Debate the Number of the Mentally Ill Homeless," *New York Times*, November 14, 1985, B11.

11. Josh Barbanel, "Saving Homeless from Themselves: A New Policy Creates New Disputes," *New York Times*, December 7, 1985, B1.

12. Norman Siegel and Robert Levy, "Koch's Mishandling of the Homeless," *New York Times*, September 17, 1987, 35.

13. Robert Gould and Robert Levy, "Psychiatrists as Puppets of Koch's Roundup Policy," *New York Times*, November 27, 1987, 35.

14. Fernando Ferrer, Howard Golden, and Claire Shulman, "No Way to Treat the Homeless," *New York Times*, October 8, 1987, 39.

15. Josh Barbanel, "Mentally Ill Homeless Taken off New York Streets," *New York Times*, October 29, 1987, 1.

16. David Dinkins, "A Shelter Is Not a Home: A Report of the Manhattan Borough President's Task Force on Housing for Homeless Families" (New York: Manhattan Borough President's Office, March 1987), 99.

17. Josh Barbanel, "Homeless: What New York Can't Do," *New York Times*, December 14, 1988, 1.

18. Asher Arian, Arthur S. Goldberg, John H. Mollenkopf, and E. Rogowsky, *Changing New York City Politics* (New York: Routledge, 1991).

19. Don Terry, "Dinkins Expands Housing Plan to Assist the Poor," *New York Times*, May 17, 1990, B3.

20. Celia W. Dugger, "Dinkins Delays Action on Homeless Panel's Ideas," *New York Times*, May 16, 1992, 1.

21. Celia W. Dugger, "Placing Emphasis on Treatment, Dinkins Plans to Revamp Shelters," *New York Times*, September 22, 1992, 1.

22. Editorial, "At Last, a Dinkins Homeless Plan," *New York Times*, September 23, 1992, 26.

23. Sam Roberts, "Homeless Timetable: Under Pressure, Efforts to Overhaul Shelter System Takes on New Urgency," *New York Times,* September 23, 1992, B3.

24. Celia W. Dugger, "Setbacks and Surprises Temper a Mayor's Hopes to House All," *New York Times,* July 5, 1993, 1.

25. Celia W. Dugger, "Giuliani Calls Dinkins Indecisive on Housing and Homeless," *New York Times,* August 5, 1993, B1.

26. Celia W. Dugger, "Giuliani to Call for Curtailing Services for Some Homeless," *New York Times,* September 17, 1993, 1.

27. Alan Finder, "New York Poll Sees Grim View of Quality of Life in City," *New York Times,* October 8, 1993, 1.

28. Committee of Fifteen, *The Social Evil, with Special Reference to the Condition in the City of New York* (New York: Committee of Fifteen, 1902).

29. Thomas Mackey, *Pursuing Johns: Criminal Law Reform, Defending Character, and New York City's Committee of Fourteen, 1920–1930* (Columbus: Ohio State University Press, 2005).

30. J. Anthony Lukas, "City Revising Its Prostitution Controls," *New York Times,* August 14, 1967, 1.

31. Sidney Zion, "Loitering Cases Dismissed Here," *New York Times,* September 27, 1967, 60; Sidney Zion, "Judge Orders Police to Call Off Midtown Prostitution Crackdown," *New York Times,* November 10, 1967, 54.

32. Edward Burks, "New Prostitution Law Increases Maximum Penalty to 90 Days," *New York Times,* August 31, 1969, 38.

33. This remained the case until the Giuliani administration changed the city's zoning laws, giving the city the right to close down many of these businesses.

34. Murray Schumach, "Prostitution, and Opposition, Growing," *New York Times,* March 29, 1976, B1.

35. Jane Jacobs, *The Death and Life of Great American Cities* (New York: Vintage Books, 1961).

36. Frank Prial, "Bus and Subway Vandals Cost City 2.6 Million in '70," *New York Times,* March 30, 1971, B1.

37. Richard Goldstein, "The Graffiti 'Hit' Parade," *New York Magazine,* March, 1973, 33–39.

38. George Jochnowitz, "Graffiti: Offenses against Public Space," *New York Times,* April 19, 1973, 42.

39. David Dinkins, *Mayor's Management Report, 1989* (New York: City of New York, 1989).

40. Gene D. Palmer, "Hearing Held to Rub out Graffiti," *Newsday,* November 5, 1990, 25.

41. New York Police Department, "Combat Graffiti: Reclaiming the Public Spaces" (New York: New York Police Department, 1996).

NOTES TO CHAPTER 5

1. Michael Harloe, Peter Marcuse, and Neil Smith, "Housing for People, Housing for Profits," in *Divided Cities. New York and London in Contemporary World,* edited by Susan Fainstein et al. (Cambridge, Mass.: Blackwell, 1992), 175–202.

2. Alex Schwartz, "New York City and Subsidized Housing: Impacts and Lessons of the City's $5 Billion Capital Budget Housing Plan," *Housing Policy Debate* 10, no. 4 (1999): 839–77.

3. Carol Bellamy, "Homeless Should Be Rehoused," *New York Times,* May 18, 1984, 31.

4. William Sites, *Remaking New York: Primitive Globalization and the Politics of Urban Community* (Minneapolis: University of Minnesota Press, 2003).

5. Barry Bluestone and Bennett Harris, *The Deindustrialization of America* (New York: Basic Books, 1982).

6. Paul Lerman, *Deinstitutionalization and the Welfare State* (New Brunswick, N.J.: Rutgers University Press, 1982).

7. Josh Barbanel, "Mentally Ill Homeless Taken off New York Streets," *New York Times,* October 29, 1987, 1.

8. Editorial, "The Mental Health Sieve," *New York Times,* October 2, 1988, 24.

9. Thomas Morgan, "Views Divided over a New Plan on the Homeless," *New York Times,* November 23, 1990, 14.

10. Fox Butterfield, "By Default, Jails Become Mental Institutions," *New York Times,* March 5, 1998, B1.

11. Paul von Zielbauer, "Rikers Houses Low-Level Inmates at High Expense," *New York Times,* January 16, 2004, 1.

12. Jason DeParle, "Clinton Considers Taxing Aid to Poor to Pay for Reform," *New York Times,* February 13, 1994, 1.

13. Edward B. Lazere, Paul A. Leonard, Cushing N. Dolbeare, and Barry Zigas, *A Place to Call Home: The Low Income Housing Crisis Continues* (Washington, D.C.: Center on Budget and Policy Priorities and Low Income Housing Information Service, 1991), 38.

14. Ibid., 39.

15. Ibid., 31.

16. Christopher Jencks, *The Homeless* (Cambridge, Mass.: Harvard University Press, 1994).

17. See Ash Amin, *Post Fordism: A Reader* (Oxford: Blackwell, 1994).

18. Amin, *Post Fordism*; and Scott Lash and John Urry, *The End of Organized Capitalism* (Cambridge: Polity Press, 1987).

19. Kevin R. Cox, "Globalization, Competition and the Politics of Local Economic Development," *Urban Studies* 32, no. 2 (1995): 213–24.

20. David Harvey, "From Managerialism to Entrepreneurialism: The Transformation in Urban Governance in Late Capitalism," *Geografiska Annaler* 71B, no. 1 (1989): 3–17; Dennis Judd and Randy Ready, "Entrepreneurial Cities and the New Policies of Economic Development," in *Reagan and the Cities,* edited by George Peterson and Carol Lewis (Washington, D.C.: Urban Institute, 1986), 209–47; and Tim Hall and Phil Hubbard, *The Entrepreneurial City: Geographies of Politics, Regime and Representation* (New York: Wiley, 1998).

21. John Logan and Harvey Molotch, *Urban Fortunes: The Political Economy of Place* (Berkeley and Los Angeles: University of California Press, 1987).

22. Harvey, "From Managerialism to Entrepreneurialism," 7.

23. Graham Burchell, Colin Gordon, and Peter Miller, eds., *The Foucault Effect: Studies in Governmentality* (Chicago: University of Chicago Press, 1991); and Mitchell Dean, *Governmentality: Power and Rule in Modern Society* (New York: Sage, 1999).

24. For a discussion of urban regime theory's strengths and weaknesses, see Jason Hackworth, *The Neoliberal City: Governance, Ideology, and Development in American Urbanism* (Ithaca, N.Y.: Cornell University Press, 2007), 61–78.

25. Saskia Sassen, *The Global City: New York, London, Tokyo* (Princeton, N.J.: Princeton University Press, 1991).

26. Frances Fox Piven and Richard Cloward, *The Breaking of the American Social Contract* (New York: Norton, 1997).

27. Regional Plan Association, *The Second Regional Plan* (New York: Regional Plan Association, 1968).

28. New York City Planning Commission, *Plan for the City of New York* (New York: City of New York, 1969).

29. See Eric Lichten, *Class, Power and Austerity: The New York Fiscal Crisis* (South Hadley, Mass.: Bergin & Garvey, 1986); Martin Shefter, *Political Crisis Fiscal Crisis: The Collapse and Revival of New York City* (New York: Columbia University Press, 1992); and William Tabb, *The Long Default: New York City and the Urban Fiscal Crisis* (New York: Monthly Review Press, 1982).

30. Joshua Freeman, *Working Class New York: Life and Labor since World War II* (New York: New Press, 2001).

31. Les Ledbetter, "Community Board 5 Calls for Building Moratorium," *New York Times,* October 14, 1979, 46.

32. John Mollenkopf, *A Phoenix in Ashes* (Princeton, N.J.: Princeton University Press, 1992).

33. Ibid.

34. James McKinley, "Dinkins Pledges 4-Year Corporate Tax Freeze," *New York Times,* October 20, 1992, B9.

35. Twentieth Century Fund, *The Global City* (New York: Twentieth Cen-

tury Fund, 1981); and State of New York, *The New York State Economy for Economic Growth and Opportunity* (Albany: State of New York, 1981).

36. Robert Fitch, *The Assassination of New York* (New York: Verso Press, 1993), 282.

37. Richard Schaffer, *Planning and Zoning in New York City: Yesterday, Today and Tomorrow* (New York: Center for Urban Policy, 1993), 3.

38. Good Jobs New York, *New York City's Biggest Retention Deals* (New York: Good Jobs New York, 2005).

39. Ian Gordon and Saskia Sassen, "Restructuring the Urban Labor Markets," in *Divided Cities: New York and London in Contemporary World*, edited by Susan Fainstein et al. (Cambridge, Mass.: Blackwell, 1992), 116.

40. Isaac Shapiro and Robert Greenstein, "Where Have All the Dollars Gone: A State by State Analysis of Income Disparities over the 1980s," *Center on Budget and Policy Priorities*, August 1992.

41. David Dinkins, "A Shelter Is Not a Home: A Report of the Manhattan Borough President's Task Force on Housing for Homeless Families" (New York: Manhattan Borough President's Office, March 1987), 37.

42. New York State Department of Social Services, *Homelessness in New York State: A Report to the Governor and Legislature* (Albany: New York State Department of Social Services, 1984), 36.

43. Fiscal Policy Institute, *Learning from the '90s* (New York: Fiscal Policy Institute, 2002), 6.

44. Ibid., 7.

45. Ibid., 19.

46. Ibid., 20.

47. Dinkins, "A Shelter Is Not a Home," 41. See also Coalition for the Homeless, "Single Room Occupancy Hotels: Standing in the Way of the Gentry" (New York: Coalition for the Homeless, March 1985).

48. Frank DiGiovanni and Lorraine Minnite, "Patterns of Neighborhood Change," in *Dual City: Restructuring New York*, edited by John H. Mollenkopf and Manuel Castells (New York: Russell Sage, 1991), 267–311.

49. Citizens Budget Commission, "New York City's Housing Crisis: Public Spending and Its Results, 1984–1987" (New York: Citizens Budget Commission, 1988, September), 19.

50. Coalition for the Homeless, "Single Room Occupancy Hotels," 19.

51. Oliver Avens, "The Rich Get Richer: J-51 Tax Breaks in New York City 1981–1982" (New York: New York Public Interest Research Center, 1984), i.

52. Ibid.

53. Bellamy, "Homeless Should Be Rehoused."

54. Anthony Blackburn, *Single Room Living in New York City* (New York: New York City Department of Housing Preservation and Development, 1996).

55. Winston Smith, "An Economic Evaluation of the J-51 Tax Incentive Program of New York" (PhD diss., Century University, 1993), 22.

56. James McKinley, "New York City Council Votes Tax Breaks for Huge Towers," *New York Times,* December 22, 1993, A1.

57. Citizens Budget Commission, "New York City's Housing Crisis," 19; and Smith, "An Economic Evaluation," 22.

58. Smith, "An Economic Evaluation," 22.

59. Dinkins, "A Shelter Is Not a Home," 40.

60. Coalition for the Homeless, "A History of Modern Homelessness in New York City" (New York: Coalition for the Homeless, 2003), 5.

61. Sheila Rule, "17,000 Families in Public Housing Double Up Illegally, City Believes," *New York Times,* April 21, 1983, A1.

62. Dinkins, "A Shelter Is Not a Home," 48.

63. Schwartz, "New York City and Subsidized Housing," 840.

64. Don Terry, "Dinkins Expands Housing Plan to Assist the Poor," *New York Times,* May 17, 1990, B3.

65. Dinkins, "A Shelter Is Not a Home, 60.

66. Schwartz, "New York City and Subsidized Housing," 840.

67. Coalition for the Homeless, "A History of Modern Homelessness in New York City," 7.

68. Schwartz, "New York City and Subsidized Housing," 846.

69. Smith, "An Economic Evaluation," 22.

70. Blackburn, *Single Room Living in New York City,* 15.

71. Celia W. Dugger, "Dinkins Delays Action on Homeless Panel's Ideas," *New York Times,* May 16, 1992, 1.

72. Coalition for the Homeless, "A History of Modern Homelessness in New York City," 5.

NOTES TO CHAPTER 6

1. Jerome Skolnick and David Bayley, *The New Blue Line: Police Innovation in Six American Cities* (New York: Free Press, 1986); James Q. Wilson, *Varieties of Police Behavior: The Management of Law and Order in Eight Communities* (1968; repr., Cambridge, Mass.: Harvard University Press, 1978).

2. For an extended discussion of the forces leading to the adoption of quality-of-life policing in New York, see Alex S. Vitale, "Innovation and Institutionalization: Factors in the Development of 'Quality of Life' Policing in New York City," *Policing and Society* 15, no. 2 (2005): 99–124.

3. William Bratton, *Turnaround: How America's Top Cop Reversed the Crime Epidemic* (New York: Random House, 1998); Wayne Barrett, *Rudy! An Investigative Biography of Rudolph Giuliani* (New York: Basic Books, 2000);

Andrew Kirtzman, *Rudy Giuliani: Emperor of the City* (New York: HarperCollins, 2000); Rudolph Giuliani, *Leadership* (New York: Miramax Books, 2002).

4. Phyllis McDonald, Sheldon Greenberg, and William Bratton, *Managing Police Operations: Implementing the NYPD Crime Control Model Using COMPSTAT* (Belmont, Calif.: Wadsworth, 2001); Vincent Henry and William Bratton, *The Compstat Paradigm: Management Accountability in Policing, Business and the Public Sector* (New York: Looseleaf Law Publications, 2002).

5. Eli Silverman, *NYPD Battles Crime: Innovative Strategies in Policing* (Boston: Northeastern University Press, 1999).

6. Wilson, *Varieties of Police Behavior.*

7. Samuel Walker, *A Critical History of Police Reform: The Emergence of Professionalism* (Lexington, Mass.: Lexington Books, 1977).

8. President's Commission on Law Enforcement and Administration of Justice, "The Challenge of Crime in a Free Society" (Washington, D.C.: U.S. Government Printing Office, 1967).

9. Edwin Schur, *Deviant Behavior and Public Policy: Abortion, Homosexuality, Drug Addiction* (Englewood Cliffs, N.J.: Prentice-Hall, 1965).

10. President's Commission, "The Challenges of Crime."

11. Debra Livingston, "Police Discretion and the Quality of Life in Public Places: Courts, Communities, and the New Policing," *Columbia Law Review,* April 1997, 551–672.

12. *Papachristou v. City of Jacksonville,* 405 U.S. 156 (1972).

13. For a review of relevant court decisions, see Livingston, "Police Discretion and the Quality of Life of Public Places."

14. Edward Burks, "New Prostitution Law Increases Maximum Penalty to 90 Days," *New York Times,* August 31, 1969, 38.

15. J. Anthony Lukas, "City Revising Its Prostitution Controls," *New York Times,* August 14, 1967, 1.

16. Ibid.

17. Sidney Zion, "Loitering Cases Dismissed Here," *New York Times,* September 27, 1967, 60; Sidney Zion, "Judge Orders Police to Call off Midtown Prostitution Crackdown," *New York Times,* November 10, 1967, 54.

18. Fred Siegel, *The Future Once Happened Here: New York, D.C., L.A., and the Fate of America's Big Cities* (New York: Free Press, 1997).

19. Andrew Golub, Bruce D. Johnson, Angela Taylor, and John A. Eterno, "Quality of Life Policing: Do Offenders Get the Message?" *Policing* 26, no. 4 (2003): 690–707; Bernard Harcourt, *Illusion of Order: The False Promise of Broken Windows Policing* (Cambridge, Mass.: Harvard University Press, 2001); Charles M. Katz, Vincent J. Webb, and David R. Schaefer, "An Assessment of the Impact of Quality of Life Policing on Crime and Disorder," *Justice Quarterly* 18, no. 4 (2001): 825–77; Robert J. Sampson and Stephen Raudenbush,

"Systematic Social Observation of Public Spaces: A New Look at Disorder in Urban Neighborhoods," *American Journal of Sociology* 105, no. 3 (1999): 603–51; Ralph Taylor, *Breaking Away from Broken Windows* (Boulder, Colo.: Westview Press, 2002).

20. Herman Goldstein, *Problem Oriented Policing* (Philadelphia: Temple University Press, 1990); James Q. Wilson and George Kelling, "The Police and Neighborhood Safety," *Atlantic Monthly,* March 1982, 29–38.

21. Roger Burke, *Zero Tolerance Policing* (Leicester: Perpetuity Press, 1998); Norman Dennis, *Zero Tolerance: Policing a Free Society* (London: IEA Health and Welfare Unit, 1998); John A. Eterno, "Zero Tolerance Policing in Democracies: The Dilemma of Controlling Crime without Increasing Police Abuse of Power," *Police Practice* 2, no. 3 (2001): 189–217.

22. Katz, Webb, and Schaefer, "An Assessment of the Impact."

23. Golub, Johnson, Taylor, and Eterno, "Quality of Life Policing."

24. Sometimes the enforcement practices are not strictly legal, as when young people are ordered off a street corner.

25. George Kelling and Catherine Coles, *Fixing Broken Windows: Restoring Order and Reducing Crime in Our Communities* (New York: Free Press, 1996); Bratton, *Turnaround.*

26. Bratton, *Turnaround.*

27. Kelling and Coles, *Fixing Broken Windows*; Lawrence C. Sherman, "Police Crackdowns: Initial and Residual Deterrence," in *Crime and Justice: A Review of Research,* vol. 12, edited by Michael Tonry and Norval Morris (Chicago: University of Chicago Press, 1990), 1–48.

28. Jack Maple, *The Crime Fighter* (New York: Broadway, 1999).

29. Kelling and Coles, *Fixing Broken Windows.*

30. Elliot Spitzer, *The New York City Police Department's "Stop and Frisk" Practices: A Report to the People of New York State from the Office of the Attorney General* (Albany: Attorney General of the State of New York, Civil Rights Bureau, 1999).

31. For a discussion of the parochial and co-opted nature of most resident-based crime control efforts, see Steve Herbert, *Citizens, Cops, and Power: Recognizing the Limits of Community* (Chicago: University of Chicago Press, 2006); and Patrick J. Carr, *Clean Streets: Controlling Crime, Maintaining Order, and Building Community Activism* (New York: New York University Press, 2005).

32. Selwyn Raab, "Crime Increases According to FBI Figures," *New York Times,* March 15, 1977, 23.

33. Richard Meislin, "Rising Concern Found over Crime in City," *New York Times,* December 22, 1981, B1.

34. Ibid.

35. Richard Meislin, "Fear of Crime Is Now Woven into the Fabric of City Lives," *New York Times,* January 31, 1982, 1.

36. Barbara Basler, "Serious Crime Nearing Record in New York," *New York Times,* November 18, 1980, B1; Meislin, "Fear of Crime."

37. Robert McFadden, "Homeless Pose Problems at Grand Central," *New York Times,* February 11, 1985, B10.

38. Stephen Kinzer, "Call to Arm in the Home Is Debated," *New York Times,* January 6, 1983, B3.

39. Roger Starr, *The Rise and Fall of New York City* (New York: Basic Books, 1985), 114.

40. David Dinkins, "A Shelter Is Not a Home: A Report of the Manhattan Borough President's Task Force on Housing for Homeless Families" (New York: Manhattan Borough President's Office, March 1987).

41. George James, "Crime Totals Confirm Fears in Queens," *New York Times,* April 21, 1998, B1.

42. Kirk Johnson, "Metro-North Police Division Is Demoralized, Report Says," *New York Times,* October 12, 1988, B2.

43. Michael Freitag, "New Barriers to Homeless at Station," *New York Times,* September 17, 1989, 50.

44. Ned Kilkelly, "Homeless Being Kicked Out of Subway, Advocates Say," *New York Times,* October 29, 1989, B1.

45. Sara Rimer, "Pressed on Homeless, Subways Impose Rules," *New York Times,* October 25, 1989, B1.

46. Jacques Steinberg, "Coaxing Grand Central's Homeless into the Light," *New York Times,* March 17, 1992, 1.

47. Mitchell Duneier, *Sidewalk* (New York: Farrar, Straus & Giroux, 1999).

48. Alex S. Vitale, 1998. "Taming Urban Fear: The Politics of Community and Homelessness," *Found Object* 7 (winter 1998): 71–87.

49. Interview with Harry Laughlin, November 1994.

50. Ibid.

51. Jane Cowen, "Community Backs Midtown Homeless Outreach Program," *Our Town,* March 10, 1994, 11.

52. Christian Parenti, "Sidewalk Mercenaries vs. the Homeless," *Z Magazine,* November 1994, 23–30.

53. Interview with William Bratton, November 11, 2000.

54. James Hawkins, *The Guardian Angels* (Hillside, N.J.: Enslow, 1983).

55. Lynn Zimmer, "Operation Pressure Point: The Disruption of Street-Level Drug Trade on New York's Lower East Side" (New York: Center for Research in Crime and Justice, New York University Law School, 1987).

56. Volker Madry, "These Residents Fight against Drug Plague," *Villager,* September 3, 1987, 3.

57. Lili Wright, "Unite to Fight East Village Crack," *Villager*, April 7, 1988, 2.

58. Ibid.

59. Interview with Howard Hemsley, February, 23, 1999.

60. Ibid.

61. Betsy Herzog, "Pressing Produces Promise of Change for Conditions around 3rd St. Men's Shelter," *Villager*, September 15, 1988, 1.

62. Ibid.

63. Betsy Herzog, "Push for a Drug Free Zone," *Villager*, July 28, 1988, 1.

64. Heidi Beghosian, "Merchants of Menace," *East Villager*, June 1988, 2.

65. Ibid.

66. Heidi Beghosian, "Vendors Bizarre: A Public Nuisance," *East Villager*, July 1988, 3.

67. Ibid.

68. Ibid.

69. Interview with Michael Julian, January 30, 2001.

70. Holly Leit, "Sidewalk for Sale," *East Villager*, May 1989, 3.

71. Interview with Michael Julian, January 30, 2001.

72. Interview with William Bratton, November 11, 2000.

73. Lee Brown, "Staffing Needs of the New York City Police Department" (New York: NYPD, 1990).

74. Ibid., 20.

75. David Dinkins, *Safe Streets, Safe City: An Omnibus Criminal Justice Program for the City of New York* (New York: City of New York, 1991), 7.

76. His wife, Yvonne Brown, died of cancer in December 1992.

77. Bratton, *Turnaround*.

78. George Kelling, Michael Julian, and Steven Miller, "Managing 'Squeegeeing': A Problem-Solving Exercise" (New York: New York Police Department, 1994).

79. Ibid.

80. Ibid., p. 4.

NOTES TO CHAPTER 7

1. For a discussion of the efforts by community groups in the South Bronx to provide affordable housing, see Alexander Van Hoffman, *House by House, Block by Block: The Rebirth of America's Urban Neighborhoods* (New York: Oxford University Press, 2003), 19–76.

2. Chris Archer, "Group Says 'Enough' over Plan for a New Shelter," *Villager*, January 29, 1987, 2.

3. Interview with Howard Hemsley, February 23, 1999.

4. Ibid.

5. Ibid.

6. Volker Madry, "Board Says 'No' to Plan for First Street Shelter," *Villager,* June 11, 1987, 3.

7. Archer, "Group Says 'Enough.' "

8. Madrey, "Board Says 'No.' "

9. Ibid.

10. Claire Keller, "Change Ahead for 3rd St. Shelter," *Villager,* October 13, 1988, 2.

11. Saul Alinsky, *Rules for Radicals* (New York: Vintage Books, 1971).

12. Betsy Herzog, "Push for a Drug Free Zone," *Villager,* July 28, 1988, 1.

13. Interview with Howard Hemsley, February 23, 1999.

14. Heidi Beghosian, "Merchants of Menace," *East Villager,* June 1988, 2.

15. Ibid.

16. Heidi Beghosian, "Vendors Bizarre: A Public Nuisance," *East Villager,* July 1988, 3.

17. Editorial, "I Want This Park Back," *New York Times,* July 8, 1989, 22.

18. Ibid.

19. Kate Walter, " 'Village' Anarchists: Master Intimidators," *New York Times,* July 26, 1989, 23.

20. Betsy Herzog, "Some Neighbors Speak Out about Conditions in Park," *Villager,* October 26, 1989, 1.

21. Steven Vincent, "On the Edge: The Lowdown on New York's Lower East Side," *In These Times,* March 13, 1990, 18–19.

22. James Barron, "Removal of Tompkins Square Homeless Is Set," *New York Times,* November 16, 1989, B1.

23. Interview with Steve Vincent, March 12, 1999.

24. John Kifner, "Neighbors' Attitudes Shift as Park Declines," *New York Times,* December 7, 1989, B1.

25. Interview with Steve Vincent, March 12, 1999.

26. Ibid.

27. Vincent, "On the Edge."

28. Sam Roberts, "What Led to Crackdown on Homeless," *New York Times,* October 28, 1991, B1.

29. Nashua, "Who Is Antonio Pagan?" *Shadow,* August/September 1991, 6.

30. "Ideological Issues Are Focus of Challenge to Friedlander by Pagan," *Villager,* June 27, 1991, 4.

31. Ibid.

32. Ibid.

33. Robert McFadden, "Homeless Pose Problems at Grand Central," *New York Times,* February 11, 1985, B10.

34. Ibid.

35. Suzanne Daley, "Grand Central Ends Night Shelter," *New York Times,* February 12, 1985, B1.

36. Ibid.

37. Richard Levine, "24 Arrested at Grand Central Criticized," *New York Times,* March 14, 1987, 31.

38. Richard Levine, "Grand Central May Bid Homeless to Travel On," *New York Times,* March 22, 1987, B1.

39. Kirk Johnson, "Court Says Homeless Loitering in Stations Cannot Be Arrested," *New York Times,* March 13, 1987, A1.

40. Editorial, "Help for Grand Central Homeless," *New York Times,* November 15, 1990, 26.

41. Michael Freitag, "Plan to Push Unruly Homeless out of Subways Is Failing," *New York Times,* January 24, 1990, B1.

42. Thomas Morgan, "Views Divided over a New Plan on the Homeless," *New York Times,* November 23, 1990, B14.

43. Jacques Steinberg, "Coaxing Grand Central's Homeless into the Light," *New York Times,* March 17, 1992, B1.

44. Terry Golway, "Get Off the Streets: Homeless Aid Center or 'Para-Cop' Precinct," *New York Observer,* January 17, 1994, 1; and Jesse Drucker, "Thanks for Nothing: Homeless Sue Boss," *New York Observer,* November 21, 1994, 1.

45. Drucker, "Thanks for Nothing."

46. Bruce Lambert, "Group Bullied the Homeless, Agency Finds," *New York Times,* July 6, 1995, B1.

47. Duneier, *Sidewalk.*

48. Jane Cowen, "Community Backs Midtown Homeless Outreach Program," *Our Town,* March 10, 1994, 11.

49. Interview with Harry Laughlin, October 19, 1995.

50. Interview with Tudor City resident, October 29, 1995.

51. Interview with Ella Kurt, October 29, 1995.

52. Dena Kleiman, "Hard Times in Brooklyn: How 2 Neighborhoods Have Coped," *New York Times,* July 4, 1985, B1.

53. "Coalition Organizes for Safer New Lots Avenue," *Link,* September/October, 1988, 3.

54. William Greer, "Squatters and City Battle for Abandoned Buildings," *New York Times,* August 2, 1985, B1.

55. "Temporary Shelters No Solution to Homelessness," *Link,* February 1987, 2.

56. "Shelters Not the Answer," *Link,* March 1988, 3.

57. Susan Chira, "New York's Poorest Neighborhoods Bear the Brunt of Social Programs," *New York Times,* July 16, 1989, 1.

58. Interview with Anthony Mammina, February, 12, 2001.

59. "Shelter Plan for People with Aids Hurts Homeless and E.N.Y.," *Link,* November/December 1988, 1.
60. "Shelters Not the Answer."
61. Chira, "New York's Poorest Neighborhoods."
62. Ibid.
63. Ibid.
64. Alan Finder, "Plan Would Reassign Power and Land Use," *New York Times,* October 20, 1989, B1.
65. Interview with Mel Grizer, February 26, 2001.
66. Interview with Eze Van Buckley, February 26, 2001.
67. Interview with Mel Grizer, February 26, 2001.
68. Interview with Zachary Brown, February 20, 2001.
69. Ibid.

NOTES TO THE CONCLUSION

1. Mike Davis, *Planet of Slums* (London: Verso, 2006).
2. For a discussion of a progressive urban economic development agenda, see Todd Swanstrom, *The Crisis of Growth Politics* (Philadelphia: Temple University Press, 1985).
3. For a discussion of methods of enhanced community involvement in government, see Archon Fung, *Empowered Participation: Reinventing Urban Democracy* (Princeton, N.J.: Princeton University Press, 2004).

Bibliography

Alinsky, Saul. *Rules for Radicals*. New York: Vintage Books, 1971.

Amin, Ash. *Post Fordism: A Reader*. Oxford: Blackwell, 1994.

Arian, Asher, Arthur S. Goldberg, John H. Mollenkopf, and E. Rogowsky. *Changing New York City Politics*. New York: Routledge, 1991.

Avens, Oliver. "The Rich Get Richer: J-51 Tax Breaks in New York City 1981–1982." New York: New York Public Interest Research Center, 1984.

Barrett, Wayne. *Rudy! An Investigative Biography of Rudolph Giuliani*. New York: Basic Books, 2000.

Baxter, Ellen, and Kim Hopper. *Private Lives/Public Spaces: Homeless Adults on the Streets of New York City*. New York: Community Service Society, 1981.

Becker, Howard. *Outsiders: Studies in the Sociology of Deviance*. New York: Free Press, 1963.

Ben-Chieh, Liu. *Quality of Life Indicators in U.S. Metropolitan Areas, 1970: A Statistical Analysis*. New York: Praeger, 1976.

Berube, Maurice, and Marilyn Gittell. *Confrontation at Ocean Hill–Brownsville: The New York School Strikes of 1968*. New York: Praeger, 1969.

Blackburn, Anthony. *Single Room Living in New York City*. New York: New York City Department of Housing Preservation and Development, 1996.

Bluestone, Barry, and Bennett Harris. *The Deindustrialization of America*. New York: Basic Books, 1982.

Bratton, William. *Turnaround: How America's Top Cop Reversed the Crime Epidemic*. New York: Random House, 1998.

Brown, Lee. "Staffing Needs of the New York City Police Department." New York: New York Police Department, 1990.

Burawoy, Michael. "Introduction: Reaching for the Global." In *Global Ethnography: Forces, Connections, and Imaginations in a Postmodern World*, edited by Michael Burawoy et al., 1–41. Berkeley and Los Angeles: University of California Press, 2000.

Burchell, Graham, Colin Gordon, and Peter Miller, eds. *The Foucault Effect: Studies in Governmentality*. Chicago: University of Chicago Press, 1991.

Burke, Rodger. *Zero Tolerance Policing*. Leicester: Perpetuity Press, 1998.

Caro, Robert. *The Power Broker: Robert Moses and the Fall of New York.* New York: Vintage Books, 1974.

Carr, Patrick J. *Clean Streets: Controlling Crime, Maintaining Order, and Building Community Activism.* New York: New York University Press, 2005.

Citizens Budget Commission. "New York City's Housing Crisis: Public Spending and Its Results, 1984–1987." New York: Citizens Budget Commission, 1988, September.

Coalition for the Homeless. "A History of Modern Homelessness in New York City." New York: Coalition for the Homeless, 2003.

———. "Single Room Occupancy Hotels: Standing in the Way of the Gentry." New York: Coalition for the Homeless, 1985, March.

Committee of Fifteen. *The Social Evil, with Special Reference to the Condition in the City of New York.* New York: Committee of Fifteen, 1902.

Cox, Kevin R. "Globalization, Competition and the Politics of Local Economic Development." *Urban Studies* 32, no. 2 (1995): 213–24.

Cuomo, Mario. *Forest Hills Diary.* New York. Vintage Books, 1974.

Davey, Joseph. *The New Social Contract: America's Journey from Welfare State to Police State.* Westport, Conn.: Praeger, 1995.

Davis, Mike. *Planet of Slums.* London, Verso, 2006.

Dean, Mitchell. *Governmentality : Power and Rule in Modern Society.* New York: Sage, 1999.

Dennis, Norman. *Zero Tolerance: Policing a Free Society.* London: IEA Health and Welfare Unit, 1998.

DiGiovanni, Frank, and Lorraine Minnite. "Patterns of Neighborhood Change." In *Dual City: Restructuring New York,* edited by John H. Mollenkopf and Manuel Castells, 267–311. New York: Russell Sage, 1991.

Dinkins, David. *Mayor's Management Report, 1989.* New York: City of New York, 1989.

———. "Safe Streets, Safe City: An Omnibus Criminal Justice Program for the City of New York." New York: City of New York, 1991.

———. "A Shelter Is Not a Home: A Report of the Manhattan Borough President's Task Force on Housing for Homeless Families." New York: Manhattan Borough President's Office, 1987, March.

Duneier, Mitchell. *Sidewalk.* New York: Farrar, Straus, & Giroux, 1999.

Eterno, John A. "Zero Tolerance Policing in Democracies: The Dilemma of Controlling Crime without Increasing Police Abuse of Power." *Police Practice* 2, no. 3 (2001): 189–217.

Etzioni, Amiti. *New Communitarian Thinking: Persons: Virtues, Institutions, and Communities.* Charlottesville: University of Virginia Press, 1995.

———. *The New Golden Rule: Community and Morality in a Democratic Society.* New York: Basic Books, 1996.

Fiscal Policy Institute. *Learning from the '90s.* New York: Fiscal Policy Institute, 2002.

Fitch, Robert. *The Assassination of New York.* New York: Verso, 1993.

Freeman, Joshua. *Working Class New York: Life and Labor since World War II.* New York: New Press, 2001.

Fung, Archon. *Empowered Participation: Reinventing Urban Democracy.* Princeton, N.J.: Princeton University Press, 2004.

Garland, David. *The Culture of Control: Crime and Social Order in Contemporary Society.* New York: Oxford University Press, 2001.

Giuliani, Rudolph W. 2002.*Leadership.* New York: Miramax Books.

———. "The Next Phase of Quality of Life: Creating a More Civil City." Archives of Rudolph W. Giuliani, 1998.

Goldstein, Herman. *Problem Oriented Policing.* Philadelphia: Temple University Press, 1990.

Goldstein, Richard. "The Graffiti 'Hit' Parade." *New York Magazine,* 1973, 33–39.

Golub, Andrew, Bruce D. Johnson, Angela Taylor, and John A. Eterno. "Quality of Life Policing: Do Offenders Get the Message?" *Policing* 26, no. 4 (2003): 690–707.

Good Jobs New York. *New York City's Biggest Retention Deals.* New York: Good Jobs New York, 2005.

Gordon, Ian, and Saskia Sassen. "Restructuring the Urban Labor Markets." In *Divided Cities: New York and London in Contemporary World,* edited by Susan Fainstein et al., 105–28. Cambridge, Mass.: Blackwell, 1992.

Hackworth, Jason. *The Neoliberal City: Governance, Ideology, and Development in American Urbanism.* Ithaca, N.Y.: Cornell University Press, 2007.

Hall, Tim, and Phil Hubbard. *The Entrepreneurial City: Geographies of Politics, Regime and Representation.* New York: Wiley, 1998.

Harcourt, Bernard. *Illusion of Order: The False Promise of Broken Windows Policing.* Cambridge, Mass.: Harvard University Press, 2001.

Harloe, Michael., Peter Marcuse, and Neil Smith. "Housing for People, Housing for Profits." In *Divided Cities: New York and London in Contemporary World,* edited by Susan Fainstein et al., 175–202. Cambridge, Mass.: Blackwell, 1992.

Harvey, David. *A Brief History of Neoliberalism.* New York: Oxford University Press, 2005.

———. "From Managerialism to Entrepreneurialism: The Transformation in Urban Governance in Late Capitalism." *Geografiska Annaler* 71B, no. 1 (1989): 3–17.

Hawkins, James. *The Guardian Angels.* Hillside, N.J.: Enslow Publishers, 1983.

Henry, Vincent, and William Bratton. *The Compstat Paradigm: Management*

Accountability in Policing, Business and the Public Sector. New York: Loose-leaf Law Publications, 2002.

Herbert, Steve. *Citizens, Cops, and Power: Recognizing the Limits of Community.* Chicago: University of Chicago Press, 2006.

Hirschi, Travis. *Causes of Delinquency.* Berkeley and Los Angeles: University of California Press, 1969.

Hollinger, Robert. *The Dark Side of Liberalism: Elitism vs. Democracy.* Westport, Conn.: Praeger, 1996.

Jacobs, Jane. *The Death and Life of Great American Cities.* New York: Vintage Books, 1961.

Jencks, Christopher. *The Homeless.* Cambridge, Mass.: Harvard University Press, 1994.

Johnson, Lyndon Baines. *Problems and Future of the Central City and Suburbs: Message from the President of the United States Relative to the Problems and Future of the Central City and Its Suburbs: Hearings before the House Subcommittee on Housing,* 89th Cong., 1st sess., March 2, 1965.

Judd, Dennis, and Randy Ready. "Entrepreneurial Cities and the New Policies of Economic Development." In *Reagan and the Cities,* edited by George Peterson and Carol Lewis, 209–47. Washington, D.C.: Urban Institute, 1986.

Katz, Charles M., Vincent J. Webb, and David R. Schaefer. "An Assessment of the Impact of Quality of Life Policing on Crime and Disorder." *Justice Quarterly* 18, no. 4 (2001): 825–77.

Kelling, George, and Catherine Coles. *Fixing Broken Windows: Restoring Order and Reducing Crime in Our Communities.* New York: Free Press, 1996.

Kelling, George, Michael Julian, and Steven Miller. "Managing 'Squeegeeing': A Problem-Solving Exercise." New York: New York Police Department, 1994.

Kirtzman, Andrew. *Rudy Giuliani: Emperor of the City.* New York: HarperCollins, 2000.

Kleiman, Dena. "Hard Times in Brooklyn: How 2 Neighborhoods Have Coped." *New York Times.* July 4, 1985, B1.

Koch, Edward. *Mayor's Management Report, 1981.* New York: City of New York, 1981.

———. *Mayor's Management Report, 1984.* New York: City of New York, 1984.

Lash, Scott, and John Urry. *The End of Organized Capitalism.* Cambridge: Polity Press, 1987.

Lazere, Edward B., Paul A. Leonard, Cushing N. Dolbeare, and Barry Zigas. *A Place to Call Home: The Low Income Housing Crisis Continues.* Washington, D.C.: Center on Budget and Policy Priorities and Low Income Housing Information Service, 1991.

Lerman, Paul. *Deinstitutionalization and the Welfare State.* New Brunswick, N.J.: Rutgers University Press, 1982.

Levine-Waldman, Oren. *Reconceiving Liberalism: Dilemmas of Contemporary Liberal Public Policy.* Pittsburgh: University of Pittsburgh Press, 1996.

Lichten, Eric. *Class, Power and Austerity: The New York Fiscal Crisis.* South Hadley, Mass.: Bergin & Garvey, 1986.

Livingston, Debra. "Police Discretion and the Quality of Life in Public Places: Courts, Communities, and the New Policing." *Columbia Law Review* 97, no. 3 (1997): 551–672.

Logan, John, and Harvey Molotch. *Urban Fortunes: The Political Economy of Place.* Berkeley and Los Angeles: University of California Press, 1987.

Mackey, Thomas. *Pursuing Johns: Criminal Law Reform, Defending Character, and New York City's Committee of Fourteen, 1920–1930.* Columbus: Ohio State University Press, 2005.

Macleod, Gordon. "From Urban Entrepreneurialism to a 'Revanchist City'? On the Spatial Injustices of Glasgow's Renaissance." *Antipode* 34, no. 3 (2002): 602–24.

Maple, Jack. *The Crime Fighter.* New York: Broadway, 1999.

McDonald, Phyllis, Sheldon Greenberg, and William Bratton. *Managing Police Operations: Implementing the NYPD Crime Control Model Using COMPSTAT.* Belmont, Calif.: Wadsworth, 2001.

Merton, Robert. *Social Theory and Social Structure.* New York: Free Press, 1957.

Mitchell, Don. "Postmodern Geographical Praxis? Postmodern Impulse and the War against Homeless People in the 'Postjustice' City." In *Postmodern Geography: Theory and Praxis,* edited by Claudio Minea, 57–92. Oxford: Blackwell, 2001.

Mollenkopf, John. *A Phoenix in Ashes.* Princeton, N.J.: Princeton University Press, 1992.

Morris, Charles. *The Cost of Good Intentions: New York City and the Liberal Experiment, 1960–1975.* New York: Norton, 1980.

National Law Center on Homelessness and Poverty. "No Homeless People Allowed: A Report on Anti-Homeless Laws, Litigation and Alternatives in 49 United States Cities." Washington, D.C.: National Law Center on Homelessness and Poverty, 1994, December.

New York City Planning Commission. *Plan for the City of New York.* New York: City of New York, 1969.

New York Police Department. 1996. "Combat Graffiti: Reclaiming the Public Spaces." New York Police Department.

———. "Police Strategy No. 5: Reclaiming the Public Spaces of New York." New York: New York Police Department, 1994, July 6.

New York State Department of Social Services. *Homelessness in New York State: A Report to the Governor and Legislature.* Albany: New York State Department of Social Services, 1984.

O'Flaherty, Brendan. *Making Room: The Economics of Homelessness.* Cambridge, Mass.: Harvard University Press, 1996.

Ong, Aihwa. *Neoliberalism as Exception: Mutations in Citizenship and Sovereignty.* Durham, N.C.: Duke University Press, 2006.

Parenti, Christian. "Sidewalk Mercenaries vs. the Homeless." *Z Magazine,* November 1994.

Perkins, James. *Quality of Life.* Ithaca, N.Y.: Cornell University Press, 1968.

Piven, Frances Fox, and Richard Cloward. *The Breaking of the American Social Contract.* New York: Norton, 1997.

Podair, Gerald E. *Blacks, Whites and the Ocean-Brownsville Crisis.* New Haven, Conn.: Yale University Press, 2002.

Poppendieck, Janet. *Sweet Charity? Emergency Food and the End of Entitlement.* New York: Viking, 1998.

President's Commission on Law Enforcement and Administration of Justice. "The Challenge of Crime in a Free Society." Washington, D.C.: U.S. Government Printing Office, 1967.

Prial, Frank. "Bus and Subway Vandals Cost City 2.6 Million in '70." *New York Times,* March 30, 1971, B1.

Regional Plan Association. *The Second Regional Plan.* New York: Regional Plan Association, 1968.

Rieder, Jonathan. *Canarsie: The Jews and Italians of Brooklyn against Liberalism.* Cambridge, Mass.: Harvard University Press, 1985.

Sampson, Robert J., and Stephen Raudenbush. "Systematic Social Observation of Public Spaces: A New Look at Disorder in Urban Neighborhoods." *American Journal of Sociology* 105, no. 3 (1999): 603–51.

Sassen, Saskia. *The Global City: New York, London, Tokyo.* Princeton, N.J.: Princeton University Press, 1991.

Schaffer, Richard. *Planning and Zoning in New York City: Yesterday, Today and Tomorrow.* New York: Center for Urban Policy, 1993.

Schansberg, D. Eric. *Poor Policy: How Government Harms the Poor.* Boulder, Colo.: Westview Press, 1996.

Schmandt, Henry, and Warner Bloomberg. *The Quality of Urban Life.* Beverly Hills, Calif.: Sage, 1969.

Schur, Edwin. *Deviant Behavior and Public Policy: Abortion, Homosexuality, Drug Addiction.* Englewood Cliffs, N.J.: Prentice-Hall, 1965.

Schwartz, Alex. "New York City and Subsidized Housing: Impacts and Lessons of the City's $5 Billion Capital Budget Housing Plan." *Housing Policy Debate* 10, no. 4 (1999): 839–77.

Schwartz, Joel. *The New York Approach: Robert Moses, Urban Liberals, and Redevelopment of the Inner City.* Columbus: Ohio State University Press, 1993.

Shapiro, Isaac, and Robert Greenstein. "Where Have All the Dollars Gone: A

State by State Analysis of Income Disparities over the 1980s." *Center on Budget and Policy Priorities,* August 1992.

Shefter, Martin. *Political Crisis Fiscal Crisis: The Collapse and Revival of New York City.* New York: Columbia University Press, 1992.

Sherman, Lawrence C. 1990. "Police Crackdowns: Initial and Residual Deterrence. In *Crime and Justice: A Review of Research,* edited by Michael Tonry and Norval Morris, vol. 12, 1–48. Chicago: University of Chicago Press.

Siegel, Fred. *The Future Once Happened Here: New York, D.C., L.A., and the Fate of America's Big Cities.* New York: Free Press, 1997.

Silverman, Eli. *NYPD Battles Crime: Innovative Strategies in Policing.* Boston: Northeastern University Press, 1999.

Sinacore, John. *Health, a Quality of Life.* New York: Macmillan, 1968.

Sites, William. *Remaking New York: Primitive Globalization and the Politics of Urban Community.* Minneapolis: University of Minnesota Press, 2003.

Skogan, Wesley. *Disorder and Decline: Crime and the Spiral of Decay in American Neighborhoods.* New York: Free Press, 1990.

Skolnick, Jerome, and David Bayley. *The New Blue Line: Police Innovation in Six American Cities.* New York: Free Press, 1986.

Sleeper, Jim. *The Closest of Strangers: Liberalism and the Politics of Race in New York.* New York: Norton, 1990.

Smith, Neil. "Giuliani Time." *Social Text* 57 (1998): 1–20.

———. *The New Urban Frontier: Gentrification and Revanchist City.* New York: Routledge, 1996.

Smith, Winston. "An Economic Evaluation of the J-51 Tax Incentive Program of New York." PhD diss., Century University, 1993.

Spitzer, Elliot. *The New York City Police Department's "Stop and Frisk" Practices: A Report to the People of New York State from the Office of the Attorney General.* Albany: Attorney General of the State of New York, Civil Rights Bureau, 1999.

Starr, Roger. *The Rise and Fall of New York City.* New York: Basic Books, 1985.

State of New York. *The New York State Economy for Economic Growth and Opportunity.* Albany: State of New York, 1981.

Swanstrom, Todd. *The Crisis of Growth Politics: Cleveland, Kucinich, and the Challenge of Urban Populism.* Philadelphia: Temple University Press, 1985.

Tabb, William. *The Long Default: New York City and the Urban Fiscal Crisis.* New York: Monthly Review Press, 1982.

Taylor, Ralph. *Breaking Away from Broken Windows.* Boulder, Colo.: Westview Press, 2002.

"Time of Reckoning Nears for a City $13 Billion in Debt." *U.S. News & World Report,* June 2, 1975, 43.

Twentieth Century Fund. *The Global City.* New York: Twentieth Century Fund, 1981.

U.S. Department of Housing and Urban Development. 1966. *Improving the Quality of Urban Life: Program Guide: Model Neighborhoods in Demonstration Cities. Title I of the Demonstration Cities and Metropolitan Development Act of 1966.*

U.S. Environmental Protection Agency. *The Quality of Life Concept: A Potential New Tool for Decision-Makers.* Washington, D.C.: Environmental Studies Division, Environmental Protection Agency, 1973.

U.S. Government. *The Kerner Report: The 1968 Report of the National Advisory Commission on Civil Disorders.* New York: Pantheon, 1968.

Van Hoffman, Alexander. *House by House, Block by Block: The Rebirth of America's Urban Neighborhoods.* New York: Oxford University Press, 2003.

Vincent, Steven. "On the Edge: The Lowdown on New York's Lower East Side." *In These Times,* March 13, 1990, 18–19.

Vitale, Alex. S. "Innovation and Institutionalization: Factors in the Development of 'Quality of Life' Policing in New York City." *Policing and Society* 15, no. 2 (2005): 99–124.

———. "Taming Urban Fear: The Politics of Community and Homelessness." *Found Object* 7 (winter 1998): 71–87.

Walker, Samuel. *A Critical History of Police Reform: The Emergence of Professionalism.* Lexington, Mass.: Lexington Books, 1977.

Wilson, James Q. *Varieties of Police Behavior: The Management of Law and Order in Eight Communities.* 1968. Reprint, Cambridge, Mass.: Harvard University Press, 1978.

Wilson, James Q., and George Kelling. "The Police and Neighborhood Safety." *Atlantic Monthly,* March 1982, 29–38.

Young, Jock. *The Exclusive Society: Social Exclusion, Crime and Difference in Late Modernity.* Thousand Oaks, Calif.: Sage, 1999.

Zimmer, Lynn. *Operation Pressure Point: The Disruption of Street-Level Drug Trade on New York's Lower East Side.* New York: Center for Research in Crime and Justice, New York University School of Law, 1987.

Index

About the Author

Alex S. Vitale is an associate professor of sociology at Brooklyn College, City University of New York.